Interviewing for
the Helping Professions

Related books of interest

Understanding and Managing the Therapeutic Relationship
Fred R. McKenzie

Theory and Practice with Adolescents: An Applied Approach
Fred R. McKenzie

Research Methods for Social Workers, Second Edition
Samuel S. Faulkner and Cynthia A. Faulkner

Empowering Workers and Clients for Organizational Change
Marcia B. Cohen and Cheryl A. Hyde

Social Work Practice with Families: A Resiliency-Based Approach,
Second Edition
Mary Patricia Van Hook

Child and Family Practice: A Relational Perspective
Shelley Cohen Konrad

Getting Your MSW: How to Survive and Thrive in a Social Work Program, Second Edition
Karen M. Sowers and Bruce A. Thyer

Social Service Workplace Bullying: A Betrayal of Good Intentions
Kathryn Brohl

Policy, Politics, and Ethics: A Critical Approach, Third Edition
Thomas M. Meenaghan, Keith M. Kilty, Dennis D. Long, and
John G. McNutt

Social Work with HIV and AIDS: A Case-Based Guide
Diana Rowan and Contributors

Interviewing for the Helping Professions

A Relational Approach

Fred R. McKenzie
Aurora University

LYCEUM
BOOKS, INC.

Chicago, IL 60637

© 2014 by Lyceum Books, Inc.

Published by
LYCEUM BOOKS, INC.
5758 S. Blackstone Avenue
Chicago, Illinois 60637
773-643-1903 fax
773-643-1902 phone
lyceum@lyceumbooks.com
www.lyceumbooks.com

6 5 4 3 2 1   14 15 16 17 18 19

ISBN 978–1-935871–35–4

Printed in the United States of America.

Library of Congress Cataloging-in-Publication Data

McKenzie, Fred R.
   Interviewing for the helping professions : a relational approach / Fred R. McKenzie, PhD, Aurora University.
      pages cm
   Includes bibliographical references and index.
   ISBN 978-1-935871-35-4 (pbk. : alk. paper)
    1. Social service—United States.   2. Interviewing—United States.   3. Human services—United States.   4. Professional ethics—United States.   5. Social service—Canada.   6. Interviewing—Canada.   7. Human services—Canada.   8. Professional ethics—Canada.
I. Title.
HV91.M376   2013
001.4'33—dc23
                                                                            2013015829

I dedicate this book to my many clients for their patient contribution to the interviewing process and for teaching me so much, and to my wife, Tamela, who has enabled me to accomplish so much in life.

Contents

Foreword

All professions, including the human service professions, are ultimately tied to the assumption that portions of the human experience are knowable, understandable, and subject to rational intervention by a given professional. While this assumption justifies professional behavior, the assumption is in turn severely influenced by the reality of two philosophical phenomena: human beings are by nature relational, and human beings are somewhat discrete in their existence.

Within this context of assumption and philosophical phenomena, the subject of interviewing must be seen as something other than just the professional asking questions so as to discern the right strategy for subsequent intervention. Gathering information from a client is rarely linear and never simple. Selected informational questions are often enmeshed in a variety of contextual factors: the theoretical perspectives of the helper; the chosen role relationship between the client and professional; the similarities and differences between the client and professional in terms of social factors such as age, gender, race, and class; and the structure of programming within a given organization.

McKenzie's book is the first book on interviewing that successfully appreciates the dynamism and complexity within which any professional interviewing takes place. Further, McKenzie's book builds the presentation of how to think and conduct interviews within a perspective that stresses the centrality of building a process of relationship between client and professional. McKenzie's book clearly suggests that interviewing without achieving a positive relationship between client and professional runs the risk of severely limiting the amount of functional information to support rational professional responses. In short, discreteness between client and professional dominates, and relevant information may not be shared with the professional, thus producing a less than appropriate response by the professional.

In McKenzie's view, there is a case for the requisite integration of thought and behavior associated with the "differential use of self" in the unfolding of the interview and the interview process. Because McKenzie does such a wonderful job of dealing with the complexity of interviewing, he affirms the wonderment of the human experience, especially the client-professional relationship, and he is totally successful in avoiding a cookbook approach to interviewing. McKenzie, in short, helps us understand that interviewing is a critical aspect of the noble process called helping.

Thomas M. Meenaghan
New York University

Preface

A successful professional interview depends on the development of a generally positive human interaction. Without a positive base, the interview can be fraught with difficulties and road-blocks. This is true regardless of the discipline, be it social work, psychology, human services, nursing, criminal justice, medicine, psychiatry, or other disciplines. From the earliest contributions of Sigmund Freud to the latest writings and research of neuroscience, the initial connection has been emphasized as the most significant precursor to an effective interpersonal encounter in human services.

Human beings are social animals. Successful early attachment dictates the extent to which subsequent development will be either a positive or negative experience. The interview carries with it that same significance. Obviously both interviewer and client always have predispositions based upon inherent constitution and life circumstances. (For the purposes of this book, the term *client* will be used instead of *interviewee*. The term *interviewer* will be used because of its generic usefulness in examining an interdisciplinary encounter.) However, the positive outcome of an interview can sometimes powerfully alter those circumstances.

Most books on interviewing are filled with helpful recommendations regarding technique, and perhaps even the theory behind those approaches. Unfortunately, most books on interviewing do not emphasize the emotional underpinnings that make an interview successful. Chief and foremost among those elements is trust. Trust forms the basis of all human relationships, especially as it relates to interviewing and any therapeutic relationship. This book goes beyond most others in its emphasis on the emotional foundation of interviewing. Any interviewing technique is only as good as its emotional value to the interviewer and client, and the genuineness that is conveyed and accepted.

Beginning interviewers may have learned solid technique, but often are initially focused more on thinking about what they will say next, than on understanding or even listening to the interviewee/client. As a result, that critical initial interview, whose success affects the future of most professional encounters, is often disrupted by a failure to truly listen and understand.

Interviewing for the Helping Professions: A Relational Approach can help both the beginning professional and the veteran interviewer understand the nature and purpose, technique, meaning, emotions, and outcomes of the interviewing process. This text also provides a comprehensive overview of the theory and technique so crucial to meaningful interviewing. More important, it emphasizes the emotional significance of the interaction, and grounds that process in contemporary attachment, relational, and neuroscience theory, and empirical research. Rich case examples from a variety of disciplines are used to demonstrate the subtle complexity of interviewing. Each chapter ends with a list of recommended readings, media, and Internet sources.

Chapter 1 lays the groundwork for all subsequent chapters. It presents a thorough and comprehensive review of the historical literature as it relates to interviewing. Tracing this history from Freud, neo-Freudians, ego psychologists, object relations theorists, and humanist, cognitive, behavioral, and developmental approaches, the reader will develop a solid background and understanding of what constitutes a successful interview. Of special importance are the most recent literature in neuroscience and empirical research on the interviewing process.

Chapter 2 focuses on the nature of interviewing and the many contexts in which it is performed. It emphasizes technique, but with a constant eye toward maintaining the relationship with the client regardless of the type of interview.

Chapter 3 delves into the different types of interviewing within the professions, such as assessment, crisis intervention, social/medical histories, and engagement in therapy.

Chapter 4 covers the complex issue of diversity in the interviewing process. Although diversity is an inherent element in all interviewing, and is implicitly infused throughout the book, this chapter provides much greater detail, case examples, and approaches to this important topic. This text is intended for professional interviewers in both the US and Canadian systems. There are tremendous similarities in both arenas, but each audience can learn from the other. This chapter sheds light on that subject for professionals in both countries.

Chapter 5 examines how the interview process changes relative to the specific modality in which it is provided. Interviewing an individual is, and should be, different than interviewing a couple, family, or group.

Chapter 6 examines the variations in interviewing with different age groups. Interviewing children demands a very different approach and skill set than interviewing adults. Interviewing children also necessitates at least some involvement with caretakers. Interviewing adults varies with the life stage of that adult. Older adults require a different approach in an interview than do people in their early twenties.

Chapter 7 addresses how to integrate a variety of interviewing approaches, depending on different situations. For example, an interview with an adolescent may appear to be going well until it moves into an area that threatens him or her. If the adolescent becomes defensive, the interview may require a much more delicate and skillful use of empathy and even use of self-disclosure by the interviewer in order to be successful.

Chapters 8 and 9 explore interviewing approaches in a wide spectrum of mental health situations. Case examples illustrate how the interview process shifts according to the situation.

Interviewing people with addictions and dual-diagnosis problems is the focus of chapter 10. This controversial area has historically been separated from interviewing centered on mental health issues. Contemporary professional wisdom has come to recognize that the two are almost always inseparable: hence the term *dual diagnosis*. This chapter will help the interviewer navigate through this delicate process.

The case examples in chapter 11 bring together the content areas of the earlier chapters. This detailed material combines and explores numerous real-world interviewing situations that all professionals will face throughout their careers.

Chapter 12 explores the essential elements of ethical interviewing, including comprehensive case examples, supervision, and consultation.

Acknowledgments

I want to thank the following people who have been so instrumental in helping me with this text. Lyceum publisher David Follmer and his expert staff were always there for me and provided ongoing support in every step of the process. Tom Meenaghan has become a trusted friend and mentor whose wisdom and experience have been invaluable in all of my writing with Lyceum. I can't find the words to show my appreciation for Tom's time and effort with me. I want to thank all of the reviewers who have taken the time to read and reread my manuscript and provided important feedback that has helped shape this text. I could not have written this book were it not for the knowledge and experience I have gained from all of my students and clients. It is they who have taught me how to interview and how to teach it. Finally, I could not have completed this work without the ongoing patience and support of my first editor, my wife, Tamela. She has been with me at every step in all my professional writing. Her generous critiques, skillful guidance, and unconditional love have kept me engaged throughout this process.

Theoretical Foundations of Interviewing

This chapter examines the theoretical and clinical history under which today's interviewing theory, styles, and rationale have developed. It provides a bird's-eye view of many of the most important psychological theorists who have affected interviewing. This review establishes a context for the essential style, skills, and approaches so important in interviewing. (References for all the theorists discussed here appear at the end of the chapter.)

PSYCHOANALYTIC THEORY

Sigmund Freud (1856–1939): Topographic, Tripartite, and Transference Theories

Sigmund Freud is probably the first and best-known theorist and contributor to the understanding and meaning of the interviewing process. Freud developed his theories in the late nineteenth and early twentieth centuries. His contributions were monumental and far too numerous and expansive to cover in this text. He is considered to be the father of psychology, and many of his concepts, ideas, and theories have withstood the test of time and are being validated by neuroscience research (Cozolino, 2002). Three of his key theories (the topographic, tripartite, and transference theories) will be discussed here because of their particular relevance to understanding the human condition and the implication for interviewing.

Topographic Theory

Freud's topographic theory posits the idea that the human mind consists of conscious, unconscious, and preconscious areas that together manage thought and emotion, and the resulting behaviors. Freud believed that human beings are driven by innate instincts. These instincts are what motivate all human beings to function in the world. Freud believed that there are two such instincts, the libidinal or love instinct, and the aggressive instinct. He believed that all human activity derives from these two instincts interacting with the environment. The instincts were believed to be housed in an area of the mind that is completely out of awareness of the individual. In other words, they are unconscious (S. Freud, 1960).

The instincts can be somewhat managed in the unconscious by a force that Freud called the repression barrier. This barrier is analogous to a mental force field that helps protect the individual from uncomfortable or overwhelming instinctual thoughts and emotions by containing them in the unconscious. Because human beings are driven by the instincts, however, we must find suitable and acceptable ways to express them in life. The repression barrier was considered to be weakest when an individual is asleep and at other stressful and vulnerable times.

Above the repression barrier is the area of mental functioning that is in the conscious awareness of the human being. The consciousness of the individual enables him or her to carry out everyday functions of life, such as work, play, love, and other pragmatic aspects of existence. All human activity, even thinking, according to Freud, is driven by the instincts. In normal life, this process is not problematic. Aggressive instincts fuel the desire for success and work. Libidinal instincts lead to love relationships, marriage, and children. Occasionally, however, some of these conscious activities become tied to the drives in a dysfunctional way. If this attachment is too powerful, or forbidden in both positive and negative ways, the thoughts and emotions surrounding these activities are put back into the unconscious through a process called repression.

For example, a small child may become so angry with one of her parents, and the emotions become so unbearable, that repression puts the emotions into the unconscious in order to keep them out of the awareness of the child. This protects the child emotionally, but does not eliminate the conflict, which could return in other ways later in life. Freud believed that anything that was put into the unconscious became symbolically disguised and changed in order to protect the individual. Yet there is often a need to express these elements, because of the tension related to the drive conflict. A slip of the tongue is an example of unconscious and forbidden material seeping into everyday life. "Accidentally" calling your wife by your mother's, or even ex-wife's, name is an example of a Freudian slip of the tongue. Freud believed that dreams are another example of the mechanism by which emotional conflicts can become metaphors and symbols. Expression of these symbols in dreams allows the conflict(s) to move past the weakened sleep state of the repression barrier and safely into relative dream consciousness, producing some relief.

The topographic theory's metaphor is that of an iceberg floating in a body of water. The unconscious is everything beneath the surface. The repression barrier contains the forces of the unconscious and under certain circumstances allows unconscious elements to come into consciousness (S. Freud, 1960). Consciousness is everything above the repression barrier.

This complex concept is worth a bit more explanation, especially because of its relevance to human functioning and the effect it has on the interviewing process. Freud discovered in his psychoanalytic interviewing and treatment of clients that many of the emotional distresses of life were managed by repression, placing them in the unconscious. As mentioned above, a child may experience a traumatic event, and in order to emotionally protect herself, push it out of awareness, through repression, into the unconscious. Although it is in the unconscious, the experience is still tied to emotions related to the two drives of love and aggression. This unresolved conflict searches for an outlet, which, if severe enough, can become an emotional symptom such as depression, a physical complaint, or socially unacceptable behavior and discomfort. Freud believed that a rewarding and happy life depends on the successful management of the instincts. Clients came to analysis because of emotional conflicts related to the unsuccessful management of the instincts.

Tripartite Theory

The topographic theory eventually evolved and expanded into Freud's tripartite theory, which explains the function and development of id, ego, and superego. The id houses the drives, and its contents are unconscious. The ego, according to Freud, develops out of the id's interaction with the world and serves as a mediator with the environment. A common metaphor for the ego/id interaction is a horse and rider. The horse is the id, and the rider is the ego. More specifically, this horse and rider are inseparable. The best that the rider, or ego, can do is to somewhat manage and contain the horse, or id, throughout life. The ego is the seat of conscious functioning in life. Aspects of the ego can be repressed and become unconscious, given a severe emotional conflict at any point in life.

The superego, much like the ego, forms in childhood as part of the id and ego. It serves as a moral conscience to the individual. According to Freud, all conflicts and aspects of life are a function of the interaction of these three entities and their interaction with the two drives (S. Freud, 1960).

The unconscious (id) contains the drives, while the ego and superego attempt to manage, suppress, and uncover conflicts in order to help the individual function in life. The role of the analyst is to help the client gain insight and relative mastery over emotional conflicts in order to live a better life. The process of psychoanalysis or the psychoanalytic interview served as the vehicle through which the client could be cured. Free association was the technique, along with carefully timed interpretations aimed at insight. This was one of the very first professional interviewing processes (S. Freud, 1940). Freud discovered that if clients, through psychoanalytic interviewing, relaxed and talked about whatever came to their minds, invariably the emotional conflicts would rise to the surface, through the repression barrier, and be available for interpretation by the analyst. This insight allowed the client to be free of this conflict. This is a very simplistic description of the complex process of psychoanalysis, but it helps explain some of the historical origins of Freud's interviewing process.

Transference Theory

Freud's theory of transference is perhaps his most famous, and in many ways the most relevant to contemporary interviewing. He discovered this phenomenon through psychoanalytic work with clients. As mentioned above, free association was the fundamental technique in psychoanalytic interviewing. This process did not include the mutually interactive exchange customary in most modern-day interviewing. Psychoanalysis was a very strict and stilted process with a specific aim (S. Freud, 1940).

Through extensive psychoanalytic interviewing, Freud discovered that many clients resisted free association. The analyst dealt with this resistance by urging the client to free associate and break through the resistance. This was easier with some clients than with others. One client in particular resisted to such an extent that she began focusing her attention on Freud, to the exclusion of everything else. Her only communication was about him and her thoughts and ideas about his person, life, thoughts, emotions, and so on. Despite Freud's constant urging and determination, the client stayed on this course during her treatment.

After a prolonged struggle with this type of resistance, and thorough examination of these thoughts and emotions, Freud arrived at an important hypothesis. He realized that the client was reenacting earlier emotional struggles, scenarios, and situations symbolically in her analysis. The client was actually transferring these emotional situations onto Freud. With this insight Freud was able to help the client realize that she was reliving earlier emotional difficulties in the analytic interview with him. This eventual insight by the client enabled her to resolve these conflicts in much the same way as in free association alone. Freud came to recognize that not only was transference the most powerful element of psychoanalytic interviewing, it was the essential foundation for successful work. The relationship focus in the psychoanalytic interview held the seeds of the cure (S. Freud, 1940).

In addition to the transference theory, Freud discovered that the psychoanalyst may contribute to distortion and emotional entanglement through the unconscious introduction of his own unconscious emotional difficulties. The psychoanalyst, like the client, may react to, understand, and respond to the client as if she were some important figure from his own past. This potential difficulty can have devastating implications for any interview, and is probably as powerful and influential as the client's transference distortions. Freud stressed the importance of psychoanalysts' undergoing analysis themselves in order to minimize these difficulties. For the potential interviewer, having a basic understanding of the relational implications of the theory of transference can be an invaluable instrument in the interviewer's toolbox. Simply attempting to interview without a sufficient theoretical background, introspective awareness, and training can even be considered unethical. Because human relationships are complex and highly subjective, interviews of any type can be fraught with idiosyncratic distortions (S. Freud, 1940).

NEO-FREUDIAN THEORY

As Freud's psychoanalytic theories evolved, they became popular and attracted many followers. This group of theorists and practitioners worked with Freud and discussed many of his ideas. From these discussions came a number of new variations, modifications, and theoretical constructs. These theorists historically became known as the neo-Freudians (*neo* meaning new).

There were quite a number of neo-Freudians, far too many to adequately cover in this text. However, several are of particular importance to the interviewing process.

Alfred Adler (1870–1937)

Adler departed from many of Freud's ideas while developing and emphasizing the conscious life of the individual. Many believe that Adler was the first cognitive and family theorist, as well as the first clinical social worker. He emphasized the influence of the family and childhood experiences in shaping the personality of the individual. Adler did not believe it is necessary to delve deeply into the unconscious to resolve emotional conflicts, but instead focused more on the here and now as it is affected by family. He believed that one of the most important struggles in life is between feelings of inferiority and superiority and the need to have a balance between them. All problems in life, according to Adler, stem from occupational, social, and sexual challenges. He recognized that human beings live in a social and environmental world that strongly influences who they become and how they live. His intervention technique of exploring the client's first memory set the stage for all future work and has been used by many others in the field to this day (Adler, 1931).

Carl Jung (1875–1961)

Jung was especially well known for his theory of the collective unconscious, the life and death fear, the anima and animus, and the light and dark (shadow) sides of all human beings. Jung's interviewing technique was psychoanalytic, like Freud's: the client lay on a sofa in front of and facing away from the analyst, to facilitate free association without the distraction of seeing the analyst. Like Freud, Jung stressed the importance of the examination of dreams, and the spiritual nature of humanity in life. His theories give important insight into the human condition, especially as it relates to interviewing.

Jung believed that the unconscious is a much more expansive and universal phenomena than Freud originally proposed. The collective unconscious contains the entire emotional history of humanity in the form of symbolic characterizations Jung called archetypes. These archetypes are derived from primordial images that contain universal themes such as hero, villain, lover, mother, father, and sibling. The archetypes defy any specific definition, but contain a generalized form that emotionally resonates with every human being. In addition, Jung believed that each human being's experience contains elements of the archetypes and collective unconscious that are experienced, are modified, and contribute to the further evolution of the collective unconscious. In other words, all humanity is connected through the stable, yet personally dynamic and ever changing, collective unconscious. An individual's life is influenced by the specific archetypal process that is unique to his or her experiences. Jungian psychoanalytic technique was steeped in interpretive use of the collective unconscious and the archetypes.

Jung also believed that human beings struggle with a life and death fear. A pronounced life fear inhibits an individual's ability to trust, take risks, and move forward in a confident manner throughout life. The death fear is the more natural of the two, and something that all human beings come to terms with throughout life, but it does not necessarily drastically inhibit their life's journey.

The anima and animus concepts were also cornerstones of Jung's theories. He believed that contained within the collective unconscious and within all men and women are complementary male (animus) and female (anima) aspects of the personality. Women and men contain both feminine and masculine aspects. Furthermore, there is both a light and dark side to the collective unconscious as well as in every human being. Jung called the dark side the shadow. Jung believed that insight into one's shadow side enables one to live more freely and with less conflict. Put much more simply, being aware of one's aggressive possibilities and anger (without inappropriately acting on them) can be freeing. Knowing oneself is the key to knowing others and to a successful and fulfilling life (Jung, 1959).

Otto Rank (1884–1939)

Rank's main contribution to the development of psychological theory was his notion of the will as the guiding force in life. A human being's major struggle is between his or her will and the counterwill of society. He also emphasized the importance of birth as a source of anxiety and consequent struggles in development throughout life. Individual development for Rank was a three-step process. First, the individual comes to terms with his or her own will and the subsequent desires and process it exerts on life in the form of wants and needs. Second is the realization of the societal counterwill and the individual struggle to reconcile and compromise with it in order to exist in a manner that both conforms to society and meets the needs of the individual's will. Finally, the individual is able through this process to develop an integrated self that can function sufficiently and in a psychologically healthy manner. Problems in life arise from the difficulties in this three-step process (Rank, 1936).

Karen Horney (1885–1952)

Horney was one of the very few female neo-Freudians and perhaps the first psychoanalytic theorist to emphasize female development and the influence of culture on the individual. Like Adler and Rank, Horney focused the analytic process more on the problems of everyday life, while minimizing the conflicts of unconscious drives as the core issue of emotional difficulties. She, like several other theorists of her time, believed that life's problems are caused by anxiety that originates in infancy and early care. Neurosis, Horney believed, is contextual and influenced by culture and environment. However, she also stressed that early relationships with key caretakers shape, and to some extent solidify, personality styles that form the basis of potential problems in life and fundamental conflicts with others. For Horney, there are four main personality styles that can lead to neurotic difficulties (Horney, 1945).

First are those individuals who move toward others. In a psychologically healthy way, this style is adaptive and leads to cooperation, mutual dependence, and productive and satisfying social, occupational, and family life. Taken to its extreme, moving toward people can result in extreme dependence, personal uncertainty, and severe problems with autonomy.

The second personality style is moving away from others. In health this can be evidenced by confidence, autonomy, and the ability to successfully negotiate life on all levels in mutually satisfying ways. Taken to its negative extreme, moving away from others emphasizes detachment and estrangement in development and can result in an inability to connect with others on the personal, occupational, and societal levels, resulting in a lonely, isolated, and perhaps even schizoid existence.

The third personality style is moving against others. In a psychologically healthy way, this style leads to individuals capable of confident and socially appropriate assertiveness, similar to the moving away from others. When problematic, moving against others evolves from a basic lack of trust and can lead to severe interpersonal difficulties, lack of cooperation, and destructive relationships in life. In many ways, moving against people could be considered the most problematic style. Horney believed that these individuals tend to have minimal insight into their personality and as a result project and externalize their problems, that is, they are always someone else's fault.

The fourth personality style is the most positive, the idealized image. Although no one can ever be perfect, the idealized image emphasizes the individual's awareness that life and self are not perfect, and that healthy self-development consists of self-awareness and the realization and working through of the aspects of all three previous styles.

EGO PSYCHOLOGY

The ego psychologists followed the neo-Freudians. The main contribution of ego psychology was to further the examination and expansion of the concept, properties, and function of Freud's notion of the ego. Many theorists and practitioners were in the ego psychology camp. We see with the ego psychologists an even more pronounced move away from the more distant interviewing of traditional psychoanalysis, less focus on drive theory, and a broader expansion of development across the life span. One of the key differences between

Freud's notion of the ego and the ego psychologists' was that Freud believed the ego evolves from the id, whereas the ego psychologists believed that human beings are born with a primitive and rudimentary form of the ego, predisposed to certain developmental functions.

Harry Stack Sullivan (1892–1949): Anxiety in Development and Pathology

Sullivan focused extensively on the importance of anxiety as the defining and primary influence on development. Anxiety, he believed, begins at birth and defines the human personality through the way in which it is managed (and instilled) by the primary caretakers. Sullivan emphasized the importance of the influence of primary caretakers in shaping the form, content, and emphasis of anxiety in development. This is in some ways similar to Horney's focus on personality styles evolving from the relationship with others (Sullivan, 1953).

Sullivan believed that if anxiety is not managed successfully, it can lead to schizoid and perhaps even schizophrenic conditions. Extreme anxiety manifested in early primary relationships might cause the infant to turn inward and away from others as a form of self-protection. Pathologically, this process can result in a schizoid individual.

The adolescent period was of great importance to Sullivan because of the precarious way in which young people manage anxiety and the early development of mature personality. He believed that the adolescent maturation process includes a strong tendency to fantasize, daydream, and dissociate in the process of understanding and defining one's identity. This type of mental functioning is not possible prior to adolescence because the brain does not have the capacity for abstract thought. Adolescents spend a great deal of time in their own minds, contemplating a variety of key concepts, ideas, wishes, and so forth. They also use this time to solve many of life's challenges. Sullivan believed that, taken too far, this dissociative process can turn inward and result in pathology, such as psychotic or schizophrenic conditions, as the adolescent begins to actually live in that inner world instead of real life. This is an important insight in light of what we now know, that the schizophrenic condition develops in adolescence and young adulthood. Although schizophrenia is most likely an organic condition, Sullivan's ideas provide a possible explanation of the inner emotional process of the development of psychosis at this stage of life.

Heinz Hartmann (1894–1970): Conflict-Free Ego Sphere and Adaptation

Along with Erik Erikson, Heinz Hartmann is one of the most influential ego psychologists. Hartmann's monumental contribution came from his book *Ego Psychology and the Problem of Adaptation* (1958). Prior to Hartmann's work, Freud defined the processes and development of the ego as manifested in drive conflict and resolution. In other words, all functions in life are connected in some way with drive impulses and the instincts. Hartmann postulated that parts of the ego are inherently conflict-free. He called them "Conflict-Free Ego Spheres." In other words, they do not develop from the instincts or a drive conflict: these functions evolve apart from the drives. Perception, memory, mobility, and other key functions in life develop on their own, Hartmann believed, without any attachment to instincts. Although many functions were believed to be primarily conflict-free, they can become secondarily attached to the drives through emotional conflicts in life. Hysterical blindness due to trauma might be an example of this type of secondary conflict.

This key theoretical concept expanded the realm of ego development and the way in which adaptation could be understood as a process that did not always include drive discharge or conflict resolution. Hartmann believed that human beings have some capability to function independently of the drives (Hartmann, 1958). In many ways this resonates with Rank's notion of the will (Rank, 1936).

Anna Freud (1895–1982): Defense Mechanisms and Therapeutic Play

Besides being Sigmund Freud's daughter, Anna Freud's major claims to fame were her expansion of the definition and understanding of ego defense mechanisms, and establishing the importance of play as a therapeutic vehicle in assessing, understanding, and working with children (A. Freud, 1936).

Although Sigmund Freud and many of his followers discussed the defensive functions of the ego in managing drive conflicts in everyday life, Anna Freud expanded and refined those specific functions. She devoted much of her writing to delineating the primitive ego defenses, for example, projection, splitting, and denial, as well as the more mature and psychologically healthy ways in which human beings manage their emotions in life, for example, sublimation, intellectualization, and rationalization (A. Freud, 1936). This expansive and detailed repertoire enables interviewers to have a more comprehensive understanding of the management of emotions in the interviewing process.

Another major contribution was Anna Freud's work with children in play therapy. Unlike other theorists of her time, Freud believed that children's difficulties can be understood and helped through the examination of the symbolic features of their play. Play, Freud believed, represents a safe, displaced, and symbolic format in which to reenact and work through emotional conflicts in the real world. By actually playing with children and allowing them in the interview to unknowingly (unconsciously) symbolize situations through the use of dolls, stuffed animals, toys, and drawings, the underlying meanings (and solutions) can be ascertained by a skillful interviewer. In fact, Freud demonstrated that this clinical process can produce relief without any discussion of the actual events in real life. In other words, the therapeutic playing itself is curative (A. Freud, 1936). This process of play therapy has withstood the test of time and is used today in a variety of disciplines and fashions, especially for children with special needs such as autism.

Erik Erikson (1902–94): The Eight Ages of Man and Ego Development

Undoubtedly the most influential of the ego psychologists was Erik Erikson. He was the first theorist beyond Freud who developed a comprehensive theory of human emotional development throughout the life cycle. Erikson studied many cultures and worked extensively as a psychoanalyst to derive his theory of the epigenetic "Eight Ages of Man" (Erikson, 1950).

Building upon Freud's psychosexual stages, Erikson proposed that human beings are compelled by drives, emotions, and society to move through discrete yet overlapping stages defined by key life challenges. The successful resolution of the challenges within each of these stages affects individuals' success in meeting the next stage as well as their overall success in life. Human beings, Erikson felt, can become fixated (emotionally stuck or unresolved) in any stage, but are still compelled by life to move into the next stage because of their age, physiology, and societal pressure. For example, an adolescent may not successfully resolve the stage of "identity versus role confusion," but she will chronologically be pushed into adulthood regardless of the emotional work left over from the previous stage. This difficulty obviously presents some challenges in entering subsequent stages and inevitably signals a need to go back and work through that previous stage.

Erikson's eight stages are (1) trust versus mistrust, (2) autonomy versus shame and doubt, (3) initiative versus guilt, (4) industry versus inferiority, (5) identity versus role confusion, (6) intimacy versus isolation, (7) generativity versus stagnation, and (8) integrity versus despair. The continuum of life challenge inherent in each stage is compelling and represents the wide range of possible outcomes. Each stage or phase is somewhat fluid, indicating the possibility of revisiting and reworking all of them throughout life's experiences. The epigenetic chart also represents the possibility that previous stages can be influenced by subsequent ones in both positive and negative ways. Erikson's contribution dramatically and dynamically broadened the understanding of human emotional life (Erikson, 1950).

OBJECT RELATIONS THEORY

The next historical shift in psychological theory came with the advent of the so-called object relations theorists and practitioners. Until this group arose, interviewing and practice focused on the drives and the ego. The object relations theorists believed that the primary driving force in life is the need for an emotional connection or attachment to another, the object. They did not dismiss or ignore the drives, but relegated them to a subordinate position relative to the need for object relationships with others. Through a successful emotional relationship with the primary caretaker(s), the human infant gradually internalizes the ability to self-soothe as well as to develop relative autonomy and independence in life. The extent, quality, and nature of this process dictate and predict the emotional health and well-being of the individual throughout life. The focus in interviewing is on helping a client recognize and repair deficits in object relations, by providing a nurturing therapeutic environment in which new object structures (starting with the relationship with the interviewer) can be established and carried on with others.

The object relationists are far too numerous a group to be covered in this text. Two key theorists, D. W. Winnicott and Margaret Mahler, are discussed here.

D. W. Winnicott (1896–1971): Early Relationships

Winnicott is responsible for a variety of significant object relations theories, all of which delve into the importance of the early relationship with the primary caretaker(s). In order for the infant to successfully develop an emotional self, capable of self-soothing and object constancy (relative emotional autonomy), she must be provided with a "good enough holding environment." The holding environment, according to Winnicott, is the physical and emotional space that helps the infant feel safe and secure enough to be relatively spontaneous in her interactions with others. If the holding environment does not provide this safety, the infant is too overwhelmed with issues of safety and emotional security to develop a healthy ability to function in the world. Instead, her sense of self would develop in an uncertain world of anxiety, stress, and even trauma.

The mirroring role in development is a concept that Winnicott developed to explain the way in which infants come to know their emotions and through this process develop a stable and secure sense of self. Specifically, the look in the caretaker's eyes and his or her facial expressions in response to the infant's gestures reflect the infant's emotions. In other words, an infant without this consistent and reliable process does not know what she is feeling. That ability comes from the mirror of reflection in the caretaker's face, a reliable recognition of the infant's affect (Winnicott, 1965). This theory has been recently verified through contemporary neuroscience research and the discovery of mirror neurons (Cozolino, 2002).

Transitional Objects, Space, and Transitional Phenomena

According to Winnicott, if the holding environment is "good enough," infants gradually develop a sense of confidence that allows them to act with relative spontaneity in their environment. Spontaneous gestures are typically in the form of play, usually around the feeding process in the transitional space between infants and caretakers. In fact, Winnicott believed that this process enables infants to feel a sense of omnipotence in their environment and creates the illusion that everything comes to them as they need it. Ultimately, there are inevitable frustrations and anxiety (Winnicott called them impingements), but the successful development of this confidence helps infants manage them. This came about, Winnicott hypothesized, because infants can create a transitional object that serves a self-soothing function in the absence of the caretaker. This transitional object is "found" or "created" in play and was called the "first NOT ME" possession by Winnicott. The transitional object can be virtually anything: a teddy bear, blanket, piece of cloth, self-made sound or touch, and so on. What is important is that it represents the emotional functions of caretakers and serves to successfully transition or emotionally soothe infants when alone and in the absence of the primary caretakers until they return (Winnicott, 1971). This transitional object is needed as infants gradually learn to self-soothe and become relatively "object constant" (emotionally autonomous). Winnicott believed that the transitional object is "abandoned" and unnecessary once infants internalize its qualities and develop the ability to provide what the transitional object once did for them. In other words, those object functions become a part of the self.

Key for Winnicott was the inherent creative ability derived from the transitional phenomena process. He believed that once infants successfully acquire the ability to have confidence in their capacity to relatively manage themselves, that process becomes the cornerstone of creativity, confidence, and success in life. In other words, the infants' experience helps them to feel a sense of belief in themselves and to trust life (Winnicott, 1971).

The Capacity to Be Alone

In a process similar to that of transitional objects and phenomena, infants or young children can feel comfortable being alone only if they first have that experience in the presence of a trusted caretaker. Once again, play is the vehicle for this process. The child lost in play in the presence of a trusted other "forgets" that the other is there, and eventually can feel relative comfort in being alone. The key, however, according to Winnicott, is earlier establishment of a sense of trust in the presence of another (Winnicott, 1965).

The Capacity for Concern

Winnicott also contributed the theory of the capacity for concern in the child. He believed that children's sense of moral development is in many ways shaped by the extent to which they internalize and become dependent upon trusted caretakers. Winnicott believed that the realization of the possibility and fear of losing those caretakers influences the extent to which the child demonstrates concern for them (Winnicott, 1965).

Ego Distortion in Terms of True and False Self

Finally (though not necessarily in this order), Winnicott developed the theory of "ego distortions in terms of true and false self" (1965). Like many of his other theories, the continuum of a true and false self in ego development centers upon infants' ability to have experienced a consistent, reliable, and "good enough" holding environment early in life. With this experience, infants find the ability to function at times in relative spontaneity, expressing their true self as it is realized through socially acceptable aspects of the id. In other words, the child is able to live authentically and in a socially acceptable way. For example, a college student might not want to be in class listening to what he feels to be a boring lecture, but instead back at his dorm playing video games with his friends. This person realizes that his college education is important, however, and that proper behavior in class is required for a good/passing grade. So even though he may really not want to be in class, he comes, acts appropriately, and may even doodle on a piece of paper to feign attentiveness, all the while watching the clock in anticipation of leaving class. This behavior demonstrates his ability to function in society while still being himself and recognizing his "true self" needs (video gaming), which will come later. By the same token, an unhealthy false self may develop when infants cannot find ways of expressing spontaneity, but instead are forced to comply with the wishes of others, never finding expression of their authenticity. Abused and neglected children are classic examples of the unhealthy false self, but many other more subtle forms of relationship can create the same type of personality. Winnicott did not believe that anyone could live in a genuine and ongoing "true self" state, because it would be an uncensored version of the id. That type of raw instinctual be-havior would be socially unacceptable. However, emotionally sound individuals do learn how to use their "healthy" false self to meet emo-tional and physical needs while operating at a socially acceptable level.

All of Winnicott's theories discussed above center on the concept of object relations and the process by which the self forms through the internalization of emotional objects in the real world. Trust, safety, confidence, authenticity, concern for others, self-soothing, and object constancy are all by-products of the object relations scenarios of early life.

Margaret Mahler (1897–1985): The Separation-Individuation Process

Mahler, like Winnicott, believed in and studied the emotional process of separation-individuation as a cornerstone of life. Whereas much of Winnicott's work consisted of the examination of anecdotal case stud-ies and interviews with children and adults, Mahler was one of the first to study the real-time interactions of mothers and infants in the separation-individuation process. Through a series of highly structured laboratory experiments with mothers and infants, Mahler demonstrated that there seem to be specific stages in the separation-individuation process that ultimately lead to object constancy. Specifically, Mahler studied the ways in which infants reacted to being temporarily separated (usually a matter of minutes) from their mothers at different developmental periods in the first few years of life. This groundbreaking research led to Mahler's theory of the separation-individuation timetable, which hypothesized specific emotional states and behaviors in infants that depend upon where infants are on those timelines. The separation-individuation process moves from a period of total dependence, which Mahler called symbiosis, to a state of relative emotional autonomy, called object constancy. This crucial developmental timetable occurs over approximately the first three years of life. Generally, infants move from a total dependence on the mother to a gradual ability to venture away, returning for emotional refueling and safety, eventually achieving a relative state of emotional autonomy or object constancy.

One of the most pivotal phases in Mahler's theory is the rapprochement phase. During this period, around eighteen months to three years, the infant is in a continual process of moving toward and away from the mother in order to test his independence and autonomy. The mother's key role in this process is to allow the infant to negotiate it. In other words, when the infant wants to be dependent, the mother should be empathic, understanding, and permissive (within reason). What is important is to not reject or push the infant away when he seems to need to be dependent. By the same token, when the infant wants to be independent, the mother should also be accepting and tolerant (within reason) of this need, and not interrupt or cling to him. Mahler theorized (and demonstrated through her research) that what is happening emotionally and psychologically within infants is the internalization and ability to develop a sense of confidence in negotiating the world around them without debilitating anxiety. Infants learn through the relationship with empathic caretakers that the world is relatively safe, and that they can feel confidence in themselves through becoming object constant.

Like Winnicott, Mahler demonstrated through her research the actual process by which object constancy might be accomplished. Both Winnicott and Mahler emphasized the importance of consistent and reliable caretaking, as well as the crucial necessity for the development of object constancy as a key to emotional and psychological life. Implicit in their work as well is that pathology can develop if object constancy is not achieved (Mahler, Pine, & Bergman, 1975; Winnicott, 1965, 1971).

HUMANISTIC APPROACH

The humanistic approach to psychology developed in the midtwentieth century. This approach focuses on the holistic nature of the individual and a belief in human beings' actualizing tendency (Rogers, 1965). The focus on the relationship with the interviewer is paramount, and essential in the curative process. It was during this period that many, if not all, of the important interviewing techniques used today were identified and tested. There were many influential theorists in this time period, including Maslow (1943), who developed the theory of human beings' "hierarchy of needs," from basic survival needs to the self-actualizing tendency; but in terms of the interviewing process, there was probably no one more important than Carl Rogers.

Carl Rogers (1902–87): Client-Centered Therapy

Rogers, like Maslow, believed in the self-actualizing tendency of all human beings. He believed that we are goal directed and hold the capacity within ourselves to be successful. Problems in living, or so-called pathology, Rogers felt, are the result of experiences in life that create cognitive dissonance among the beliefs, values, and ideals of the individual. For example, a young child growing up with an alcoholic father may initially feel good about herself and her capabilities, but come to doubt those qualities as a result of the unfounded, insecure, and self-centered criticisms of her father. These beliefs can form the core of the child's identity, which affects the confidence with which she approaches life. A corrective emotional therapeutic experience in client-centered therapy can help the client overcome the cognitive dissonance between her inherent self-concept and that which has been imposed upon her from childhood because of her alcoholic father's diminishment of her abilities and self-esteem.

Rogers believed in the curative power of empathy and the capacity of the client to change, through a nonjudgmental therapeutic relationship. The role of the interviewer in client-centered therapy is to listen carefully to the client's perspective or viewpoint, without judgment, offering advice, or guidance. Interviewing responses or "techniques" are aimed at providing empathy alone. That process allows the client to feel understood, not critiqued, interpreted, or analyzed. Rogers truly believed that clients know best what they feel and the meaning of their lives, not the interviewer. The interviewing process of client-centered therapy may sound simple, but it requires a well-trained and dedicated interviewer. Suspending one's judgment, values, and opinions (even in one's mind) takes a great deal of restraint and discipline. Rogers called upon the interviewer to provide "active listening," a process of vicarious introspection, in order to truly understand clients and reflect that empathy to them. It is also important to have "unconditional positive regard" for clients. This means truly believing in the clients' capacity to know themselves and their difficulties, and to improve their lives. This process does not happen in isolation; it requires a client-centered interviewer with a special belief system and a set of interviewing skills aimed at providing an empathic relationship and process that facilitates change in the client (Rogers, 1965).

Rogers's client-centered theory/therapy has withstood the test of time and has been incorporated into many mainstream therapy models, such as motivational interviewing (Miller & Rollnick, 2002). What is presently called person-centered therapy stems from Rogers's original work. Most social work and psychology textbooks use some form of Rogerian principles and techniques in training students on both the graduate and undergraduate levels (Hollis & Woods, 1964; Hepworth,

Rooney, Rooney, Strom-Gottfried, & Larsen, 2006; Zastrow, 2010). One of the main reasons for this is that Rogers was one of the first to test the effectiveness of empathy through studying actual cases of client-centered therapy (Rogers, 1965). This research, combined with extensive anecdotal and verbatim interviewer-client interactions, provided compelling evidence of the power and effectiveness of empathy and the role of the interviewer in facilitating improvement (Rogers, 1965).

SELF PSYCHOLOGY

Like object relations theory, self psychology emphasizes the importance of the relationship with early caretakers in the development of the emotional self. Self psychologists believed that through a successful internalization process, the infant is able to establish a relatively secure sense of self that helps manage life. Heinz Kohut was the theorist and practitioner who developed self psychology.

Heinz Kohut (1913–81): Self Psychology

In his traditional psychoanalytic work with "so-called" narcissistic personality disordered clients, Kohut discovered that strict interpretation was not helpful and in many instances seemed to disrupt and even damage the therapeutic relationship. Through trial and error, much like Sigmund Freud before him, Kohut modified his interviewing techniques to be more empathically focused, which appeared to be more helpful to his clients.

This shift in technique led Kohut to create an entirely new theory of development of the self that, in many ways, was drastically different from Freud's psychoanalytic theory (Kohut, 1971). Kohut believed (much like the ego psychologists and object relation theorists) that the infant is born with a rudimentary nuclear self. This nuclear self develops in accord with the way in which the primary caretakers respond to the child in the first few years of life. Kohut theorized that all human beings are driven by three basic relational needs: mirroring, merger, and twinship. These basic needs were defined by Kohut as self-object needs. They are provided initially by the primary caretaker(s), and are continually provided to a lesser extent through relationships with significant others throughout life. The caretakers are the self-objects for the infant, as are many others to a greater or lesser extent in life. Mirroring is the self-object need to feel admired and appreciated through the eyes of the caretakers and their genuine positive reflection (mirroring) of the infant's accomplishments and abilities. This self-object need corresponds to what Kohut called the grandiose self in the infant. Successful mirroring enables the grandiose self to become established in the infant. Merging is the self-object need to feel connected with an idealized other. It corresponds to the idealized parental imago. Initially, infants possess only an archaic sense of narcissism or self-worth. The provision of merging self-object functions by the primary caretakers gradually helps infants internalize a sense of their own value as it is gleaned from the primary caretakers and internalized into the nuclear self. Finally, Kohut postulated that infants also have a self-object need for twinship, which is provided by the primary caretakers in the form of the alter-ego self-object function. Twinship self-object needs are defined as the ability to feel like another: to recognize shared experiences, talents, ideas, emotions, and so forth. Like the grandiose self and idealized parental imago, the alter-ego self-object functions provide the infant's nuclear self with the emotional sustenance needed to eventually internalize those abilities and become a part of a cohesive self capable of providing those self-object needs without the continual presence of caretakers (Kohut, 1971).

Kohut identified the process by which self-objects become sufficiently internalized into the infant's nuclear self, resulting in a cohesive self. He called it transmuting internalization. Simply put, the process of taking in self-objects is not a perfect process. There are inevitable disappointments or disruptions in all three self-object areas (mirroring, merging, and twinship). If the frustration that results from these inevitable disruptions is "optimal," however, infants will be able to rely upon and draw from their rudimentary self-object formations (already provided by the primary caretakers) in order to weather the disruption. In essence, according to Kohut, this is how a healthy cohesive self develops. By the same token, constant disruptions and inconsistencies in self-object provision by the primary caretakers can lead to self-object deficits, as well as fragile, incomplete, and fragmented individuals. These types of people will have narcissistic deficits and disturbances that, taken to the extreme, evidence themselves as narcissistic personality traits or disorders (Kohut, 1971).

Individuals with these deficits may be mirror-, merger-, or twinship-hungry throughout life. Kohut believed that the need for self-objects is most pronounced in infancy, but they are needed to some extent throughout life, in much the same way human beings need food, oxygen, and other forms of sustenance to survive. The dynamic balance in life depends on a successful combination of the grandiose self, idealized parental imago, and alter-ego self-object properties. Kohut described this as the "Tension-Arc." The extent to which these needs were successfully accomplished dictates an individual's confidence in his or her abilities (grandiose self), belief in self (idealized parental imago), and a feeling of connection to others (alter-ego; Kohut, 1971).

From a self psychology perspective, clients come to the interview with a basic need to be repaired because of the nature, quality, and quantity of self-object deficits in life. The self psychology interviewer's role is to help repair and create new self-objects through an empathic therapeutic relationship. The interviewer can become the mirroring, merging, and twinship self-objects for the client. The therapeutic process is aimed at identifying these needs and providing optimal gratification for clients in order to help them live a more satisfying life. This was accomplished through mirroring, merging, and twinship transferences (where needed) with the client (Kohut, 1971).

COGNITIVE-BEHAVIORAL THEORY AND THERAPY

Behavioral and cognitive theories and approaches were initially viewed and developed as separate entities. Pavlov, B. F. Skinner, and other behaviorists focused primarily on the importance of stimulus-response and various forms of conditioning as a key explanation for human behavior (Pavlov, 1927; Skinner, 1976). On the other hand, cognitive theorists such as Beck and Ellis believed that problems in the human condition are the result of faulty or irrational beliefs (Beck, 1975; Ellis, 1973). Bandura (1962) in many ways attempted to bridge the two theories through his emphasis on social learning theory, which seemed to combine aspects of both behavioral and cognitive approaches. Most present-day interviewers and practitioners who use behavioral and cognitive theories combine them into a cognitive-behavioral model.

Albert Ellis (1913–2007): The Rational Emotive Behavioral Approach

Albert Ellis is best known for his rational emotive behavior therapy, or humanistic psychotherapy, as he called it. He believed that problems in living can be traced to irrational belief systems, which in turn result in faulty or self-defeating behaviors. Although Ellis was influenced by many earlier theorists, he did not focus on the unconscious or instincts. Instead, he developed a very directive approach to interviewing and instructing the client to think and act in different ways. He believed that by changing one's thinking, behavior will also change. For example, if someone felt insecure in his or her life, Ellis would not go to great lengths to explore the origins of that insecurity in the past. Instead, he would examine the current, specific, and immediate problems, and help instruct clients to realize that they alone were the cause of their problems, due to an irrational belief system, regardless of its historical origins or duration. His approach was a "here and now" interviewing and therapeutic model (Ellis, 1973).

Aaron Beck (1921–): Cognitive-Behavioral Therapy

Aaron Beck, like Ellis, focused on the thinking process and resulting behaviors as the reason for problems in human functioning in life. More specifically, he theorized that the origins of emotional problems stem from a core belief system that influences thoughts and behaviors starting early in life. Although Beck did not focus on the unconscious as Freud defined it, he did believe in what he called cognitive "schemas" (Beck, 1975). These schemas are the basis for the core belief system. Some of them can easily be accessed by clients—in other words, are more in their awareness—while others are at a deeper level and require greater exploration to uncover. For example, a surface-oriented schema might be "I am not a good worker." The deeper schema related to that complaint might be "I am worthless and will never amount to anything." The interviewer in Beck's cognitive-behavioral therapy builds a relationship with the client in whom these belief systems can be identified, and helps construct behavioral plans and exercises to help stop the negative thinking and change the subsequent behaviors (Beck, 1975).

Alfred Bandura (1925–): Social Learning Theory

Another theorist in the cognitive-behavioral camp is Alfred Bandura. Bandura developed social learning theory. Like Ellis, Beck, and other cognitive-behavioral theorists, Bandura emphasized the importance of thoughts and behavior as they are influenced by significant others. One of his most important concepts is that of "modeling." Bandura believed that children learn to act and behave through imitating the behaviors of the people around them. He did not, for example, believe that human beings are necessarily predisposed to certain behaviors, as in Freud's drive theory. The interviewer in Bandura's approach helps clients identify the modeling source of their difficulties in order to adopt more socially acceptable forms of behavior. Social learning theory has far-reaching implications and applications to parenting, teaching, coaching, and other influential relationships in life (Bandura, 1969).

SYSTEMS THEORIES

Surprisingly, most if not all psychological theory from the late 1800s to the mid-1960s focused almost exclusively on the individual. Although the parents, family, significant others, and environment were inferred to be important elements in developmental life, there were virtually no significant, comprehensive theories that attempted to explain them at any great length. This gap has been filled by a number of models. The ecological approach and family therapy models are discussed here.

Carel Germain (1916–95): The Ecological Approach

Carel Germain, a social worker, developed the ecological approach through her studies of systems theory. The ecological approach, or life model as it later came to be known, emphasized the importance of the "person in their environment." The ecological approach was not a comprehensive theory, but an important framework with which to understand the influence of the environment in the life of any individual (Gitterman & Germain, 1980).

Germain and her colleague Alex Gitterman emphasized the importance of the interviewer's examination of the client's "fit with the environment" as a crucial assessment factor in any type of treatment. One of the important interviewing tools, especially for the social work and nursing professions, that grew out of the ecological assessment is the ecogram, or eco-map. An eco-map is a diagram with a series of circles depicting the client's (individual or family) life environment. The client is represented as a circle in the center of the diagram, with various types of circles connected to the client's circle by a series of lines of different intensity, length, and so forth that represent the nature and importance of their influence in the client's life. For example, work, friends, school, church, family, and other key areas of life can all be drawn to emphasize the nature of their impact on the client's life. The eco-map helps the interviewer gain a comprehensive overview of clients' fit with their environment and important areas of possible exploration in the helping process (Gitterman & Germain, 1980).

Murray Bowen (1913–90): Differentiation in Family Systems

Murray Bowen and most other family therapy theorists were trained as psychoanalysts. All of them were well steeped in Freudian theory and psychoanalytic technique. What led them to develop family therapy theories was the frustration they experienced in trying to apply psychoanalysis to family situations. As a result, each family theorist developed a particular version of family systems concepts as they related to his or her practical experiences.

Bowen's family systems theory is arguably the most complex and sophisticated of all family therapy approaches. Bowen's concepts illuminated the individual's process of development within the family and, moreover, the emotional health of the family system itself. Perhaps the key concept in Bowen's work is that of "differentiation." Differentiation is the process by which children develop an identity that is distinct from the family, to the extent to which it allows them to function in a state of healthy autonomy. Although similar to theories of separation-individuation, Bowen's emphasis was not on object constancy or emotional autonomy apart from the caretaker. Instead, Bowen stressed the importance of feeling a sense of self apart from being a member of the family. In addition, he created a number of key concepts such as "triangulation," "emotional cut-off," and "family projection process," which will be considered at length in chapter 5 (Bowen, 1978).

The genogram, an assessment tool similar to the eco-map described above, is a diagram of the structure of the family generational system, including marriages, children, divorce, adoption, death, and many other pivotal family dynamics. The interviewer uses the genogram to help the family visualize and discuss not only the reality of the family constellations, but also the inherent strengths and weaknesses in the family itself and the individuals within it. The genogram is a powerful and instructive tool in working with families. Interviewers from a Bowenian perspective are educational in their approach, believing that once the family had insight regarding their dynamics, they would be able to change them (Bowen, 1978).

Salvador Minuchin (1913–90): Joining the Family System

A contemporary of Bowen's, Salvador Minuchin also became frustrated with traditional psychoanalysis as an approach to helping families. Minuchin, like Bowen and others, developed key theoretical concepts to help explain, assess, and work with families. He focused on the power differential within the family, using concepts such as "subsystems," "boundaries," "enmeshment," and "scapegoating" to describe, assess, understand, and work with the family. Minuchin believed it was important to become a part of any family system with which he worked, in a process he called "joining." Through this very active process, he was able to help the family experience the family dynamics and subsequently change their behaviors. Some of Minuchin's interviewing techniques were highly controversial, including provocatively challenging family interactions and instructing family members to unwittingly act in paradoxical ways with each other in order to "experience" family difficulties (Minuchin, 1974). Minuchin's approach is further explored in chapter 5.

ATTACHMENT AND RELATIONAL THEORIES

The attachment theorists focused on the particular styles of emotional relatedness that form in early infancy and childhood and the implications of these attachments styles throughout life. Although there are many classic and contemporary attachment theorists and practitioners, the focus here is on John Bowlby's contributions because his work set the stage for all subsequent attachment theory.

The relational theorists are a more recent group of contributors to the understanding of the interviewing process and relationship. Most of their work stems from an expansion of countertransference theory. Countertransference concepts as well as the understanding and application of them to interviewing have been evolving since Freud's original development of the concept in unison with the theory of transference (S. Freud, 1940). The "classical" position on countertransference posited that the interviewer (analyst) must be aware of her own emotional conflicts and the possible ways in which these unresolved conflicts might pollute the interviewing process. Once successfully analyzed, the interviewer could eliminate the possibility of having her emotional conflicts disrupt the process with the client. The advent of object relations and self psychology theories, with their emphasis on the therapeutic importance of the relationship, introduced the notion of the "totalist" position on countertransference. This expansive group of practitioners and theorists recognized that countertransference contributions were ubiquitous, inevitable, and a necessary and (if properly handled) helpful aspect in interviewing. Although the interviewer may be aware of and have insight regarding her emotional conflicts, the effects of those conflicts can never be entirely eliminated from the interviewing process. The totalists believed it is important to be continually cognizant of their own contributions to the interviewing process. Finally, the "specialist" camp further expanded the countertransference phenomena by acknowledging that all interviewing is an intermingling of the emotional, cognitive, and behavioral contributions of both the interviewer and client. Each relationship is unique, as is the exchange between the interviewer and client, based upon their life circumstances and emotional constitution (Tansey & Burke, 1989). It was out of this understanding that the relational approach developed.

The attachment and relational models are grouped together here because of their special emphasis on the mutual contributions of interviewer and client. The ways in which these individuals interact is especially influenced by their unique histories and capabilities.

John Bowlby (1907–90): Attachment Theory

Bowlby's most important contribution to the interviewing process was his identification of the various attachment styles that infants develop early in life. As mentioned above, all human beings come into this world with a certain predisposition or constitution for certain types of attachment to others. The seminal work of Bowlby and others identified four main attachment styles as well as the process of attachment in infancy and early childhood (Bowlby, 1969).

Secure attachment is the most emotionally healthy state, derived from a positive relationship with the primary caretaker. Infants with secure attachment styles negotiate their emotional world with relative ease, leading to the development of adults who are capable of so-called "normal emotional autonomy and object constancy." Anxious attachment infants can be irritable and need a great deal of reassurance. They are often very dependent in their interactions and emotionally unstable unless reassured and soothed by key others. Adults with anxious attachments are typically nervous individuals in most key areas of life, especially in important emotional relationships. Avoidant infants tend to move away from others as a way of protecting themselves, not in the normal sense of autonomy development. These individuals tend to become much more oppositional, distant, and even schizoid in adulthood. Finally, some infants demonstrate a combination of these more dysfunctional styles, called "disorganized attachment." These infants are the most emotionally challenged, shifting from anxious to avoidant styles with chronic unpredictability. In adulthood this may evidence itself in what could be considered personality disorders.

Key to understanding the attachment styles and process is the fact that constitution and caretaking are the crucial intermingling factors that shape the infant. Some infants are simply born with a certain emotional predisposition, while others have an attachment style that can be heavily influenced by their interactions with caretakers and the environment in which they live. It is of great importance to remember that attachment is a complex, multifaceted process.

Daniel Stern (1934–2012): Infant Research

The work of Daniel Stern is of pivotal importance to interviewing. Along with other key developmental theorists, Stern's contributions expand upon earlier theories of human development and provide important connections among the work of attachment theorists such as Bowlby, relational theorists and practitioners, and recent advances in neuroscience. The significance of Stern's work lies in its base empirical infant research; it has profound implications for understanding development and clinical practice, especially interviewing. Through the study of infants, he postulates a developmental progression of overlapping and ongoing phases: the sense of an emergent self, sense of a core self, sense of a subjective self, and sense of a verbal self.

The emphasis in Stern's work is on the very early importance of the intersubjective experience of the infant with the primary caretaker, especially pre- and nonverbal communication such as vitality affects, and how those experiences shape a sense of self almost from the moment of birth. He believed and demonstrated, through performing and examining infant research studies in the late twentieth century, the myriad of ways in which infants process and understand their world. Stern's work challenges the long-held assumptions of psychoanalytic, ego psychology, and object relations theorists that an infant's symbiotic merger with the primary caretaker at birth presupposes the inability to have a self until many months into development (Stern, 2000). His ideas will be explored in greater length through the practical interviewing examples in subsequent chapters.

Fred McKenzie (1951–): Relational Therapy

In *Understanding and Managing the Therapeutic Relationship* (2011), I focused extensively on the mutual contributions of both interviewer and client in the therapeutic process. That work combines contemporary countertransference, relational, attachment, and neuroscience theories and technique. Its theory and technique are more tightly aligned with relational models than with anything else. The key emphasis is to understand the environment and the essential emotional contributions from the interviewer and client, in order to develop an effective relationship and therapeutic process.

Of utmost importance to the success of interviewing and therapeutic work in general, regardless of discipline, is a comprehensive understanding of the dynamic of both interviewer and client. Dynamics include the physical constitution, emotional makeup, developmental contributions, and subtle intersubjective matrix that come to life in the professional interview and therapeutic relationship. The interviewer uses working models of interviewer and client, bringing constant awareness and sensitivity to the ongoing contributions and evolving intersubjective nature of the relationship with the client (McKenzie, 2011).

NEUROSCIENCE

For decades, interviewers could provide little or no empirical or research evidence of the success of their work. The case study and other anecdotal forms of information tended to be relied upon to demonstrate effectiveness. Cognitive-behavioral forms of interviewing were most successful in this process, because of the relative ease of operationalizing and measuring successful work. In other words, a particular problem could be identified (e.g., fear of flying); an intervention was performed (e.g., desensitization by gradual exposure); and the problem was resolved. The more complex psychological problems, even those with somatic components, were far too difficult to operationalize for definitive research explanation (Heineman Pieper, 1981). As a result, for years interviewing processes and clinical work were considered as much an art form as they were a science. Carl Rogers and others helped further the understanding of the potential success of interviewing, especially the role of empathy, but their methods were also empirically weak in many respects (Rogers, 1965).

Daniel Stern's study of infant research and the advance of neuroscience over the past decade has changed that perception. Through the empirical study of the brain, we now know and understand much more about how the brain functions, and more important, how the process of interviewing and clinical work can actually change and heal the brain. This new information has provided important empirical evidence regarding the success of interviewing (Cozolino, 2002). Louis Cozolino's work and the important contributions of the *Psychodynamic Diagnostic Manual* (PDM) are explored here to give a small taste of this valuable work.

Louis Cozolino (1953–): Neuroscience

In his 2002 book, *The Neuroscience of Psychotherapy: Building and Rebuilding the Human Brain*, and the 2010 revised edition, *The Neuroscience of Psychotherapy: Healing the Social Brain*, Cozolino used a careful and comprehensive discussion of neuroscience research to dramatically demonstrate the actual changes that can occur in the brain through a carefully targeted interviewing process. He discussed a wide range of approaches that, if used in informed differential ways, can heal the brain. This information and insight regarding important neuroscience concepts such as neurogenesis, neural plasticity, mirror neurons, and neural networks in general has elevated the empirical and scientific knowledge of the interviewing process (Cozolino, 2002, 2010).

Psychodynamic Diagnostic Manual: *Contemporary Diagnosis*

For decades the *Diagnostic and Statistical Manual of Mental Disorders* (DSM) has been a widely applied standard used to assess and diagnose clients for medical purposes. There have been five or more versions of this manual. The DSM is a derivative of the International Classification of Diseases (ICD) manual, which is used by medical personnel worldwide in treating all physical conditions.

After the fourth edition of the DSM was published, some of the most influential writers of the DSM developed the *Psychodynamic Diagnostic Manual* (PDM; 2006), which has been heavily influenced by neuroscience research. The significance of the PDM for interviewing is that it greatly expands and elaborates upon the understanding of emotional functioning in order to better assess, plan, and carry out the interviewing process. The DSM contains five diagnostic areas: axis I, "Clinical Disorders"; axis II, "Personality Disorders and Mental Retardation"; axis III, "General Medical Conditions" (related to mental disorders); axis IV, "Psychosocial and Environmental Problems"; and axis V, "Global Assessment of Functioning." The PDM, informed by cutting-edge neuroscience research, has expanded and modified the DSM. The manual is broken down into three sections: part 1, "Classification of Adult Mental Health Disorders"; part 2, "Classification of Child and Adolescent Mental Health Disorders"; and perhaps most important, part 3, "Conceptual and Research Foundations for a Psychodynamically Based Classification System for Mental Disorders" (PDM, 2006).

The material within the PDM is far too lengthy and comprehensive to cover in this text. However, its value and importance lie in the fact that it is one of the few, if not the only, recent diagnostic tools that provide a major shift in understanding based upon empirical neuroscience research. It goes to great lengths to include many of the major scientific studies that validate its principles. Of particular note is the addition of several new axes with which to understand the client.

Part 1 of the PDM, "Classification of Adult Mental Health Disorders," is divided into three axes. The P axis examines personality patterns and disorders, the M axis provides a comprehensive profile of mental functioning, and the S axis looks at symptom patterns and the subjective experience of the client.

Part 2, "Classification of Child and Adolescent Mental Health Disorders," includes three axes. The MCA axis examines mental functioning in children and adolescents, the PCA axis looks at personality patterns and disorders in this group, and the SCA axis explores the subjective symptom patterns for children and adolescents. Numerous case examples demonstrate and elaborate upon the axes in parts 1 and 2.

Part 3 of the PDM comprehensively examines the historical and conceptual foundations for mental disorders and grounds them in contemporary research. Taken together, the three parts provide an invaluable lens with which to enhance, broaden, and develop the interviewing process.

RESEARCH IMPLICATIONS AND BASIS OF PRACTICE

Practice Focused Research: Integrating Human Service Practice Research by Powers, Meenaghan, and Toomey (1985) provides a comprehensive process with which to examine the efficacy of any given practice theory or approach. This model is an excellent measure of the empirical understanding of interviewing as well.

The authors described four levels of research knowledge with which to examine theories, frameworks, models, and so forth. All four are important to understanding and empirically validating practice work, and each level has unique value. The first level of research is *intuitive knowledge*, the most fundamental and probably the first form of validation that occurs in any research process. *Intuition* means that one "knows" that something works simply by the nature of the concept. There has been no empirical testing or perhaps even much practice experience to validate intuition, but there is an inherent logic to its value. *Practice wisdom* comes from "testing" intuitive hunches through one's own clinical experience and arriving at anecdotal validation. The case study is a good example of this process. *Theoretical knowledge* evolves from intuition and practice wisdom. The development of theory is a much more rigorous and comprehensive attempt to explain and eventually validate any concept or set of experiences, including interviewing. The fourth and final level is *validated knowledge*, which comes in many forms. Historically, validated knowledge was derived primarily from a quantitative experimental design as developed in classical scientific experimentation. Over time, evolving from that design, a variety of quantitative, qualitative, and mixed methods of research have been used to study the clinical process. Because most aspects of clinical process, including interviewing, do not lend themselves well to a purely quantitative research design, they are better investigated through mixed methods, including anecdotal intuition, practice wisdom, and theoretical formulations. All the theories discussed in this chapter have been evaluated by one or more of these four levels of practice-focused research (Powers, Meenaghan, & Toomey, 1985; McKenzie, 2008, 2011).

The theories and practice methods examined above provide a broad range of research validation for the interviewing process. The early theorists such as Sigmund Freud, the neo-Freudians, and the ego psychologists used the range of intuition, practice wisdom, and theoretical formulation. Each in their own way varied in the extent to which their ideas and contributions regarding the interviewing process rose to the level of theoretical knowledge. Mahler's laboratory studies of the separation-individuation process with mothers and infants clearly are validated knowledge, although some of her methods and conclusions could certainly be challenged, as is true of *all* research to some extent. Carl Rogers's study of the empathic process in interviewing also incorporates all four levels of research knowledge. Some of the family therapy theorists, such as Bowen, used sophisticated research methods to examine the strength of their ideas. The cognitive-behavioral practitioners were able to apply validated knowledge level because of the relative simplicity of measuring change in the stimulus-response interviewing process. However, the most advanced validated knowledge appears to be coming from Daniel Stern and the neuro-science theorists and practitioners. The continuum of intuition, practice wisdom, theoretical formulation, and validated studies is beginning to demonstrate the value of the differential use of interviewing methods to help clients in very specific ways.

SUMMARY

This chapter covered the broad range of theoretical and practice knowledge that has contributed to the development and success of the interviewing process in professional disciplines. Although certainly not exhaustive, this chapter provided a highly relevant and important cross section of key theorists and practitioners who must be known and understood in order to become an effective interviewer. From Freud's psychoanalytic theories to contemporary neuroscience, the interviewing process has evolved into a sophisticated and informed discipline. Any professional interested in using interviewing in their profession can greatly benefit from the theoretical and technical knowledge presented here. Having this information in hand prepares the reader to move on to the specifics of the actual interviewing situation.

RECOMMENDED READING

Psychoanalytic Theory

Freud, S. (1940). *An outline of psychoanalysis*. New York: W. W. Norton.

Freud, S. (1960). *The ego and the id*. New York: W. W. Norton.

Freud's work is vast, complex, and extremely comprehensive. These two books will provide the seasoned or beginning interviewer with a wonderful snapshot of some of Freud's major theories. These concepts are extremely helpful in approaching and understanding the interviewing process with the client.

Neo-Freudian Theory

Adler, A. (1931). *Alfred Adler: What life could mean to you.* Center City, MN: Hazelden.

Horney, K. (1945). *Our inner conflicts.* New York: W. W. Norton.

Jung, C. J. (1959). *The archetypes and the collective unconscious.* Princeton, NJ: Princeton University Press.

Rank, O. (1936). *Will therapy.* New York: W. W. Norton.

This small selection of writings from the neo-Freudians will help expand and sharpen the interviewer's understanding of basic Freudian concepts and the implications for work with clients.

Ego Psychology

Erikson, E. (1950). *Childhood and society.* New York: W. W. Norton.

Freud, A. (1936). *The ego and the mechanisms of defence.* New York: International Universities Press.

Hartmann, H. (1958) *Ego psychology and the problem of adaptation.* New York: International Universities Press.

Sullivan, H. S. (1953). *The interpersonal theory of psychiatry.* New York: W. W. Norton.

The ego psychologists were an enormous group of theorists and practitioners. This small sample of key contributors captures essential elements of their theories. Sullivan, though considered by many to be an object relations theorist, falls into the gray area in terms of his designation. Of primary importance to interviewers is the work of Erik Erikson and Anna Freud. Erikson's epigenetic life stages and Freud's work on refining the understanding of defense mechanisms are pivotal areas of knowledge for the interviewer.

Object Relations Theory

Mahler, M. S., Pine, F., & Bergman, A. (1975). *The psychological birth of the human infant.* New York: Basic Books.

Winnicott, D. W. (1965). *The maturational processes and the facilitating environment*. Madison, CT: International Universities Press.

Winnicott, D. W. (1971). *Playing and reality*. New York: Routledge.

The object relations theorists expanded the understanding of emotional development through emphasizing the crucial relationship with the primary caretaker as the driving force in life and subjugating the drives to that process. Winnicott and Mahler are arguably two of the most important contributors to object relations theory.

Humanistic Approach

Rogers, C. (1965). *Client-centered therapy*. Boston: Houghton Mifflin.

This classic book by Rogers provides a comprehensive guide to client-centered interviewing as well as anecdotal and empirical research on that process. To this day, many of the Rogerian principles and techniques are taught in some form as foundational interviewing material.

Self Psychology

Kohut, H. (1971). *Analysis of the self*. Chicago: University of Chicago Press.

This important initial work from Kohut postulates a new line of development of the self. His emphasis on the use of empathic responsiveness to the client is a very helpful addition to the interviewer's understanding and skill set.

Cognitive-Behavioral Theory and Therapy

Bandura, A. (1962). *Social learning through imitation*. Lincoln: University of Nebraska Press.

Beck, A. T. (1975). *Cognitive therapy and the emotional disorders*. Madison, CT: International Universities Press.

Ellis, A. (1973) *Humanistic psychotherapy: The rational emotive approach*. New York: Julian Press.

These cognitive-behavioral theorists provide the interviewer with a comprehensive view of useful principles and techniques in interviewing.

Systems Theory

Bowen, M. (1978). *Family therapy in clinical practice*. New York: Aronson.

Gitterman, A., & Germain, C. (1980). *The life model of social work practice*. New York: Columbia University Press.

Minuchin, S. (1974). *Families and family therapy*. Cambridge, MA: Harvard University Press.

The family therapy theorists were and are an immense group. However, Minuchin's and Bowen's theoretical contributions are probably the most notable. Having a family systems conceptualization in the interviewing process is essential and an invaluable skill. The ecological approach of Gitterman and Germain is one of, if not *the*, original environmental frameworks from which to understand clients in their world. The eco-map should be a skill in every interviewer's toolbox.

Attachment and Relational Theories

Bowlby, J. (1969). *Attachment and loss:* Vol. 1, *Attachment*. New York: Basic Books.

McKenzie, F. (2011). *Understanding and managing the therapeutic relationship*. Chicago: Lyceum Books.

Stern, D. (2000). *The interpersonal world of the human infant: A view from psychoanalysis and developmental psychology*. New York: Basic Books.

These three texts give an essential overview of attachment and relational theory. Daniel Stern's work in particular is essential reading for any interviewer, because of his ability to explain the necessity of being with the client.

Neuroscience

Cozolino, L. (2010). *The neuroscience of psychotherapy: Healing the social brain*. New York: W. W. Norton.

Psychodynamic diagnostic manual. (2006). Silver Spring, MD: Alliance of Psychoanalytic Organizations.

The current advances in neuroscience research and their implications for interviewing and clinical practice in general are nothing short of amazing. Both Cozolino and the PDM provide a thorough and compelling case for the use of neuroscience concepts in the interviewing process.

MULTIMEDIA SOURCES

The following films, television series, and Internet sites are helpful additions and enhancements to the understanding of the interviewing process. They provide a variety of interviewing examples and sources for delving more deeply into some of the theories presented in the chapter. The films and television series are not presented as definitive illustrations of correct interviewing; rather, they are intended to provide thought-provoking examples of how interviewing can be done. These items are important because they illustrate successful and not-so-successful interviewing, reminding us that the interviewing process is in many ways idiosyncratic and dynamic.

A Dangerous Method. (2011). David Cronenberg (Director). Sony Pictures Classics.

Taken from the real-life events of Sigmund Freud and Carl Jung, this intense and fascinating film presents a powerful picture of the early psychoanalytic process and gives food for thought about interviewing in general.

Good Will Hunting. (1997). Gus Van Sant (Director). Miramax Films.

Robin Williams's portrayal of a therapist working with a troubled young adult man provides many poignant examples of traditional and unconventional approaches to interviewing.

Girl, Interrupted. (1999). James Mangold (Director). Columbia Pictures.

On several levels this film is a helpful addition to interdisciplinary interviewing. Whoopi Goldberg's portrayal of a psychiatric nurse and Vanessa Redgrave's role as the institution's main psychiatrist provide helpful examples of the interview from several helping-profession vantage points.

Huff. (2004–6). Showtime.

Hank Azaria stars in this dark dramatic comedy about a psychoanalyst dealing with difficult patients and a challenging life. For the interviewer there are many helpful examples of both successful and not-so-successful ways of interacting.

In Treatment. (2008–11). HBO.

This series starring Gabriel Byrne is a powerful example of the ways in which a relational therapist struggles with his own emotions in understanding, evaluating, and deciding how best to proceed in interviewing his clients.

American Psychoanalytic Association, www.apsa.org.
Society of Modern Psychoanalysts, http://smp.memberlodge.org.

For interviewers interested in exploring psychoanalytic theory in greater depth as well as the contemporary practice of it, these two sites are quite useful.

C. G. Jung Institute of Chicago, www.jungchicago.org/index.php.

The Chicago institute is a good example of what can be found at almost every Jungian institute around the world, listed here. For interviewers looking to broaden their understanding and use of Jungian theory, concepts, and techniques, this link is quite comprehensive.

Erikson Institute, www.erikson.edu.

The Erikson Institute provides the interviewer with extensive information about the famous ego psychologist, as well as training and educational information relevant to interviewing.

Self Psychology Page, www.selfpsychology.com/.
International Association for Psychoanalytic Self Psychology,
     www.psychologyoftheself.com/iapsp/.

These Internet sites are very useful sources for expanding the interviewer's understanding of this important theory.

Society for Neuroscience, www.sfn.org.

Neuroscience is probably the most important contemporary source of information in understanding how interviewing affects the brain and how to differentially decide upon specific interviewing approaches with the client. This source provides comprehensive information about neuroscience.

What Is Interviewing and How Is It Done?

This chapter starts with a case example and examines the interviewer's interventions and responses, step by step, in order to show the relational process that develops. Where appropriate, the case example is examined through specific theoretical lenses. The knowledge base developed in chapter 1 helps guide interviewers in their attempts to understand the client.

CASE EXAMPLE: LINDA

Linda, a forty-year-old married woman with four children (ages 7, 9, 11, and 13), called a social worker in private practice for an individual appointment. During the phone conversation with the social worker, Linda explained that she was having difficulty with her marriage and life in general, and needed help and support in sorting out what to do next. The following dialogue captures the essence of that first interview.

> **Interviewer**: Well, Linda, I remember from our phone conversation that you wanted to come in to talk about your marriage and some general concerns about your life. Did I understand that correctly?

Linda: Yeah, that's right.

Interviewer: OK, good. Could you tell me a little more about the concerns on your mind?

Linda: Well, where would you like me to start?

She seems to the interviewer to be very open, interested, and willing to talk.

Interviewer: Anywhere you want. I would just like to be able to know more about what brought you here. You mentioned your marriage on the phone. Is that a good place to start?

Linda: OK. I'm really not happy in my marriage. My husband and I have been married for twenty years. He's very distant with me, and I think he is somewhat verbally abusive to me and the children . . . mostly the children though. I don't know if I want to stay married to him sometimes, but I worry about the kids and how they'll react if I leave.

She seems very conflicted, and the interviewer senses this frustration.

Interviewer: So let me see if I understand you. You and your husband have been married for twenty years, and during that time you have come to experience him as distant and also are concerned about his being somewhat verbally abusive with you, but mostly the children. You've also been thinking about divorcing him, but are worried about how that might affect your children. Am I getting that right?

The interviewer wants to be sure that he has understood what the client is thinking and feeling to the best of his ability before moving on to something else.

Linda: Yeah, I think so.

She seems to feel completely understood.

Interviewer: Linda, when you say your husband is distant, can you help me understand what you mean by that?

Words can convey multiple meanings, and the interviewer wants to get some clarity as to exactly what Linda means about being "distant."

Linda: Well, I think I told you that we have been married over twenty years, and almost from the beginning of our marriage, John didn't seem to want to spend much time with me, and besides getting me pregnant, he also doesn't seem very interested in having sex with me.

Interviewer: When you do spend time together, what is that like?

Linda: Sometimes we'll watch TV together, but that's about it except for the occasional sex.

Interviewer: And how often would you say that is?

The interviewer senses this may be an important point of discussion, so getting clarity is essential.

Linda: Oh, maybe a couple of times a year. Even when we have sex, John is very distant. He seems to just want to do his business. He doesn't focus on me at all except to get off.

Interviewer: You seem very frustrated by that.

The interviewer is trying to convey empathy as he senses Linda's feelings.

Linda [*starting to cry*]: I have felt so alone for so long. I don't know what to do. If it weren't for the kids, I think I'd have left him a long time ago.

The interviewer senses that Linda is very vulnerable and really wants to share these deep feelings of sadness, confusion, and frustration.

Interviewer: You've mentioned your concerns about your children a couple of times.

The interviewer feels that this is all he needs to say to convey his understanding of Linda's concerns and encourage her to continue this point of discussion if she'd like.

Linda: They're really not close to him, and he hardly pays any attention to them, like me. John is also very mean to them. He calls them names, like my nine-year-old "fatso," and my oldest "stupid." It's so hard to take. I try to stop him, and sometimes he will just leave the room and let them alone, but sometimes he just turns on me then . . . which is OK with me. I can take it and I'd much rather save them from any abuse.

Once again Linda is being extremely open and vulnerable, which signals to the interviewer that there is some trust building in their relationship.

> **Interviewer:** That must be so difficult for you to watch and handle, and yet it sounds like you've been able to really protect your kids a lot of the time.

The interviewer feels that all he needs and wants to do right now is validate and respond empathically to Linda's thoughts and feelings.

> **Linda:** I hope so; I really love them so much and want them to have a better life than I did growing up.

Linda is very expressive and emphatic in this statement.

> **Interviewer:** Unless you feel we might be getting off track, would you like to tell me a little bit about your growing up?

The interviewer does not want to veer away from the clearly important topic that Linda is discussing, but also senses that she might want to talk about her upbringing in this context. His question allows Linda to choose where she wants to go next rather than being instructed or directed to change topics. This shows respect for her.

> **Linda:** I didn't really have a father growing up. My mother was not married to my biological father. She worked hard in a factory all day, and I was alone well into the evening because she would drink at the bar, or come home and drink until she passed out. I did most of the cooking and cleaning. I saw my dad off and on when I was a little girl, but he never seemed very interested in me when we got together. He stopped seeing me when I was around ten. I was really alone.
>
> **Interviewer:** Sounds like you might feel that way sometimes even now.

This may be a leap or premature response because it begins to take the interview to an even deeper emotional layer, but the interviewer's instincts are that the feelings from childhood are perhaps similar to what Linda is going through in the present.

> **Linda:** I hadn't really thought about it that much, but now that you mention it, those feelings are very familiar.

The interview continues in this manner for most of the rest of the session, with Linda elaborating further on her feelings in the present and their connections to the past.

> **Interviewer:** I think I can understand why this certainly seems to be a very difficult time in your life. Linda, I notice that we are coming near the end of our time. I'm not sure if you would like to come back to talk more about your situation?
>
> **Linda:** Yeah, this has been helpful, I think I would. How does this work?
>
> **Interviewer:** Well, I think the way we discussed things today is pretty much how I work. Of course as time goes on, we can talk more specifically about what you might like to do to handle your life right now. Do you have any questions about me or this process that could help you understand it better or feel more comfortable with me?
>
> **Linda:** I don't think so right now. We talked about your credentials, and you came highly recommended. I really felt comfortable with you.
>
> **Interviewer:** Good, I felt comfortable with you too and sense we might work well together. Let's set up another time.
>
> **Linda:** OK.

DISCUSSION OF INTERVIEWING TECHNIQUE

The preceding vignette is based upon an actual case. It is a fairly accurate, although somewhat condensed, version of a first interview in a counseling situation. From an interviewing perspective, a lot was happening. The interviewer used specific types of questions or interventions aimed at gathering information and demonstrating understanding of this client. What was most important in this interview, however, is that a relationship was established. The relationship was established through a structured professional interview, but it felt natural, not stilted or contrived. The client opened up and seemed to feel understood and helped. The interviewer seemed to really engage with the client and was interested in knowing and helping her. This is what successful interviewing is all about.

Was this interview perfect? No, there are no perfect interviews. Interviewing is a process that is filled with successful and unsuccessful moments in the same way that any human interaction ebbs and flows. However, it seemed to be good enough to help this client feel understood and want to return for help. What exactly was happening in this interview? How can it be understood from a technical, theoretical, and relational standpoint?

Many books on interviewing stress theory or technique, or some form of both; but few, if any, emphasize the relationship and emotional connection between the client and interviewer (Hollis & Woods, 1964; Miller & Rollnick, 2002; Hepworth, Rooney, Rooney, Strom-Gottfried, & Larsen, 2006; James, 2008; Halgrin & Whitbourne, 2010; Zastrow, 2010; Wilkinson & Treas, 2011). That connection is the heart of interviewing in any helping profession. Most beginning interviewers from any professional discipline worry more about what they are or should be saying next rather than paying attention to and following the client. That very common experience can obviously be disruptive to the interview process and, more importantly, to establishing a connection with the client.

The major secret to successful interviewing is "following the client." This means that the interviewer's questions and interventions should naturally flow from an interest and curiosity about wanting to know the client and her situation better. Basically it's as simple as that. However, a myriad of essential and useful techniques and theories are used throughout the helping profession to promote successful interviewing. The key point here is that an interview is a human interaction. Human beings need others, and they also need emotional connection and support throughout life to thrive. Family relationships, friendships, work relationships, and other important human ties are based upon the ability to communicate genuinely and be understood. The professional interview is no different, except that it has a unique purpose based upon the discipline and circumstance. Crisis intervention is a different process than long-term therapy. A professional intake is obviously much briefer and more succinct than psychoanalysis. However, the relationship between the client and interviewer dictates the success of that process regardless of the type of interview.

Neuroscience validates this process. It has been found that mirror neurons within the brain help us understand and anticipate the thoughts, emotions, and actions of others. In other words, we are pre-wired toward empathy (Cozolino, 2010). That innate ability is what is used in interviewing. It allows the interviewer to take in the client, that is, listen to the words, feel the emotions, notice the outward signs of physical expression (facial expression, body language, etc.). This common ongoing human communication is part of the road map for the interviewer. It can go unnoticed if the interviewer is too focused on technique or theory. Really being with the client allows for a natural flow of interviewing, based upon a solid observation of and empathic understanding of the client.

Revisiting key lines from the interviewing vignette above helps provide a thorough explanation of the relational process, technique, and theoretical implications and direction.

> **Interviewer:** Well, Linda, I remember from our phone conversation that you wanted to come in to talk about your marriage and some general concerns about your life. Did I understand that correctly?
> *Linda:* Yeah, that's right.
> **Interviewer:** OK, good. Could you tell me a little more about the concerns on your mind?

The opening of any type of interview is a potentially challenging situation. Several types of questions are evident in the first step of this particular interview. From a relational standpoint, the interviewer in lines 1 and 3 is gently conveying his understanding of the client's interest in coming in, while encouraging her to begin to discuss whatever may be on her mind. From a technical perspective there are at least two types of questions here: a clarification or summarizing, and an open-ended invitation to begin where the client is at. These are technical interview techniques, to be sure, but come across as genuine attempts to understand and respect the client.

> **Linda:** Well, where would you like me to start?

She seems to the interviewer to be very open, interested and willing to talk.

> **Interviewer:** Anywhere you want. I would just like to be able to know more about what brought you here. You mentioned your marriage on the phone. Is that a good place to start?

The client is looking to the interviewer for direction, yet the interviewer responds with another relatively open-ended question about the client's marriage. The interviewer does not direct per se, but does provide a general lead that is based upon what the client has already presented. This may seem obvious, but the gentle and supportive nature of the interviewer's question continues to set a tone of respect and interest in the client and her process. Some interviewers might take this question from the client as an opportunity to lead the interview in a certain direction that may not be where the client wants to go. Depending on the type of interviewing—for example, intake, crisis intervention, social history, and even certain models of therapy—this may be appropriate and even necessary. However, for an initial counseling session like this one, clients are more likely to open up if they feel safe and experience a genuine sense of trust and encouragement.

> **Linda:** OK. I'm really not happy in my marriage. My husband and I have been married for twenty years. He's very

distant with me, and I think he is somewhat verbally abusive to me and the children . . . mostly the children though. I don't know if I want to stay married to him sometimes, but I worry about the kids and how they'll react if I leave.

She seems very conflicted, and the interviewer senses this frustration.

Interviewer: So let me see if I understand you. You and your husband have been married for twenty years, and during that time you have come to experience him as distant and also are concerned about his being somewhat verbally abusive with you, but mostly the children. You've also been thinking about divorcing him, but are worried about how that might affect your children. Am I getting that right?

The interviewer wants to be sure that he has understood what the client is thinking and feeling to the best of his ability before moving on to something else. Clearly the client feels at least an initial sense of trust because of the way in which she jumps right in to describe her situation. There even appears to be some fairly intense affect/emotion being expressed. The interviewer responds with what might be called a summarizing response. He doesn't jump to any conclusions, but instead is careful to convey to the client that he wants to be sure that he understands her before going any further. This type of interview response is crucial and often overlooked, especially by the beginning interviewer. The response is an attempt to convey understanding before moving on, because any misunderstanding can derail the interviewing process. This is a natural way of following the client's lead as well as encouraging more input from her.

Linda: Yeah, I think so.

Linda seems to feel completely understood.

Interviewer: Linda, when you say your husband is distant, can you help me understand what you mean by that?

Words can convey multiple meanings, and the interviewer wants to get some clarity as to exactly what Linda means about being "distant."

Linda: Well, I think I told you that we have been married over twenty years, and almost from the beginning of our marriage, John didn't seem to want to spend much time with me, and besides getting me pregnant, he also doesn't seem very interested in having sex with me.

Interviewer: When you do spend time together, what is that like?

Linda: Sometimes we'll watch TV together, but that's about it except for the occasional sex.

Interviewer: And how often would you say that is?

The interviewer senses this may be an important point of discussion, so getting clarity is essential.

Linda: Oh, maybe a couple of times a year. Even when we have sex, John is very distant. He seems to just want to do his business. He doesn't focus on me at all except to get off.

This exchange begins to move the interview into an exploration of the details of the client's concern. It seems to be a natural flow because of the client's acknowledgment that the interviewer understands her. This natural exchange opens the door for a series of clarifying statements that allow the client to elaborate further on the previous discussion. The feel of the session appears to be more engaged and trusting, which leads the client to open up more about her concerns. The interviewer does not do much more than simply explore with genuine curiosity the nature of the client's issues, much like a friend might want to know more about another friend's problems. An interview is not a friendship, but does contain many of the very same kinds of human compassion and support. This is a very important point. Interviewing of any kind must contain and convey that genuine sense of human concern if it is going to be successful. Clients can sense, like all human beings, when someone is insincere or uncaring in interactions.

Interviewer: You seem very frustrated by that.

The interviewer is trying to convey empathy as he senses Linda's feelings.

Linda [*starting to cry*]: I have felt so alone for so long. I don't know what to do. If it weren't for the kids, I think I'd have left him a long time ago.

The interviewer senses that Linda is very vulnerable and really wants to share these deep feelings of sadness, confusion, and frustration. After this series of clarifying interventions, the client is clearly moved to express some very painful emotions. The interviewer through his clarifying statements ultimately arrived at a point where a simple yet exact empathic statement seemed appropriate to let the client know that she is understood. Yet notice the word "seem." This simple qualifier communicates to the client that perhaps the interviewer may not have totally understood. It allows the client to disagree, modify, or avoid the question. A friend might say, "Oh, that is awful!" or "He treats you so terribly!" Those statements are certainly supportive, but also judgmental, that is, expressing the well-intended opinion of a friend. The interviewer's response, however, is focused on the client and offers a possible empathic statement that the client can accept, reject, or modify. This is one of the key differences between professional interviewing and friendship.

Interviewer: You've mentioned your concerns about your children a couple of times.

The interviewer feels that this is all he needs to say to convey his understanding of Linda's concerns and encourage her to continue this point of discussion if she'd like.

Linda: They're really not close to him, and he hardly pays any attention to them, like me. John is also very mean to them. He calls them names, like my nine-year-old "fatso," and my oldest "stupid." It's so hard to take. I try to stop him, and sometimes he will just leave the room and let them alone, but sometimes he just turns on me then . . . which is OK with me. I can take it and I'd much rather save them from any abuse.

Once again Linda is being extremely open and vulnerable, which signals to the interviewer that there is some trust building in their relationship.

> **Interviewer:** That must be so difficult for you to watch and handle, and yet it sounds like you've been able to really protect your kids a lot of the time.

The interviewer feels that all he needs and wants to do right now is validate and respond empathically to Linda's thoughts and feelings.

> **Linda:** I hope so; I really love them so much and want them to have a better life than I did growing up.

Linda is very expressive and emphatic in this statement. Lines 17 through 20 continue the process that has been so carefully developed in the professional interaction between the interviewer and client. There seems to be a natural process emerging whereby the client is intuitively recognizing the role of the interviewer as one who is genuinely invested in her and will intervene to understand and help.

> **Interviewer:** Unless you feel we might be getting off track, would you like to tell me a little bit about your growing up?

The interviewer does not want to veer away from the clearly important topic that Linda is discussing, but also senses that she might want to talk about her upbringing in this context. His question allows Linda to choose where she wants to go next rather than being instructed or directed to change topics. This shows respect for her.

> **Linda:** I didn't really have a father growing up. My mother was not married to my biological father. She worked hard in a factory all day, and I was alone well into the evening because she would drink at the bar, or come home and drink until she passed out. I did most of the cooking and cleaning. I saw my dad off and on when I was a little girl, but he never seemed very interested in me when we got together. He stopped seeing me when I was around ten. I was really alone.

Since the client has mentioned her childhood in the context of her present concerns, the interviewer is genuinely curious about the possible connection. This curiosity flows from a natural interest in understanding and helping the client. Yet the interviewer again wants to allow the client to move at her own pace, offering the leading open-ended question in such a way that the client can decide whether to pursue it. Linda's response seems to indicate that she is ready and interested in following the interviewer's lead.

Interviewer: Sounds like you might feel that way sometimes even now.

This may be a leap or premature response because it begins to take the interview to an even deeper emotional layer, but the interviewer's instincts are that the feelings from childhood are perhaps similar to what Linda is going through in the present.

Linda: I hadn't really thought about it that much, but now that you mention it, those feelings are very familiar.

The interviewer senses a connection between the client's past and the present situation, but wants to be careful not to jump to any conclusions; so again he qualifies his empathic statement with the word "might." The client appears to agree, but there is a little tentativeness in her response.

Interviewer: I think I can understand why this certainly seems to be a very difficult time in your life. Linda, I notice that we are coming near the end of our time. I'm not sure if you would like to come back to talk more about your situation?

Linda: Yeah, this has been helpful, I think I would. How does this work?

Interviewer: Well, I think the way we discussed things today is pretty much how I work. Of course as time goes on, we can talk more specifically about what you might like to do to handle your life right now. Do you have any questions about me or this process that could help you understand it better or feel more comfortable with me?

Linda: I don't think so right now. We talked about your credentials, and you came highly recommended. I really felt comfortable with you.

Interviewer: Good, I felt comfortable with you too and sense we might work well together. Let's set up another time.

Linda: OK.

As the session winds down, the interviewer uses a summarizing intervention in order to be sure once again that he understands what has been discussed. The next step in an interview of this type (a typical initial counseling session) is to explore how the client is feeling about the session and whether she wants to return. It is also an important opportunity for the interviewer to allow the client to ask any questions about the process in order to satisfy any curiosity or clarify any concerns. Explaining to the client that what was just experienced is actually what the process is all about is a very natural and immediate summary that can help put the client's mind at ease about continuing. The client appears comfortable, and a new appointment is scheduled.

THEORETICAL UNDERSTANDINGS OF THE INTERVIEW

Our discussion so far has focused on technique and looking at the interview in a relational context. Chapter 1 provided a comprehensive condensed version of many theories relevant to the interviewing process. Any one of them can be used to analyze the rationale and process of the interview presented above.

From a purely technical standpoint, it seems as if Rogerian client-centered therapy provides the most basic understanding of this vignette (Rogers, 1965). The attitude and demeanor of the interviewer as well as the interviewing techniques are textbook Rogerian concepts. The interviewer is caring, interested, genuine, authentic, and nonjudgmental. The interviewer does not lead the client, but instead tries to create an atmosphere of safety and trust, from which the client can begin to talk about her concerns and build a relationship with the interviewer. This fundamental interviewing process is common to most professional disciplines such as social work, psychology, psychiatry, nursing, and criminal justice (Miller & Rollnick, 2002; Hepworth et al., 2006; James, 2008; Halgrin & Whitbourne, 2010; Zastrow, 2010; Wilkinson & Treas, 2011).

Although various professions may have different labels for the interviewing techniques used in the vignette, the process is the same. Open-ended, closed-ended, summarizing, paraphrasing, confrontational, empathic, and other types of interviewing responses are all aimed at helping and understanding the client. They all focus on developing a trusting relationship and should flow naturally out of the interviewer's interest, caring, and curiosity regarding the client. The interviewer who focuses on technique at the expense of genuine understanding and relationship building is unlikely to be successful. Developing a trusting relationship with the client is at the heart of all professional interviewing.

One of the most fascinating aspects of applying theory to any interviewing situation is the variety of ways in which an interview can be understood and perceived. One perspective on Linda's case could be a cognitive-behavioral therapy vantage point, which might lead to a further examination of the client's thoughts, beliefs, and actions in the present—ultimately leading to a plan aimed at modifying her understanding and behavior in very specific and measurable ways. A client-centered approach would continue to move ahead in much the same way as has already been portrayed; that is, the interviewer would help the client explore her thoughts and feelings in a nonjudgmental manner, trusting that the client would arrive at a solution that she understood and defined as best for her. That type of interviewing would be nondirective compared to the more directive style of cognitive-behavioral therapy. Neither approach is necessarily better. However, the strength of any approach is based upon the best fit between the interviewer and client. That's why interviewers should be able to approach their work with flexibility and the differential use of theory. The theoretical overview provided in chapter 1 implicitly emphasizes that fact. Of course every interviewer will have a limited set of knowledge and skills. Interviewers should also continually strive to remain current and grow in their knowledge and experience of interviewing. Most professionals do this naturally as they mature and become more experienced.

MANIFEST AND LATENT CONTENT

Throughout the interviewing process, the interviewer should be aware of the multiple levels of client communication. One way of understanding, listening, and examining this process is through the notion of manifest and latent content. These concepts have been around for many decades and are basic to understanding most human communication. Manifest content is the communication in the interview that is related to what is happening in the here and now: the present focus of the interview. For instance, in the interview with Linda, her manifest content is her presenting concerns about her family, marriage, and self. These are straightforward problems that can be clearly recognized and understood.

> *Linda:* OK. I'm really not happy in my marriage. My husband and I have been married for twenty years. He's very distant with me, and I think he is somewhat verbally abusive to me and the children . . . mostly the children though. I don't know if I want to stay married to him sometimes, but I worry about the kids and how they'll react if I leave.

She seems very conflicted, and the interviewer senses this frustration.

> **Interviewer:** So let me see if I understand you. You and your husband have been married for twenty years, and during that time you have come to experience him as distant and also are concerned about his being somewhat verbally abusive with you, but mostly the children. You've also been thinking about divorcing him, but are worried about how that might affect your children. Am I getting that right?

The interviewer wants to be sure that he has understood what the client is thinking and feeling to the best of his ability before moving on to something else.

These problems are what Linda wants to work on in the present.

Latent content or communication is the deeper and underlying emotions and thoughts that could also be an important focus in the interview. These are not always clearly understood or even in the present awareness of the client, but they may be sensed by an astute interviewer.

> **Linda:** I hope so; I really love them so much and want them to have a better life than I did growing up.

Linda is very expressive and emphatic in this statement.

> **Interviewer:** Unless you feel we might be getting off track, would you like to tell me a little bit about your growing up?

The interviewer does not want to veer away from the clearly important topic that Linda is discussing, but also senses that she might want to talk about her upbringing in this context. His question allows Linda to choose where she wants to go next rather than being instructed or directed to change topics. This shows respect for her.

> **Linda:** I didn't really have a father growing up. My mother was not married to my biological father. She worked hard in a factory all day, and I was alone well into the evening because she would drink at the bar, or come home and drink until she passed out. I did most of the cooking and cleaning. I saw my dad off and on when I was a little girl, but he never seemed very interested in me when we got together. He stopped seeing me when I was around ten. I was really alone.
>
> **Interviewer:** Sounds like you might feel that way sometimes even now.

This may be a leap or premature response because it begins to take the interview to an even deeper emotional layer, but the interviewer's instincts are that the feelings from childhood are perhaps similar to what Linda is going through in the present.

> **Linda:** I hadn't really thought about it that much, but now that you mention it, those feelings are very familiar.

This section of the interview seems to imply that there may be deeper childhood themes that play an important part in Linda's situation. The interviewer does not pursue them initially, but makes a mental note of an area to perhaps examine later on. Exploring these themes might actually help the client understand and function better with her presenting (manifest) issues because of the way in which they are interrelated. In other words, the themes of Linda's presenting concerns may be rooted in or influenced by the past.

Manifest and latent content also have a bearing on understanding the whole client. Successful interviewers are continually developing an ongoing understanding of themselves as well as their client. This can be called the "working models of self and other." In *Understanding and Managing the Therapeutic Relationship*, I discuss this relational concept, which is based upon object relations countertransference theory and grounded in current attachment and neuroscience theory and research. In addition, the idea of the ongoing "theoretical template" is a useful tool for any interviewer (McKenzie, 2011).

All human beings develop internal memories or representations of significant people in their lives, starting with their primary caretakers. This extends to family members, friends, coworkers, and so forth. One concept used to describe this process is working models, the idea that all people have a stored mental "file" of different people in their lives. One's working model of Dad, for example, contains all of the memories and aspects that make up his persona. When one interacts with Dad, all of the elements of the working model are drawn upon automatically and usually without awareness. In addition, each subsequent interaction with Dad adds further information and modification of the working model of Dad. Interviewers also have a working model of themselves and their client. Developing a working model of self is a lifelong process. The working model of each client begins with practically no information, but gradually develops and expands to contain a huge amount of information, including history, emotional understanding, affect recognition, body movement and configuration: in short, everything that makes up the interviewer's working model of that unique client. During the session, this information is drawn upon to help the interviewer understand and continue work with the client (McKenzie, 2011).

The "theoretical template" is a similar principle. All interviewers begin their career with very little theoretical and technical information and experience about the process. Over time, however, an internal template develops that contains the knowledge and experience from the interviewer's professional life. Novice interviewers need to focus more on technique and specific theoretical concepts until they become second nature. This process could be compared to learning to drive a car. Initially, the beginning driver is very conscious of the technical aspects of driving and the rules about how to drive. Over time, however, the process of driving becomes so automatic that the driver is barely aware of the process. The same principle happens in interviewing. With more experience as well as technical and theoretical knowledge, the interviewer internalizes a unique theoretical template. This template can be accessed at any time, but more often than not operates automatically and virtually out of awareness. Usually the interviewer contemplates his or her theoretical template when examining sessions that have ended, in order to understand them and prepare for future work.

This process is not only theoretical; it can be explained by recent empirical neuroscience. The developmental psychologist Daniel Stern writes about the idea of representations of interactions that have been generalized (RIGs). Through research, Stern demonstrated that one's memory of another is an averaging of all specific interactions with them. For example, remembering all of one's childhood dinners is not possible. What one usually remembers is the averaging of all those experiences or representations into one RIG. This does not mean that specific memories are not available, only that the RIG seems to have prominence (Stern, 2000). This is in many ways equivalent to the notion of a working model of self and other.

Louis Cozolino, among other neuroscientists, writes about implicit and explicit memory in the human brain. Explicit memories are those thoughts, emotions, and experiences that one has easy access to and are most present in the mind. Implicit memories are those that are more out of awareness, but can be accessed through greater concentration and even strong emotional stimulation (Cozolino, 2002). Implicit memory is a helpful way of understanding the theoretical templates discussed earlier. The information is stored and utilized, but not always consciously accessed.

RESEARCH IMPLICATIONS AND BASIS OF PRACTICE

The helping professions have used interviewing for well over one hundred years. The literature has progressed from intuitive knowledge to practice wisdom to theoretical and validated knowledge. Many texts have been written about the technique and theory of interviewing. Several key theoretical practitioners have provided some strong empirical information regarding the validity of interviewing (Rogers, 1965; Hollis & Woods, 1964; Hepworth et al., 2006; O'Hare, 2005). As a general practice, interviewing is recognized as a valid and useful process. Future research, however, should expand to include more relational elements of interviewing.

SUMMARY

This chapter has examined the relational, technical, and theoretical principles of interviewing. The case example demonstrates the complex process of interweaving and understanding these elements. Successful interviewing is above all a human process that comes about through the genuine caring and undivided attention from the interviewer.

RECOMMENDED READING

Bogo, M. (2006). *Social work practice: Concepts, processes, and interviewing*. New York: Columbia University Press.

Shebib, B. (2011). *Choices: Interviewing and counseling skills for Canadians*. Don Mills, Ontario: Pearson.

Bogo's and Shebib's books about the interviewing process are considered to be standard reading for many Canadian social work students and other professionals.

Rogers, C. (1965). *Client-centered therapy.* Boston: Houghton Mifflin.

Rogers was one of the first pioneers in the study of interviewing. This text is the quintessential example of his studies.

Hollis, F., & Woods, M. E. (1964). *Casework: A psychosocial therapy.* New York: Random House.

Florence Hollis is best remembered for her seminal research in identifying and categorizing the specific types of interviewing techniques so frequently used by most interviewers.

Hepworth, D. H., Rooney, R. H., Rooney, G. D., Strom-Gottfried, K., & Larsen, J. (2006). *Direct social work practice: Theory and skills.* Belmont, CA: Brooks/Cole.

This text is a helpful primer for the beginning interviewer. Its strengths lie in the explication of specific interviewing techniques, although it is lacking in theory and an emphasis on the relationship as key to interviewing success.

O'Hare, T. (2005). *Evidence-based practices for social workers: An interdisciplinary approach.* Chicago: Lyceum Books.

O'Hare's work is an excellent collection of evidence-based research, including interviewing studies.

Stern, D. (2000). *The interpersonal world of the human infant: A view from psychoanalysis and developmental psychology.* New York: Basic Books.

Stern's book, as it relates to this chapter, comprehensively covers the RIG concept in development.

Cozolino, L. (2010). *The neuroscience of psychotherapy: Healing the social brain.* New York: W. W. Norton.

Cozolino's book wonderfully details the phenomena of explicit and implicit memory discussed in this chapter.

McKenzie, F. (2011). *Understanding and managing the therapeutic relationship.* Chicago: Lyceum Books.

This text provides a comprehensive examination of the theoretical template and working models of self and other.

MULTIMEDIA SOURCES

Notes on Communication, www.wanterfall.com/Communication
-Active-Listening.htm.

This helpful site provides an overview of Carl Rogers's basic interviewing skills.

CHAPTER THREE

Types of Interviewing

Chapter 2 illustrated the basic principles of interviewing and demonstrated the importance of technique and theory in the context of developing a relationship with the client. The interviewer's theoretical template and working models of self and client are useful tools in any type of interviewing. This chapter explores several kinds of professional interviewing while incorporating the concepts from chapter 2. In addition, it introduces a practice formulation that expands the repertoire of knowledge and skill used in interviewing.

All professional interviewing is based upon the principles discussed in chapters 1 and 2. The extent and variation of these principles are differentially applied, according to the nature of the interview. For example, in addition to traditional office visits, helping professionals from both the American and Canadian systems are involved in home visits in both rural and urban settings. The process is the same, however: helping the client through genuine caring and concern guided by focused interviewing skills that are derived from innate curiosity.

THE BIOPSYCHOSOCIAL PRACTICE FORMULATION

The practice formulation is a comprehensive biopsychosocial evaluation framework within which to understand any type of client or modality, that is, individual, couple, family, or group (McKenzie, 2011). The biopsychosocial practice formulation was originally derived from Meeks's version of the diagnostic evaluation in the classic adolescent text *The Fragile Alliance* (Meeks & Bernet, 2001). It is a comprehensive holistic expansion of Meeks's evaluation tool. This model is a helpful guideline for any interviewer and can be used in its entirety, or partially, as needed, given the type of interview and client situation. There are twelve questions aimed at providing a thorough biopsychosocial picture of the client. These questions do not need to be asked directly. They serve as an important road map by which to better understand the client. The biopsychosocial practice formulation should serve as part of the theoretical template and a backdrop for the natural interviewing process.

The following biopsychosocial questions are taken from McKenzie 2011 (pp. 73–74). The exploration areas may not be suitable for all professional disciplines, and it may not be possible to cover them all at once. They are, however, a comprehensive list of helpful areas to keep in mind in the interviewing process.

1. *Is there any evidence of "constitutional" factors that might have contributed to the present situation? If so, how have they affected the client?* This broad area of focus can include a variety of organic and genetic predispositions, such as a history of family depression, addiction problems, attention deficit disorder, bipolar disorder, schizophrenia, and cancer. Carefully and tactfully identifying these factors can have a crucial impact on both understanding and helping the client. By the same token, missing this information can lead to faulty diagnosis, intervention, and treatment.

2. *What level of psychosocial development do you believe the client has achieved? How have previous stages/phases influenced the present one? Do you believe the client is fixated or regressed at all?*

What factors lead you to believe this may true? It is important for any professional interviewer to have a basic understanding of human development in order to fully understand the client (chapter 1 provides a comprehensive condensed overview of key developmental theories). For example, a four-year-old child is developmentally different than a sixteen-year-old adolescent. They are very different from a physical and emotional standpoint, among others. These differences dictate varying approaches to interviewing and will be discussed at length in chapter 6.

3. *What type of attachment did the client have with his or her caretakers, and how did these early developmental periods affect present relationships with family, peers, and significant others?* A variety of attachment theories and models can be used to help the interviewer understand clients. The most classic view of attachment comes from the work of Bowlby and Stern, who have identified various traditional and contemporary universal attachment styles: secure, anxious, avoidant, and disorganized. For the purposes of interviewing, these particular types of interactional style can signal that the client has difficulties or challenges in relationships with others. Securely attached clients seem able to engage in the interview in a relatively comfortable fashion. They may experience and demonstrate some of the features of the other three attachment forms, but not in a disruptive or debilitative fashion that interferes with the interview. Anxious clients seem to have excessive difficulty with emotions in general; this difficulty may become a major focus of the interview, making it difficult to ask questions or pursue topics due to the intense anxiety that is aroused. Avoidant clients may seem distant, depressed, or even overtly oppositional in an interview, but this type of interaction can signal the need to protect them from perceived emotional threats. Finally, disorganized clients may move in and out of the anxious and avoidant realms as well as appearing to be altogether disconnected from an interactional process. This type of client may be more severely emotionally disturbed, and unable to have sustained and consistent contact in the interview. The interviewer who has a basic understanding of general attachment styles is much more able to understand and respond in ways that help the client. For instance, an anxious client

needs more patience, and an avoidant client may need more gentle probing, while a securely attached client poses far fewer challenges in the interviewing process.

4. *Why is the client in need of service right now? Is he self-referred, or does someone else believe he needs help?* This is a crucial question for all interviews and sets the tone for the process. A self-referred client seeking psychotherapy or psychiatric services, crisis intervention services, a medical exam, or even inpatient services will probably be much more cooperative and easily engaged in the interview. An adolescent coming to a probation interview, or a resistant adult presenting with psychotic symptoms at an emergency room may not be as cooperative. Each of these situations requires a modified set of interventions and responses by the interviewer in order to build a working and trusting relationship.

5. *Does the client see herself as being conflicted, or in need of help, despite the fact that she may not be self-referred? To what extent can she see her part in the situation?* This question is very similar to question 4, but signals that the client may be more easily engaged. The less in denial the client is, the easier the work for the interviewer in helping the client explore the situation.

6. *Does the client have the "capacity" to be introspective, and is he able to view himself "objectively"? What is the extent of his "observing ego"?* The "observing ego" is a concept that was derived from early psychodynamic theory, especially ego psychology. It simply means, does the client have the ability to metaphorically stand outside of himself and imagine how others might see him? This ability is a crucial one in life, because it allows us to take on perspectives other than our own. The crucial importance of this ability is that it also allows us to experience multiple views of reality and to see the world in shades of gray as opposed to simply black or white, or good and bad. Careful questioning from the interviewer can determine this capacity and help the client view the world in a broader and more helpful fashion.

7. *Is the client's defensive structure adaptive or maladaptive?* The interviewer is certainly not expected to be an expert in psychopathology. However, most interviewers are aware of basic psychological defenses such as denial, intellectualization, and repression.

Defenses are generally described as primitive or mature. Primitive defenses are those that distort reality. Denial is a good example: "I did not do that" (when in fact they did) is a perfect example. Intellectualization is a more mature defense, because at least clients acknowledge the event or situation, just not their part or responsibility in it.

8. *How would you assess the client's support system, and how does it affect the present situation?* The interviewer should gain some sense of the people and relationships in the client's life because they can have a tremendous positive or negative effect on the origins and outcome of any situation. It is important to remember that the client's opinion of these people may be biased, but knowing who they are and the client's opinion of them can be of great help in the initial and subsequent interviews. (Chapter 5 goes into greater detail regarding this important area.)

9. *Are there particular issues of diversity that heavily affect the client's situation?* Diversity is an immense topic and factor in interviewing. There are a myriad of ways to describe diversity and how it can affect the client, the interviewer, and the process. Diversity is far more than racial, cultural, ethnic, gender, and disability issues, to mention just a few. It encompasses all aspects of each unique individual. This important topic is covered in chapter 4. What is important to remember here is to make no assumptions about a client. Proper interviewing requires an adherence to this ongoing principle. The interviewer must strive to be culturally competent in all areas of work with clients.

10. *What environmental factors are relevant to this situation?* The environment is an enormous part of the world of the client and the interviewer. It can include, but is not limited to, where the client lives, what town or neighborhood, an apartment or a single-family home, homelessness, a large or small community, rural or urban; health challenges in the community; the racial, ethnic, and religious nature of the community; and on and on. These factors, if left unexplored, can be a huge blind spot for the interviewer.

11. *What resources are available to the client in dealing with this situation? What are the client's strengths?* The interviewer should

have an eye toward exploring the kinds of resources that can assist the client. This area is related to the environment question, but explores the specific types of help available to the client. For example, is the client poor or relatively wealthy? Is there family in the area that can be of assistance? If the client is married or has a partner, what is the nature of that relationship in terms of helping the client? All clients have strengths. Do they have a cheerful and optimistic disposition; are they spiritual, creative; do they reach out to others? These and many more strengths can be the key elements in helping the client.

12. *Based upon all of the factors above, what is your intervention plan, and what do you think the outcome might be?* This may sound like a daunting question, but it is a differential one based on the type of interview being conducted. The important point is to try to take into consideration as many of the areas cited above as possible when interviewing and working with clients.

The relational interviewing process described in this text can be used in a variety of professional disciplines and scenarios. Several case examples will help demonstrate the ways in which certain features can be used to help the client. They will help differentiate and suggest various interviewing styles that can be applied to specific situations and disciplines.

CRISIS INTERVENTION

Crisis intervention is a specific type of interviewing with one main goal: to provide immediate help to the client in a time of crisis, to stabilize the client as much as possible, and to determine the appropriate disposition (next steps) to resolve the crisis. Crisis is in many ways self-defined and comes in many forms. Examples include a client with a panic attack at a hospital emergency room, an abused woman leaving home and coming to an emergency shelter for help, a pregnant adolescent seeking help and solutions at a nearby clinic, a victim of a crime seeking help at the local police station, a homesick college student turning to the university counselor for comfort, and so forth. The type of crisis is not as important as the role of the interviewer and the resolution of the situation. The example below, a fifty-three-year-old suicidal man calling the local suicide hotline, illustrates this principle.

Around the world, suicide hotlines provide twenty-four-hour confidential phone help to anyone experiencing suicidal ideation. Some settings are designed as walk-in facilities, others have telephone hotlines, and some have both capabilities. The workers in these settings are all trained in interviewing, especially as it relates to helping clients with suicidal ideation. Most of these workers have bachelor's or master's degrees in the helping professions, but some are trained volunteers supervised by professionals. All information discussed is confidential *unless* the interviewer determines that there is an imminent risk to the client or others in the client's life. In that case, the interviewer must notify the police to intervene for the client's safety. The client is advised of this policy before the interview begins.

Frank is a fifty-three-year-old businessman who has just been let go after thirty years at his job. He is in a good marriage, with a supportive wife, and has three children: a twenty-year-old daughter in college, and two sons, fifteen and ten. Frank is an anxious and somewhat insecure man, but is intelligent and competent in his work, and has functioned relatively well in his life until this recent situation. He is calling the local suicide hotline late at night after his family has gone to sleep.

Interviewer: Suicide hotline, how can I help you?

Frank: Is this a confidential hotline?

Interviewer: Yes, everything we talk about is strictly confidential, but I am obligated by law to contact the authorities if you are seriously suicidal and are planning to hurt yourself or someone else.

The interviewer in this type of crisis situation is clarifying her role with this client. This is a very important part of helping the client understand that the interviewer will do her best to help, but also has a responsibility to protect life. This is also the beginning of building trust.

Frank: No, it's not like that, I just need someone to talk to . . .

Interviewer: Can you tell me what has happened or been happening that has prompted you to call?

Frank: It's a lot of things really, but mainly my job. You see, I was just laid off.

Interviewer: When was that?

Frank: About three weeks ago.

Interviewer: What happened?

The interviewer in a crisis situation must get to the heart of the matter quickly in order not only to provide help and support, but also to ascertain the seriousness of the situation. The questions are direct, but still demonstrate caring, empathy, and interest.

Frank: I had been working at this fairly large advertising firm for over twenty years. I started right out of college and was doing very well. I did so well on my team that I was given a series of promotions, and over the last five years or so I was in charge of my department, with a lot of responsibility. I supervised about fifteen people directly, and many of them were supervisors under me who had people that reported to them. Everything seemed to be going great until this happened.

Interviewer: Sounds like this was a big surprise.

In a typical counseling session, the interviewer might have taken more time to respond with an empathic furthering intervention aimed at validating and eliciting more in-depth information, but in a crisis, this short response conveys empathy and moves the conversation along.

Frank: Kind of . . . I have been having trouble with my boss for a while, and I think it has come to a head.

Interviewer: Tell me more about that.

Frank: I have known her for a long time. She has been with the company for about fifteen years. Until recently I had not worked directly under her. When I interviewed with her for promotion several years ago, the first thing she said to me was "So . . . you want my job?" I didn't know what to say, but her statement really caught me off guard and made me think she was threatened by me.

Interviewer: Yeah, that does sound that way.

Frank: Ever since I got the promotion, she has been very difficult to work with . . .

Interviewer: In what way?

Frank: It's kind of hard to describe exactly. She did not meet with me on a regular basis except to direct me to take on some type of task. She never asked my opinion about my area, which is a huge portion of the company. She cut me off in conversations, and just didn't seem interested in anything I have to say.

Interviewer: So let me see if I understand. You had been doing well at work, so well that you had gotten promoted to a fairly high position with a good deal of responsibility, but now your immediate supervisor seemed to be opposed to you, or perhaps even threatened?

Frank: Yeah, does that sound crazy?

Interviewer: Well, from how you describe things, it sounds like this is a huge surprise, very unexpected, and troublesome.

Frank: Exactly. There are a couple of other strange interactions I have had with her that I think you should know about.

Interviewer: OK.

Frank: The two of us were headed to a meeting awhile ago, and she told me that one of my people had mentioned that they thought it might be helpful to their team if my boss was a little more encouraging. My boss said, "Doesn't she know I don't care about people!" She also said in a small meeting of supervisors like me, "You know the problem with this country? Old people and stupid people!"

Interviewer: She doesn't sound like a very caring person.

Frank: Well, those two interactions kind of blew me away.

Interviewer: Frank, can you tell me what has led up to your calling tonight?

The interviewer is not trying to cut the client off or be insensitive, but this is not a counseling session, and getting to the crisis is important.

> *Frank:* I'm sorry, I guess I'm rambling. This is all so upsetting.
> **Interviewer:** I can certainly understand that, and I'm sorry if I'm moving too quickly.

The interviewer empathically responds to the client's worry.

> *Frank:* Can I tell you one more important part about all of this?
> **Interviewer:** Sure, take your time.

The interviewer realizes that the client needs more time before going into some of the suicidal thoughts and feelings. The interviewer also senses that the client has made a good connection and a relationship is developing.

> *Frank:* One of my teams was having trouble with their supervisor. He was not performing, and putting the blame on his hard-working team. The team members consistently complained to me with specific verifiable situations. I tried to work things out with the supervisor, but he would not cooperate with me. Ultimately I had to go to my supervisor with the problem. Even though I had very good documentation, she didn't even listen to me. She dismissed the problem and in fact told me that she was removing this particular team and supervisor from my workload in order to reduce conflict. Within a year, all the members of that team resigned and found other jobs. These were very good people. I felt powerless and inconsequential. Ever since that time I had less and less contact with my supervisor, felt less comfortable working with her, and also felt very little trust. Recently she called me into her office and told me that the agency was going through some reorganization, and they were going to let me go. I was shocked, since my teams were producing well. I am absolutely certain that she just

wanted to get rid of me, but I can't prove it, since this is the way things work in the company. I'm confused, ashamed, demoralized, angry, depressed, and don't know what I'm going to do next.

Interviewer: Wow, that's a pretty shocking story! From the way you describe it, it certainly sounds like she had it in for you. Any ideas why?

The interviewer only has the information from the client and can't be certain of the situation, but expresses empathy for the client's experience.

Frank: Ever since then, I've been getting up in the middle of the night, sitting in the living room, and just staring at the walls for hours. I just sit there. I can't sleep, I feel absolutely no motivation, and I keep going over the entire situation, trying to figure out what I did wrong or could have done differently. I'm so depressed. I don't want to live, I feel like a failure, but I don't want to kill myself.

Interviewer: The way you describe things, Frank, it sounds to me like you did the best you could. You were extremely successful until you were matched with this supervisor who appears, from how you describe it, to have had it out for you. Why wouldn't someone in this situation feel the way you do?

Here the interviewer is validating the very real and legitimate feelings of the client that seemed to have led to the depressive and quasi-suicidal feelings.

Frank: [Silence.]

Interviewer: It doesn't sound like you're actually suicidal, Frank, but feeling very hopeless and depressed.

Frank: Yeah, I just don't have the energy to do anything, even look for another job.

Interviewer: Have you thought about seeing someone for counseling?

Frank: That's why I thought I would start with you. What would you suggest?

In a crisis situation and some other types of interviewing, advice is warranted and helpful. The client doesn't appear capable in his present emotional state to make a clear decision right now.

Interviewer: It sounds to me like you're going through a situational depression right now, Frank. You've been successful, and this recent experience is a serious setback for you. I think it might help if I gave you a referral to see a psychiatrist.

Frank [*abruptly*]: A psychiatrist! Am I crazy?

Interviewer: No Frank, you're not crazy, but you are troubled by what has happened, and it seems to be interfering with your ability to function.

Frank: That's true . . .

Interviewer: A psychiatrist can evaluate you for antidepressant medication, which can really help to alleviate some of your depressed and overwhelming feelings. They can also refer you to a good therapist if you want to have someone to talk over these issues in more detail and plan for the future. I think those two things might really help getting you on the right track again.

This intervention is directive and suggestive, but needed to help the client move forward and perhaps hold onto some hope. This is a clear example of some of the main differences between the crisis intervention and therapy interviews. Crisis interviews are shorter, more to the point, yet supportive and empathic. The goal is to help the client feel understood and provide the necessary services to resolve the crisis.

The client agrees to take the referral for the psychiatrist, and the interviewer determines that Frank is not actively suicidal by asking if he has a suicide plan, has any weapons or medications in the home, and has a good support system. These are important indicators of the seriousness of suicidal ideation. Based upon this assessment, there does not seem to be a need for hospitalization or other immediate intervention.

THE PSYCHIATRIC INTAKE SESSION

Frank makes an emergency appointment to see the psychiatrist within a few days of the call to the suicide hotline. This type of interview is a follow-up to the hotline call. Usually the hotline worker will have provided the psychiatrist with a synopsis of the hotline call (with the client's signed permission) in order to expedite the helping process. The following interview is typical of a psychiatric intake in this type of situation.

> **Interviewer:** Hi Frank, I'm Dr. Wayne. I'm a psychiatrist and am here to follow up on the recent phone session you had with the hotline. I've read the notes from the hotline worker, but I would like to hear your side of the story so I don't miss anything.

The interviewer is clearly communicating to the client that he is important and that his information is vital to the helping interview. This sets a tone of respect, initial trust, and caring.

> *Frank:* Thanks for seeing me so quickly. It really helped to talk to the worker the other night. Just knowing that I was going to see you felt like a lifeline.
>
> **Interviewer:** I'm glad to hear that. Sometimes just knowing there are people who care can help take some of the edge off things.
>
> *Frank:* Where do you want me to start?
>
> **Interviewer:** Well, the worker's notes mention your situation at work and your strained relationship with your supervisor, as well as your not being able to sleep and being in a pretty steady state of worry. Maybe we could start there?

The interviewer is attempting to summarize the situation as best he knows it, validating Frank's feelings, and encouraging him to talk about them.

Frank: I'm just so down and afraid. I'm pretty sure I'll get unemployment, but that's temporary and is not going to be enough to live on. We have a little savings, but that's going to go fast. I feel so demoralized and depleted. I really don't know if I can go on. Don't get me wrong. I'm not suicidal, but I certainly wouldn't care if I didn't wake up tomorrow. My wife doesn't like to hear me talk like that, but I can't help it. I love her so much and she's been a great support, but this is not about her, it's about me feeling like a failure.

Interviewer: So you're feeling really alone with all of this and blaming yourself?

The interviewer may be reaching here, but Frank seems to be implying that he holds himself responsible for the situation. This open-ended clarifying question is aimed at that possibility.

Frank: Yeah, I keep getting up in the middle of the night when I can't sleep and go down to the living room and stare at nothing, wondering if I really am just a failure and whether everything will be OK. Right now I can't see that. I'm afraid . . . I really don't think I can go on. I mean, a part of me sort of knows that eventually I'll be OK, but I'm fifty-three and I don't know how marketable I am, and I'm worried.

Interviewer: I think I can certainly understand those feelings, Frank. You know, the way you describe your pattern of thoughts and emotions, your inability to sleep, and your generally down mood signals to me that you're probably depressed.

This is another empathic response followed by a clear diagnostic statement offered as a suggestion for Frank to consider. The interviewer does not insist or direct, but is confident and clear in stating his impressions.

Frank: I think you're right. What do I do now, take medication?

Interviewer: I think that might help, Frank, but I also think that it would be very helpful to have a professional to talk with about how to handle this situation and problem solve for the future.

Frank: Like a therapist?

Interviewer: Yeah, a social worker or psychologist would probably be the best.

Frank: Couldn't I just talk to you?

Interviewer: Well, Frank, I'm a psychiatrist and don't usually do therapy. My job is to look at the possible benefits of medication and refer you to the right person for follow-up counseling. My training and expertise is really in the area of medication management, while psychologists and social workers are experts in therapy. Does that make sense?

Frank: I guess so; it's just so many people. I want to feel better.

Interviewer: It must feel frustrating, but I can assure you this is a good way to proceed. I've seen many people with your type of situation, and a combination of medication and therapy can really help in a rather short period of time.

Once again, the interviewer is empathically reassuring Frank as well as sketching out the course of treatment.

Frank: Well, where do we go from here?

Frank's use of the word "we" signals a relational connection.

Interviewer: I would like to start you on a very good yet conservative antidepressant called Lexapro. It works quickly and has very few side effects. I would like to start you out on a small dosage to see how you handle it and perhaps increase it if you seem to need more. If there are consistent unpleasant side effects, we might switch to something else, but Lexapro is one of the newest and best, and I'd recommend it.

Frank: You're the doctor. I'm OK with trying it. You mentioned side effects. What are they?

Interviewer: Not much, really. You should start feeling the effects in about a week to ten days. You'll notice that the depression will have lifted, and you won't be consumed by those consistent negative thoughts. The medication won't make everything OK: you'll still be dealing with your situation, but you will not be as dragged down by your mood and will have more energy to tackle your problems. There are occasional sexual side effects with Lexapro, like an inability to perform, but if that happens I can give you a prescription for something like Viagra to offset that side effect.

Frank: Well, that doesn't sound like fun, but I guess if it means getting out of this down place, maybe it's worth a trade-off.

Interviewer: I don't know if you'll have any troubling side effects, but if you do, get in touch with me immediately and we'll adjust things.

Frank: OK. You mentioned seeing a therapist. Do you have any suggestions?

Interviewer: I'll give you a few names. They're all very good and I've worked with them before.

Frank: Thanks. When do I see you again?

Interviewer: Why don't we set up an appointment for about a month from now to see how you're doing with the meds and therapy? If you're experiencing any difficulties with the medication, or have any questions, please don't hesitate to call me. I'm here for you, Frank.

Frank: Thanks doctor. I feel encouraged. I hope the meds help. I'll look into the therapy.

Frank begins taking the medication and sees a therapist. His case will be revisited later in the book.

This interview demonstrates the kind of process and relationship building that is common in an intake setting. The interviewer in this case was a psychiatrist with special skills in medication assessment and management. However, it could easily have been a nurse, psychologist, social worker, or other helping professional attempting to understand the client in order to refer him to the best possible service for his situation. The interviewing skills are very similar in each of these disciplines. The goal is to help the client by developing a trusting relationship, no matter how brief. The case examples effectively illustrate this process.

INVOLUNTARY JUVENILE PROBATION INTERVIEW

The final interview example in this chapter focuses on juvenile probation. I have had extensive work with adolescents on probation, and the example illustrates how to interview and engage an involuntary and resistant adolescent juvenile. Although probation interviews are involuntary, the same interview process is necessary to engage the adolescent in a relationship that can lead to a more productive and helpful life. Chapter 6 goes into greater detail about interviewing adolescents.

John is a fifteen-year-old adolescent male who has been arrested for vandalism. He was convicted of attempting to blow up a flagpole with homemade explosives. John was sentenced to one year's probation and mandatory weekly counseling. The interviewer is required to submit monthly reports on John's progress in counseling. If John is not compliant or misses appointments, he could be required to spend time in a juvenile facility. John comes from an intact family. Both his mother and father work, and he has two older adult sisters who live outside the home. John attends high school, and spends a great deal of time alone, before and after school, because of his parents' working situation. John has few friends, and tends to alienate most of the adolescents that he tries to interact with in his life. John comes to the first session in a very uncooperative mood.

> **Interviewer:** Hi John. I read the report that was sent to me from the court, and understand that you are required to come to weekly counseling. I'm required to send in a written report once a month describing how things are going in

counseling. We can talk about that in a little while, but first, I'd really like to hear your side of the situation.

As in most interviewing situations, it is extremely helpful in building trust to ask these types of open-ended questions early, in order to communicate a genuine and sincere interest in valuing the client's opinion and to create an atmosphere that encourages mutual discussion.

John: *[Silence . . . then]* I don't know . . .

Interviewer: Well, I can imagine that you might not really want to be here, huh?

The interviewer is trying to get the process started by stating the obvious in an empathic manner, rather than assuming an authoritative position, which is already obvious.

John *[in a disgusted and angry tone]*: Yeah.

Interviewer: Do you feel like talking at all about why you were arrested?

John *[again with the same type of tone]*: No!

Interviewer: OK, I can understand that. Do you have any questions about this counseling?

John: Yeah . . . how long do I have to do this?

Interviewer: The court order says a year.

John *[sarcastically]*: Great!

Interviewer: I can tell you don't think that's going to be much fun, huh?

John: *[Silence for about two minutes.]*

The interviewer is feeling some frustration and irritation with John, but also understands and empathizes with his feelings about being forced to do something he doesn't want to do. The interviewer is also getting the sense that John, at least at this point in counseling, is probably not going to want to talk about his crime or perhaps the direct circumstances surrounding it. The interviewer decides to try to engage John in some less intrusive and conflictual conversation.

Interviewer: OK, well let me tell you how this works. We have to meet once a week for about forty-five minutes. As far as I'm concerned, we can talk about whatever you want, or we can sit here in silence. I'm OK with sitting in silence, but I'm also going to have to send in a report about our sessions. If we don't talk together at all, I'm going to have to say so, and I'm not sure how the court will react to that. Sometimes they extend the counseling; sometimes they require the person to spend some time in detention. I'm not trying to threaten or scare you, John; I just want you to know how it is.

John [*interrupting angrily*]: I'm not afraid to go to detention!

Interviewer: I believe you John, and I don't want to force you to talk.

John: [*Silence for another couple of minutes.*]

The interviewer is now debating if he should remain silent as well, or continue to coax John to talk a little.

Interviewer: I'll tell you what . . . why don't we talk a little bit about some of the things in your life that you like to do? That way I can honestly say that we're working together. Can you tell me about school?

John: I *hate* it!

Interviewer: All right, that's a start.

This is a good start. At least John is talking about his life.

Interviewer: What do you hate about it?

John: Everything!

Interviewer: Well, everything is a pretty big thing. Isn't there anything about school that's sort of OK?

John: Lunch.

Interviewer: Yeah, I could see how lunch might be OK. Anything else?

John: Seeing my friends.

Interviewer: So there are a couple of things that aren't quite so bad.

John: I guess. How much more time do I have to be here today?

Interviewer: We've got about twenty minutes left.

John: Great.

Interviewer: How about when you're not in school? What do you like to do?

John: Play guitar.

Interviewer: Oh, so you're into music. What kind do you like?

John: I like all kinds.

Interviewer: Well, give me an example.

John: I like alternative, hard rock, some jazz, and lots of stuff.

Interviewer: You're really pretty versatile.

John: What's that mean?

Interviewer: I'm sorry, it means you like a lot of different types of music.

John: Yeah, I guess.

Interviewer: That's a great thing.

The session moves on to the final minutes, and another appointment is arranged. The interviewer has begun to form some type of connection with John. John is not willing to discuss his crime yet or perhaps extenuating circumstances; however, he is talking about himself. Involuntary and resistant clients such as John need time to open up and form trust. A patient, understanding, and empathic interviewer can develop a relationship with this type of client if he persists. Interviewing with adolescents will be explored in greater detail later in the text.

RESEARCH IMPLICATIONS AND BASIS OF PRACTICE

A tremendous amount of research has demonstrated the importance, validity, and effectiveness of the interviewing process (O'Hare, 2005, 2009). There are universal interviewing techniques that are common to all the helping professions. Research has demonstrated that regardless of the theoretical model used in the interviewing process, the relationship is the most important variable for a successful outcome

(Prochaska & Norcross, 2003). Forming the relationship is crucial and sometimes a very challenging endeavor, as seen in the interview with John.

SUMMARY

The interviewing examples in this chapter demonstrate the crucial importance of building a relationship with the client. What is also emphasized is the uniformity of specific interviewing techniques, regardless of the type of interview. Empathy, caring, and the genuineness of the interviewer are essential, along with the use of intervention skills such as open-and closed-ended questions, summarizing, paraphrasing, and reflective and probing techniques. The use of these various skills must derive from the natural empathy and curiosity of the interviewer, combined with the differential use of theoretical knowledge. Chapter 4 elaborates upon the interviewing process as it relates to clients with diverse backgrounds.

RECOMMENDED READING

O'Hare, T. (2005). *Evidence-based practices for social workers: An interdisciplinary approach.* Chicago: Lyceum Books.

O'Hare, T. (2009). *Essential skills of social work practice: Assessment, intervention, and evaluation.* Chicago: Lyceum Books.

O'Hare's work is a good source for validated knowledge on interviewing.

Prochaska, J. O., & Norcross, J. C. (2003). *Systems of psychotherapy: A transtheoretical analysis.* Belmont, CA: Brooks/Cole.

This excellent source provides validated knowledge regarding the key and universal importance of the relationship in treatment outcome.

MULTIMEDIA SOURCES

Revisit the films cited in the multimedia section of chapter 1, with an eye toward the differential but universal application of common interviewing techniques.

CHAPTER FOUR

Interviewing with Cultural Competence

All clients and interviewers bring their unique history, background, culture, and experience to the relational work. Developing cultural competence is a lifelong process: it is described well in this passage from Rothman's book *Cultural Competence in Process and Practice: Building Bridges* (2008, p. 3).

> It is the author's belief, however, that cultural competence and sensitive . . . practice are not goals to be strived for, attained, and filed away for use as needed. Rather, cultural competence is a special worldview, a way of considering self and other in the context of the whole range of human experience. Cultural competence is a lifelong process, and as we grow and mature both as professionals and private individuals, the depth and breadth of our cultural competence is continually evolving. As we take in new experiences, process life events, understand others, experience history, and develop relationships, each one of these elements adds a piece to our cultural competence. We can never know too

much about cultures and differences among peoples. It is the *journey*, and not the *destination*, that we must understand and upon which we must consciously embark. We take with us the tools and worldview of our own experience, and we use those to understand the experiences of others.

Each new interviewing experience is an opportunity for both clients and interviewers to grow and develop as members of human society. The vignettes in this chapter are relevant for professional interviewers in all disciplines, but especially in the United States and Canada. They illustrate some of the similarities and subtle differences between the Canadian and US client populations. The material covered in this chapter meets and addresses the mandates of the American (National Association of Social Workers, Council on Social Work Education) and Canadian (Canadian Association of Social Workers) professional standards for practice and education (Campbell, 2003; Bogo, 2006; Hepworth, Rooney, Rooney, Strom-Gottfried, & Larsen, 2006; Strom-Gottfried, 2007; Shebib, 2011; Egan, 2013).

One of the most striking aspects of Canadian professionals' work with clients is the great amount of interdisciplinary collaboration in the health care system, as well as an emphasis on home care visits and work with primary caregivers on all case levels. In addition, the profoundly bilingual and bicultural Canadian population enhances the interviewing challenges.

The case examples in this chapter are taken from *Understanding and Managing and the Therapeutic Relationship* (McKenzie, 2011).

GENDER

Mrs. A. (we'll call her Denise) comes to the interview to work on difficulties she is experiencing with her husband (McKenzie, 2011, p. 45).

> **Interviewer:** Hi Denise. I understand you have some concerns about your marriage or relationship with your husband.

Denise: I don't think you could call it a marriage, let alone a relationship.

Interviewer: Why do you say that?

Denise: Well, he's barely involved with me. Oh yeah, he wants to have sex, but other than that, he is literally not there for me. Even in sex it's all about him.

Interviewer: So it sounds like he doesn't interact much with you. How long has this been going on?

Denise: It seems like forever.

Interviewer: How long have the two of you been married?

Denise: Almost ten years now. I guess things started to change after about three or four years.

Interviewer: And prior to that time, how was he?

Denise: He was OK, I guess. We seemed to share in the household activities, he used to sit and talk with me, and our lovemaking really seemed like love. But then it all started to change.

Interviewer: How so?

Denise: Like I said before, he just started getting more selfish and distant.

Interviewer: To help me understand better, Denise, could you talk a little bit about how the two of you dealt with these changes?

Denise: I tried to explain to him that he was acting different, and that I really needed and wanted him more involved with me and our home.

Interviewer: And how did he respond?

Denise: You know, like all men. He just couldn't see it and wasn't willing to try and change anything.

Interviewer: That must have been very frustrating [*trying to express some empathy*].

Denise: How would you know, you're a man just like all the rest.

The interviewer realizes that Denise has some preconceived ideas about men, based upon her life experiences. In order to be effective, he must not only try to understand her worldview, but also gently challenge this distortion, because, in fact, not all men, or women for that matter, are exactly the same. Furthermore, clinging to that belief will undoubtedly lead to further difficulties in life and future relationships with men. This is a delicate challenge for the interviewer in terms of his own cultural competence regarding gender.

> **Interviewer:** I'm not sure I understand what you mean, Denise, when you say I'm a man just like all the rest?
>
> *Denise:* You're all just concerned about yourselves. You know, you just want us to cook, clean, get the groceries, have sex when you want, you know.
>
> **Interviewer:** How do you know that I am that kind of man?
>
> *Denise:* You're all the same.
>
> **Interviewer:** Would it surprise you to know that I too am married, but am involved in cooking, cleaning, grocery shopping, and try to equally involve myself in my relationship with my wife?

This self-disclosure is purposely timed to challenge the client's assumptions about men, but also to begin to broaden the discussion in a way that might help Denise and her husband improve their relationship. In other words, if Denise comes to see that not all men are like her husband, she may be better able to modify her worldview and approach her interactions differently with men.

> *Denise:* I'm not sure I believe you.
>
> **Interviewer:** Why would I lie to you?
>
> *Denise:* I'm not saying you're lying, it's just I haven't experienced men like that before. I know I see them in movies and on TV, but I've always thought they weren't real.
>
> **Interviewer:** So this is kind of a different perspective for you?
>
> *Denise:* Yeah, I'm not sure what to make of it.
>
> **Interviewer:** Well, I can assure you, Denise, that I am telling you the truth. Now I'm also pretty sure that I am not

perfect, and my wife would probably tell you that there are things I could improve on, but I try to do the best I can.
Denise: Well, I'm sure she does too, but what you told me about your life gets me thinking.
Interviewer: In what way?
Denise: Well, maybe I don't have to settle for a certain kind of man.
Interviewer: I think that's a very important insight, Denise.

This client's bias about men has been successfully challenged in a sensitive way by the interviewer in order to help her understand both herself and her husband from a different perspective. This will help to move the interviewing forward, and perhaps even lead to some successful couples work. This exchange also expands the worldview of the interviewer through experiencing Denise's very different perspective on men. The use of self-disclosure here was necessary, crucial, and therapeutic, as it often is in these types of situations.

RACE

An African American female psychologist was seeing a white male interviewer with a doctorate in social work for several months in individual sessions regarding relationship and career problems. The issue of race had not yet been the focus of discussion, although it had been on the mind of the interviewer, in terms of what part, if any, their racial differences might play in the sessions. This case example picks up as the client introduces this topic.

Interviewer: Nice to see you, Marsha. How are things going?
Marsha: Pretty good. Work is OK, but I'm still struggling with the whole dating thing.
Interviewer: What do you mean, struggling?
Marsha: Well, I'm finding it hard to meet the right kind of men. I joined a special online dating service for African American professionals, but so far I just can't seem to click

with anyone. This area is basically pretty white, and so the number of prospects in general is slim.

Interviewer: Sounds frustrating.

Marsha: Kind of . . . I'm sure I'll connect with someone eventually.

Interviewer: If you don't mind my asking, Marsha, is it important to find an African American man to date?

Marsha: Well, I've dated white men and black men, but I'm really beginning to think I want to settle down and start a family. I think being with a black man is important for that.

Interviewer: Why is that?

Marsha: I really want to have kids, and I just think it will be easier if my husband and I are the same race, knowing how society will react.

Interviewer: Do you mean prejudice?

Marsha: Yeah, I guess it'll just be easier on the kids if their racial identity is clear.

Interviewer: We've been seeing each other for a while now, Marsha, and the issue of race has never really come up until now.

Marsha: Yeah, I guess I really didn't think about it much, and it didn't seem to matter. But you know, I didn't tell you this in the beginning, but I really wanted to see a white male therapist.

Interviewer: Why was that?

Marsha: Just an intuition, I think. I wanted to see what it would be like to see someone who may have a different racial perspective.

Interviewer: What has it been like so far?

Marsha: Well, it's hard to tell. I mean, we're both professionals and have a lot in common. For the most part, I think it's what you don't say that intrigues me.

Interviewer: What do you mean, the things I don't say?

Marsha: Well, like today when you asked me why I wanted to date black men.

Interviewer: What thoughts ran through your mind then?

Marsha: Well, to be honest, I thought, "Really, he doesn't know that I would be worried about the whole mixed racial thing with kids if I married a white guy."

Interviewer: So it seemed like I didn't have any idea that you might be concerned about that?

Marsha: I'm sure you did, but you didn't bring it up or talk about it. We don't really talk about race much in here, which is fine, but sometimes it feels a little like the elephant in the room.

Interviewer: That's a very good point. Now that you mention it, why did you decide to see a white male therapist rather than someone black?

Marsha: I had experiences all of my life with black family, friends, lovers, and therapists. I really wanted to know if seeing a white therapist would be different.

Interviewer: And?

The interviewer is interested and even somewhat relieved that the client is addressing this topic, because he has felt that on some level it must be meaningful. As the client had not brought it up, however, the interviewer decided that he did not want to introduce the subject as his own, thereby interfering with the client's process. Right or wrong, this was the stance of the interviewer.

Marsha: Surprisingly there hasn't been much difference.

Interviewer: Why does that surprise you?

Marsha: I guess I thought we wouldn't connect, or maybe even that I'd pick up some subtle prejudice.

Interviewer: What would that look like?

Marsha: It's hard to say. Sometimes it's a tone of voice, or a facial expression. Rarely is it overt. But as a minority you learn to be careful and observant about those things . . . it's a self-protection.

Interviewer: So far you haven't experienced that with me?

Marsha: Not so far. I think a lot of it is because, you know, we're professionals. We've got a lot in common in our professional culture. But I also think it's because we haven't talked much, if any, about race. I also think it's because I've been with a lot of white men and maybe worked out some of these issues with them.

Interviewer: What do you mean, worked out?

Marsha: Well, for me, I've discovered that there do seem to be some subtle and even overt differences between the black and white men that I've dated.

Interviewer: Like what?

Marsha: This is only my experience, mind you, so I'm not generalizing to the entire black male population, but a lot of black men I date seem to want to be in charge. I don't get that as much from the white men. I date mostly professionals, so I don't think it's a class thing. Like I said, I can't be sure, maybe it's my prejudice.

Interviewer: Well, whatever it is, it's an interesting observation.

Marsha: Yeah, and it seems to interfere a lot in my dating black guys.

Interviewer: Any thoughts about what that dynamic might be about?

The interviewer uses the word "dynamic" purposely because of his awareness and respect for the professional expertise of the client.

Marsha: I don't know if you know this, but African American men have been extremely marginalized in our society, and as a result have a very difficult time feeling good about themselves and confident in their abilities. You probably know that in a good deal of the African American communities, the woman is more dominant because of racial discrimination, economic conditions, and so forth. It stands to reason that an assertive professional woman could at least feel like a challenge to even a professional black man.

Interviewer: I see your point.

Marsha: I might be wrong. Maybe it's just my experience, but you know it's in the literature, and I do sense it sometimes.

Interviewer: How do you feel about feeling that?

Marsha: Kind of awkward actually. I almost feel like I'm being prejudiced. Sounds weird?

Interviewer: Not at all, although I can sense your guilt.

Marsha: I think that is the word.

Interviewer: Well, that's how it felt to me, I could certainly be wrong.

Marsha: No, I think you hit it right on the head.

The interviewer did take a risk in suggesting an emotional reaction by the client, but her entire conversation about this topic seemed to be intuitively leading up to it.

From this point on in sessions, the tone shifted. The interviewer and client began to learn more about each other's perspectives about race and themselves, as well as the fact that distortions and biases are a natural part of everyone's experience, regardless of race, gender, or any other form of diversity. This case example is a powerful real-world example of the importance in carefully listening and exploring all aspects of the client's and interviewer's inner world in order to be open, honest, and effective in the process, while keeping biases to a minimum.

ETHNIC GROUP OR NATIONALITY

After the 9/11 attacks, a twenty-five-year-old Middle Eastern man began seeing a forty-year-old non-Muslim male psychiatrist for anxiety. The psychiatrist recognized that he was feeling apprehensive about seeing this client because most of the suspected terrorists were presumed to be of Middle Eastern descent. The interviewer struggled with these feelings as he attempted to empathically connect with the client.

Interviewer: Nice to meet you, Sayed. I understand you've been having trouble with anxiety lately?

Sayed [*hesitantly*]: Yes.

Interviewer: You seem a little anxious right now.

Sayed: Yes, I am.

Interviewer: Do you feel like you can talk about it?

Sayed: I think I can try.

Interviewer: Good.

Sayed: Well, ever since 9/11, I have started feeling extremely anxious. I can't sleep at night. I usually will have a drink to try and relax me, and eventually fall asleep. However, I can't sleep for very long, only a few hours. I wake up in the middle of the night in a panic, sweating, and very worried. This has been happening since 9/11.

Interviewer: You seem very sure that it is the 9/11 events that are triggering your anxiety issues. What is it about 9/11 that is affecting you so strongly?

The interviewer, of course, has his own ideas about why this client of Middle Eastern descent may be feeling anxious after 9/11, but is not going to assume anything. It is very important to remain nonjudgmental, empathic, and caring in this situation despite any of the interviewer's own biases or feelings about 9/11.

Sayed: Isn't it obvious? Look at me. Everyone would think I come from a Middle Eastern background. The terrorists have been identified as almost exclusively from that part of the world. I don't feel safe right now.

Interviewer: I'm sorry if I sound naïve, Sayed, but why don't you feel safe right now?

Sayed: Because I can see how most people look at me when I leave my home, or when I'm at work. They all look at me like I'm the enemy, and I don't blame them. I am Middle Eastern.

Interviewer: But Sayed, I'm assuming you had nothing to do with the 9/11 attacks.

Sayed: Of course not, and I detest them. I feel ashamed to be a Muslim. Yet there is nothing I can do about the way I look.

Interviewer: That must be a terrible feeling.

The interviewer is feeling a genuine sense of empathy for this client.

> **Sayed:** I was worried that you would be the same way, but I really needed help and was assured by my friends that you would not judge me. I hope they were right.
>
> **Interviewer:** I'm glad you felt safe enough to come to see me.

The interviewer has ambivalent feelings in this situation. On one hand, he is comforted by the fact that this client has enough trust to see him for his problems, despite the fact that the interviewer is non-Muslim. On the other hand, the client is correct that many people probably are worried and apprehensive regarding Muslims, including the interviewer with this client. The interviewer recognizes that these reactions are irrational and prejudiced, yet very real. Does he share them with this client, or continue with the session? This is not an unusual dilemma for any interviewer with a variety of clients. All human beings have biases and reactions to everyone we encounter. The essence of cultural competence is to be aware of them and manage them in the most professional manner possible. Sometimes that may involve carefully timed self-disclosure, and at other times holding these reactions in silent contemplation can best serve the client and the process.

> **Sayed:** Do you have those feelings toward me?
>
> **Interviewer:** Well, Sayed, I have to admit when I knew I would be seeing a client of Middle Eastern background that I did feel a little anxious, as I think most people might, given the recent 9/11 events. However, after only a few minutes with you, I can honestly say I do not feel anxious, afraid, or put off by you in any way. In fact, I think I can truly sense your worries and anxiety and want to help.
>
> **Sayed:** I appreciate your being honest with me. That makes me feel much better.
>
> **Interviewer:** I will do my best to always be honest with you, Sayed.

Sayed: I just wish that Americans, of which I am one, would realize that these terrorists of Middle Eastern background are "radical" Muslim extremists. They in no way represent the mainstream Muslims. We are a peaceful people. The Koran, like your Christian Bible, teaches all Muslims to be peaceful and love all people. It does not advocate violence. Just as there are many extreme interpretations to your Bible, so too can extreme Muslims misinterpret the Koran.

Interviewer: This is a very important distinction, Sayed. It sounds like this misunderstanding is what may be at the heart of some of your anxiety?

Sayed: Yes, I'm certain it is.

Interviewer: Do you have people in your life who you can talk to about these thoughts and emotions?

Sayed: Yes, but so many of us feel the same. It's like a mass isolation. I thought coming to an objective professional would help.

Interviewer: Well Sayed, like I said, I will do my very best to help you. Have you considered taking any medication to help with this anxiety?

Sayed: Yes, but will the medication take away these worries?

Interviewer: That is a very insightful question, Sayed. No, the medication will not take away the worries, but it can help manage the anxiety and take the edge off the feelings, so you can sleep and not worry so much when you are awake.

Sayed: When will these feelings go away?

Interviewer: That's hard to say. For some people, these types of worries can be resolved relatively quickly, maybe in a few weeks or months. For others, it can take a longer time. It really depends on the person and the situation.

Sayed: What do you think about me?

Interviewer: You mean how long this might take?

Sayed: Yes.

Interviewer: I really don't know yet, Sayed.

Sayed: So what do we do now?

Interviewer: I would recommend that I start you on a mild tranquilizer that will help manage your anxiety and help you sleep at night. In addition, I think we should meet weekly for a while to talk about how you are feeling and managing things in your life. The combination of medication and talk therapy is always best for this type of problem.

Sayed: If you say so.

This case example is a good illustration of the ways in which both interviewer and client worked through potentially complicating biases, and have begun to establish a helpful and trusting relationship. It also demonstrates the essential importance of the client and interviewer working hard to continually develop a mutual cultural understanding and competence in the process.

In both Canada and the United States, many people presently identify as First Peoples. Historically this group was described in many ways, including American Indian, Native American, North American Indian, Indigenous People, and so forth. This diverse and complex population is spread throughout North America. Many of these people live on reservations, but a good number live in the major urban areas of North America, particularly larger cities. Poverty is a prevalent challenge for a good portion of this group, especially in Canada, where they live in greater numbers. The Canadian social service system works a good deal with this population in a variety of ways. Reaching out to First People families in home visits, voluntary or mandated, is an interviewing challenge because of the need to develop trust, as well as trying to work with them to meet the complex and multifaceted needs related to poverty.

The following vignette demonstrates how the interviewer can begin to engage a First People family living in poverty in a major urban area of western Canada. This type of work is not unique to Canada and could easily be translated into any type of interviewing casework with families in such circumstances. The interviewer has been mandated to visit the apartment of a family (the Smiths) because of a report of neglect. The mother (Jean) is at home with her four children. The father has not been home for a week or so. He has been out looking for work. The family has virtually no resources and is behind on their rent, and the children have been attending school inconsistently. It is the interviewer's job to assess the situation and make a recommendation to her superiors. However, it is also her opportunity to begin to work with the family to coordinate resources and help them get back on their feet. The family is likely to be defensive, afraid, and guarded.

This is quite a challenge for the interviewer, especially because she is not at all familiar with First People families. However, she has been working with the urban poor for some time. The interviewer must be careful to not judge or bring any preconceived opinions to this delicate process.

The interviewer knocks on the door and the mother answers.

Jean: Who are you and what do you want?
Interviewer: Good morning, Mrs. Smith?
Jean: Yeah, like I said, who are you?
Interviewer: I'm Susan Jones with public welfare; could I talk with you?
Jean: Is it about the rent? I know we're late, we'll get it. Good-bye! [*starts to close the door*].
Interviewer: Wait, Mrs. Smith. I'm not here about the rent. It's important.
Jean: You're not? Well, what is it?
Interviewer: My agency asked me to stop by and see how you're doing.

The interviewer is careful to approach the client with patience and the understanding that this is a delicate situation. She does not simply announce that she is investigating a neglect situation. She wants to try to establish some type of human connection with Jean.

Jean: What do you mean, how I'm doing?

Jean's voice is raised and her body posture seems rigid to the interviewer. These nonverbal expressions and vitality affects are very powerful forms of communication. In fact they communicate even more intensely than do Jean's words. In all interviewing, it is crucial to pay close attention to all aspects of communication.

Interviewer: You seem upset to me, Jean, but I could be wrong.

Jean [*a little calmer and relaxed*]: Well, I don't know you or exactly what you want. I think anyone would be a little suspicious in this type of situation.

Interviewer: I think you're absolutely right, Jean. Please let me try to explain. The department received a neglect report about your children, and I was assigned to come out to your home and investigate. This is an investigation. You are not being charged with anything, and I am certainly not assuming that you have done anything wrong. My job is actually to help people.

The more information the interviewer can give Jean that is presented in a respectful and humane fashion the better the interview will go. When working with any client, it is important to try to put oneself in her position. This empathic approach is the cornerstone to all professional helping.

Jean: Neglect, why am I being charged with neglect?

Interviewer [*calmly*]: Jean, as I just said, you are not being charged with anything. A report was made, and I was sent here to investigate it. That means just talking with you about it.

Jean: Well, who reported me?

Interviewer: In any situation like this, that information is confidential.

Jean: So I don't get to know who it is? How am I going to defend myself?

Interviewer: I know that seems kind of unfair, doesn't it? That's why I'm here, though, to help us sort this situation out. Would it be OK if we talked a little bit about it?

Once again, the interviewer is going to great lengths, but genuinely, to establish an atmosphere of trust in order to proceed. If this doesn't happen to a certain extent, the interviewing process will never be successful.

Jean: I guess so. Do you want to come in?

Interviewer: That would be great, Jean. Thanks.

Obviously this is a huge step in the interviewing process, and it demonstrates a beginning level of potential trust.

Jean: The place is a mess, I know. Neither my husband nor I are working. I'm a stay-at-home mom with four kids. Two are in school, they're eight and nine. The other two are just babies, two and four. My husband has been trying to find work since we moved here a couple of months ago. We get some help from our families back home, and our neighbors have been really nice, but it's very hard.

Interviewer: Sounds like you're doing the best you can.

This simple empathic statement can mean a great deal to any client in this type of situation. It can be easy to judge or misunderstand. There may be actual neglect occurring with this family, but the interviewer's job is to carefully explore and understand, not make any rash judgments.

Jean: I don't know, but I try. I'm pretty down, and with four kids I don't feel like I have the energy sometimes. I guess that's kind of lazy. My kids don't always look so good. We're careful with the heat and water. They don't always get a bath either. Maybe that's why someone reported me. We also don't have much to eat. I know they're hungry. I feel so bad.

Interviewer: I can see why someone might have thought your kids were being neglected, Jean, but from talking with you, I can see that you just don't have the help or resources. Maybe I can help with that.

Jean: What do you mean?

Interviewer: Well, I've got connections with a lot of agencies in the city that can help with some of the things you were talking about. There are free food pantries, organizations that can help with finances and employment for your husband. There's free day care for your kids if you need it. I really do know about a lot of places that can help. It's my job, Jean. It's what I do.

Jean: That sounds good, but am I in trouble?

Interviewer: No, Jean, that's just it. I'm here to help, not hurt you or your family. I'm even available to talk to or I can refer you to a counselor if you think that might help.

Jean: So you think I'm crazy?

Interviewer: No, of course not. But I can tell you that if I were in your situation, it might be helpful to have someone for support. It's just a thought. You certainly don't have to do it.

Jean: Well, maybe. If they were like you, I might.

Interviewer: That's nice of you to say.

Jean: Well, where do we go from here?

Interviewer: I can tell you that I'm not going to verify a neglect report, but I do think it would help if you and I and even your husband started taking advantage of some of the services I mentioned. I can help set that up and come back and talk more. Would that be OK?

Jean: Yeah, I think it might really help.

Obviously, not all situations like this resolve themselves in this way. However, the misjudging, suspicion, and lack of trust are quite common. Had the interviewer not been able to suspend her judgment and patiently and empathically respond to this woman, the situation could have been a disaster. Careful and culturally competent interviewing makes all the difference in every situation.

SKIN COLOR

A twenty-year-old biracial (African American and white) woman comes to see a forty-year-old white female social worker for general counseling related to relationship issues. The social work interviewer naïvely assumes that the young woman is African American because her skin color appears to be much more black than Caucasian. This assumption is problematic in the very first interview.

> **Interviewer:** Hi Janice. I understand that you wanted to see me to discuss some concerns you are having in a relationship?
>
> *Janice:* Yes, my boyfriend and I have been together for about six months now, and he is really pressuring me to have sex with him. I'm just not ready, but he is really pushing me. He says it's time and that everybody is doing it. He also has told me that if I don't have intercourse with him soon, he's going to start to see girls who will, or even break up with me. I think I'm starting to fall in love with him, but I'm not ready for sex.
>
> **Interviewer:** That sounds like a very difficult situation, Janice. How have the conversations gone between the two of you so far?
>
> *Janice:* Obviously not so good, or I wouldn't be here. He says he loves me and that when people love each other they should have sex.
>
> **Interviewer:** If you don't mind my asking, Janice, how intimate have the two of you been?
>
> *Janice:* We been pretty active, and done just about everything, just not intercourse.
>
> **Interviewer:** Again, I do not mean to pry—what are your feelings about premarital intercourse?
>
> *Janice:* I'm not sure . . . I don't think I'm against it, I'm just not sure this is the right time yet.
>
> **Interviewer:** So you really want to feel that it's right?

Janice: Yes, this is very important to me.

Interviewer: This is personal, but are you a virgin?

Janice: Yes I am. That's part of why this is so important to me.

Interviewer: Do you know if your boyfriend has ever had intercourse before?

Janice: He's told me that he has . . . that's why a part of me thinks, or is afraid, that he might be just using me. But he really seems to love me . . . I don't know, I'm so confused.

Interviewer: I can tell you have strong feelings for him, but are also very confused. Is your boyfriend also black?

Janice [*sounding angry*]: What!

Interviewer: Is your boyfriend also black like you?

Janice: I beg your pardon. I'm biracial, *not* black. I'm insulted that you would assume such a thing.

Interviewer: Janice, I'm terribly sorry. I just assumed because of your skin color that you were African American. That was a horrible assumption for me to make. Please forgive me.

Janice: Well, it's not the first time it's happened. It seems that so many people I meet for the first time think I'm black.

Interviewer: Well, that's no excuse for my behavior. I should never have assumed anything about you. I really hope you will forgive me.

Janice: I guess so . . . it doesn't really matter.

Interviewer: I think it does matter, Janice, especially if it happens so often. It must feel awful.

Janice: It does sometimes.

Interviewer: Like today . . . now?

Janice: Yes . . . a little.

Interviewer: I think more than a little.

Janice: You see, I was adopted by a white couple at birth. I grew up in an all-white suburban area. I went to school with all white kids, had white teachers, and really never even had any contact with black people until I went to college.

Interviewer: What was that like?

Janice: Kind of strange. I mean, I saw African Americans on TV, and my parents were very good about talking about my being biracial and all. I just never really felt like I was any kind of black person at all until I went to college.

The interviewer has realized what a terrible, prejudiced error in judgment she has made, apologized for it, and is now attempting to reengage with the client through her story.

Interviewer: You mentioned college several times, Janice. What happened there?

Janice: It seemed to happen all at once. It actually happened, just by chance, when I got a black roommate. We hit it off pretty good, but even she thought I was black, I mean all black. Anyway, we were walking back to the dorms from town one day when a car drove by and these boys yelled out the *N* word at us. I actually had never heard it in person before. I knew the word and had heard it used on TV, but never directed at me. I was totally blown away!

Interviewer: What did you do?

Janice: I was kind of scared. I wasn't sure if they were going to come after us. I didn't know what to do. My roommate just yelled back at them like it was no big deal. When we got back to the room, I just started crying. My roommate was so good to me. She really took care of me. I always thank God I had her in my life.

Interviewer: You really felt fortunate, huh?

Janice: Yeah, she's great. We've been best friends ever since.

Interviewer: That's so great!

Janice: So you can see, this black-white thing is a big deal to me. Everyone tries to get me to decide, am I black or am I white? Why do I have to pick? What if I don't want to? It's my decision, isn't it?

Interviewer: I would certainly think so.

Obviously the interviewer wants to reassure the client that her identity is her own. A definitive statement here is essential and empathic.

> ***Janice:*** Thank you, that's what I thought. You know, this has really turned out to be a pretty good session. We kind of had a bad start, but I think we're doing OK.

Although the session started out very awkwardly and could have ended abruptly, the interviewer was able to recover, demonstrate her ability to acknowledge her error, and proceed to create a caring and empathic environment in the session. In fact, one might argue that the egregious error followed by a good intervention on the part of the interviewer actually contributed to the formation of a trusting relationship. This demonstrates that potentially all professional interviewers are capable of these types of mistakes in judgment. They are inevitable because we are all human, with biases and blind spots. Cultural competence is the ability to recognize this potential and work with it to grow and develop in ways that are helpful to clients of all types.

LANGUAGE AND REGION

One of the most difficult challenges for interviewers from any professional discipline is to find common ground on which to communicate. Language capability is cultural and based upon a myriad of factors that both enhance and inhibit the speaker's ability to express his or her idiosyncratic thoughts and emotions (Lacan, 1968). The case example below is an excellent illustration of that principle.

A thirty-year-old white blue-collar worker was seeing a middle-class African American female therapist for therapy regarding a number of concerns related to his job, family, and identity in general. The area that this client comes from might be considered lower middle class by many standards, and the language of this population has its own style and terminology, especially in relationship to some key words and phrases. The following exchange between the client and interviewer happens weeks into the therapy.

Interviewer: Well, how have things been going this week, George?

George: Pretty good. The holiday coming up has me excited about spending some quality time with my wife.

Interviewer: What holiday is that?

George: You know, Valentime's Day.

The interviewer is somewhat taken aback by the client's use of the phrase "Valentime's Day" instead of "Valentine's Day." She finds herself thinking that the client is uneducated and ignorant because he used what would generally be considered an incorrect phrase. She is tempted to correct him, but upon some silent introspection realizes that this phrase is part of this client's language and does not necessarily indicate that he is uneducated, nor is it inappropriate in light of his background and the region. The interviewer decides that challenging this phrase or attempting to correct the client is her own need, and not the client's. Furthermore, doing so might alienate the client and is not really germane to the interaction or topic.

Interviewer: Is that holiday an important one for the two of you?

George: Well, we usually really celebrate. I get her flowers, some cards, we go out to a really nice restaurant, and it's a very nice time.

Interviewer: Given how things have been going lately, it sounds like the timing on this is very good.

George: Yeah, I hope so. You know how she has been saying that I don't spend enough time with her. I think this will really help her see how much I care for her.

The interviewer's instincts seem correct in this situation. The language differences between her and the client are really not an essential topic to bring up or explore, at least not at this time, if ever. Weeks later, another uneven language exchange occurs.

Interviewer: Hi George.

George: I'm really feeling like things are going so well with my wife lately.

Interviewer: You sound excited.

George: I've been working on the goals you and I have set up in the sessions, and they're really working.

During the interviewing process, the client and worker have decided upon a cognitive-behavioral approach to help improve his marital situation.

Interviewer: You mean the ones about finding something important to do or share with your wife each week to demonstrate that she is important to you and that you have been thinking about her?

George: Yeah.

Interviewer: What have you decided to do this week?

George: Well, it may sound kind of simple, but I know how much my wife likes romance novels. The libarry is right acrost the street from where I work. I went over there several times this week and found some of her favorite books. I gave them to her yesterday, and she was so excited and happy she started to cry.

Once again, the therapist is aware that she considers "libarry" and "acrost" incorrect and socially unacceptable words. The interviewer feels compelled to correct George, but she again recognizes that this is the client's language, not hers. Is this urge to correct George really an important part of the therapy? Will the correction hinder or promote the process? After more careful consideration, the interviewer decides to let these impulses go and focus instead on the obvious progress the client feels is happening.

Interviewer: I'm so happy for you, George. You've been working so hard to improve your relationship with your wife.

George: Yeah, and you know, it doesn't feel forced. I mean, once I realized that I have just been sort of expecting things to go along the way they were, of course that might make my wife feel ignored and even alone. Getting in touch with my thoughts and beliefs here with you has really helped me.

Interviewer: Well, you've done so much of that work yourself, George.

George: That's nice of you to say, but if I hadn't come here, I don't know how things would have gone in my marriage. Therapy has really been a lifesaver.

Interviewer: Sometimes I think it takes going to someone who can provide an outside objective viewpoint that can really help shed new light on a situation.

George: That's exactly what happened here. Like you said in the beginning, I just needed to look at my thinking, believe the things you said, and try to change my behaviors.

Interviewer: And you really worked hard at that, George.

George: The funny thing is that I can tell that my wife has changed too. She's so much happier. We really enjoy being together so much more now. I really think we are on the right track.

Interviewer: I'm so happy for the two of you.

This case is obviously moving in the right direction. A key to that success was the ability of the interviewer to put aside her biases about the client's language and move ahead with the process. This lesson in cultural competence for the interviewer proved to have a positive influence in the work with this particular client. Had she forced her own sense of correctness about the client's use of language, the case could have gone in a completely different direction, and maybe have been derailed altogether.

This vignette demonstrates the acceptance with which the culturally competent interviewer must approach all clients. There will always be differences to be understood and handled in a diplomatic fashion if the interviewing work is to be a success. Cultural competence is an overarching element of all interviewing work and an ongoing learning experience for the interviewer. In addition, this vignette demonstrates that individual therapy often can benefit the couple, even if both people are not present in the session.

RELIGION AND SPIRITUALITY

A couple of the Baptist faith in their thirties come to see a female pastoral counselor, also of the Baptist faith, for marital therapy. The couple's Baptist faith strongly discourages divorce, and they strictly believe in this principle. The interviewer, on the other hand, has been divorced for several years. The interviewer is struggling with whether it would be helpful to share her divorced status with the couple, or whether sharing such information would be irrelevant to their work, or perhaps even destructive to the process. On the other hand, if the information does surface in one way or another, or the couple asks directly, how will it affect the couple's work?

> **Interviewer:** Hi Mr. and Mrs. Blake. I understand that you are here due to some difficulties you have been experiencing in your marriage.
> *Mrs. Blake:* Yes, my husband has been drinking heavily, and recently I caught him surfing the Web for pictures of naked women.

In many approaches to working with couples or families, the first person to speak is often considered to be experiencing the most anxiety or to have the greatest need to start. The interviewer is recommended to go with that person in the beginning of the sessions.

> **Interviewer:** I certainly can imagine that this is probably upsetting to you, but how are you feeling about it?
> *Mrs. Blake:* I am so disappointed in him. I thought we had a good marriage, and I especially thought he was a Christian. This makes me question whether he ever was the kind of man I thought he was.
> **Interviewer:** So you really doubt your whole sense of reality when it comes to your husband?
> *Mrs. Blake:* I am very shaken up about this, but hope that counseling will help our marriage.
> **Interviewer:** Mr. Blake, can you talk a little bit about your side of this situation?

Mr. Blake: I really don't know what to say. I know I've done my wife wrong and sinned against God. I shouldn't be drinking, and the whole Internet sex thing is just unforgivable.

Interviewer: Sounds like you are feeling very bad about all of this, and apologetic, but not quite sure why this happened. Is that correct?

Mr. Blake: Yes.

Interviewer: Maybe we could talk a little about how this all started.

Mr. Blake: OK, where do you want me to start?

Interviewer: You both mentioned drinking and surfing the Internet. Did either one of those things happen first, or were they both going on at the same time?

The interviewer is trying to get a sense of the origins of these symptoms in order to help the couple begin to examine how best to proceed in repairing their relationship.

Mrs. Blake [*angrily*]: I don't know, you tell her . . .

Mr. Blake: It's hard to say, they both seemed to have started together.

Interviewer: So you really don't have sense about one preceding the other?

Mrs. Blake [*more anger*]: You really can't remember?

Interviewer: Mrs. Blake, I can see that you are really angry, but if we are going to work on this problem, I think we need to be able to discuss it openly. I'm concerned that your expressions of anger, although very real, may hinder this process.

This is a very important type of confrontation aimed at acknowledging the wife's anger, while resuming a productive path in the couple's work. Successful couples work hinges on the interviewer's being an advocate for the relationship, not either partner.

Mrs. Blake: I'm sorry, I know you're right. I just can't believe we're here.

Interviewer: It must be very difficult, but the two of you are here and seem to want to work on things, and in my experience that is one of the most positive pieces of successful work.

The interviewer is using an intervention that might be called instilling hope. Positive motivation and encouragement from the interviewer can have a very strong influence on clients.

Mrs. Blake: Really, that's so good to know.

Interviewer: So, Mr. Blake, getting back to you. What are your thoughts about these issues?

Mr. Blake: To be honest, I was beginning to feel very lonely in my marriage. My wife didn't seem to want to have sex with me, and I started drinking a little by myself, behind her back. This eventually led to me being curious about seeing if I could find pictures of naked women on the Internet. I think the drinking contributed to it, and then I'd drink more, look for more pictures, et cetera. It was kind of an endless cycle.

Interviewer: I think I understand. From your point of view, your sense of isolation led you to drink and that led you to seek out the pictures on the Internet?

Mr. Blake: Yeah.

Mrs. Blake: So that's my fault for not having enough sex with you?

Mr. Blake: No, the fault is mine. I know I was wrong.

Interviewer: Did you really think that part of this was your fault, Mrs. Blake?

Mrs. Blake: Not really, but it did cross my mind.

Interviewer: In what way?

Mrs. Blake: Well, I should be a good wife, and that means having sex with your husband, according to our religion. You're a Baptist, you know that?

Interviewer: Yes I am, but there are many types of Baptists, with various opinions on many religious issues.

Mrs. Blake: Well, I thought when we came to see you that you would agree with our religious viewpoints. Are you married?

Interviewer: No.

Mrs. Blake: Were you ever married?

Interviewer: Yes, for several years; now I'm divorced.

Mrs. Blake [*shocked*]: Divorced! I can't believe it. You have sinned, and we are coming to see someone who doesn't believe in the sanctity of marriage.

Interviewer: Just because I have been divorced doesn't mean that I can't relate to your problems.

Mrs. Blake: Well, to me it does. As far as I'm concerned this session is over.

Interviewer: I wish you would reconsider and talk this out. I think we can still work together.

Mrs. Blake: I doubt it.

The session ends abruptly on this note. What the interviewer feared most happened. She now feels that perhaps she should have gone over this important fact about her life in order to have a conversation that could have prevented this kind of rupture in the very first session. The interviewer, however, used her best judgment in deciding not to self-disclose unless necessary. Unfortunately, in this case the disparity in the couple's and interviewer's backgrounds generated an apparent impasse in what could have been a successful treatment. This is a valuable lesson in cultural competence for this interviewer. Despite good intentions, impasses of this type can happen even in the best of circumstances. The interviewer has learned from this situation, as all professionals do, and the next time she will be much better prepared for this possibility, although one can never be sure what the best choice of action is in any type of cultural-competence issue.

ABILITY OR DISABILITY

All human beings have some form of disability, or perhaps a better word is limitation. None of us is perfect. Some people perform better on IQ tests than others, which in many intellectual and academic circles is a standard measure of intelligence. It is not uncommon, however, for an individual to perform exceptionally well on an IQ test while having difficulties in the social realm. Emotion and intelligence need to work together for a truly successful life. Some people are more gifted athletically than others. Some people seem to have an innate talent for mechanics or engineering; others have a gift for working with people. There is no normal when it comes to abilities.

Individuals with so-called disabilities fall within a wide continuum as well. Some people are born with cognitive problems, or develop autism and Asperger's symptoms. Problems in living or accidents also can lead to certain types of disability. Veterans might come home from war with post-traumatic stress disorder, or might have lost arms or legs in combat. The list goes on and on.

The challenge for the interviewer is to be able to reach out and truly understand clients with disabilities in order to help them function better in life. This demands empathy and compassion, but the interviewer may also feel fear, pity, and uncertainty about the client's condition. In order to be truly successful with this type of client, interviewers must continually monitor their own emotional reactions in order to be fully present and connected to the client, and not distracted by their own conflicts.

The following case example demonstrates some of the hazards for interviewers in not staying in touch with inner cognitive and emotional reactions or presuppositions regarding clients experiencing disabilities. The client has come to see a thirty-year-old female psychologist on the insistence of his wife. David, sixty-four years old, has recently suffered a stroke and is experiencing difficulties with slurred speech and finding words in conversation as quickly as he used to. These difficulties have resulted in David's feeling a great deal of frustration and anger, which he takes out on his wife. The interviewer is familiar with strokes, but has not had much experience working with people who have had them.

Interviewer: Good morning, David. I understand that you have been recovering from a stroke and that you and your wife are having some challenges adjusting to it.

This is a typical opening intervention to summarize what information the interviewer has while leaving the door wide open for the client to clarify or expand on it.

> *David:* Sssright [*slurred*]. We . . . fight . . . a lot.
>
> **Interviewer:** David [*pause*], I can tell that you are having trouble with your speech. Are you OK?
>
> *David:* Yeah . . . It'sss . . . jussst hard to say the words . . . I can think fine.
>
> **Interviewer:** Are you getting speech therapy for this?
>
> *David* [*frustrated*]: Of cccourse.
>
> **Interviewer:** How's that going?
>
> *David:* Not so . . .
>
> **Interviewer** [*interrupts*]: Good?
>
> *David* [*angrily*]: No!
>
> **Interviewer:** Well, that must be difficult, huh?
>
> *David:* Thhhat's . . . why I'm . . . hhh . . .
>
> **Interviewer** [*finishing David's sentence*]: Here, I get it.

The interviewer is obviously trying to be helpful, but is inadvertently cutting the client off and finishing his sentences for him. This seems to be contributing to David's frustration and may be the same type of interaction that is happening with his wife. However, the interviewer does not seem to recognize this fact yet.

> *David* [*angrily*]: Don'ttt do thhhat!
>
> **Interviewer:** Do what?
>
> *David:* Finnnisssh what I say.
>
> **Interviewer:** I'm sorry, David. I was just trying to be helpful.
>
> *David:* I know, bbbut it mmmakes me mmmad.
>
> **Interviewer** [*in a somewhat patronizing manner—like speaking down to a child*]: What can I do to help you?
>
> *David* [*angrily*]: Stttop it!
>
> **Interviewer:** OK, David, I think I'm beginning to get it. I need to let you speak and go at your own pace.
>
> *David:* Thhhat would be bbbetter.

Interviewer: Got it. So how are things with your wife?

David: We fight.

Interviewer: About?

David: Stttuff like this.

Interviewer: So I'm treating you kind of like your wife does?

David: Yeah.

Interviewer: I'm very sorry, David. I can see how my interference could be very annoying. I will not interfere like that again.

David: OK.

The interviewer has essentially reenacted the very same dynamic that the client is experiencing at home with his wife. She naïvely has been trying to help David speak in the sessions, but in doing so has only frustrated and infuriated him. Slowly the interviewer is learning, the hard way, that she needs to work at the client's pace. This axiom is a fundamental concept in all professional interviewing. However, the interviewer's inexperience in working with people recovering from strokes has interfered in her ability to be with the client on his terms.

This is a very good example of how even the best intentions can cause major problems in the interviewing situation, due to a lack of understanding and cultural competence. The client is actually teaching the interviewer how to be effective with him. This is not unusual at all. The interviewer and client continually learn from each other in the process. Interviewing is relational and involves the contributions from both client and therapist.

Eventually this interviewer learned to pace herself and be with the client according to his needs. This new approach helped the client relax and work on his recovery as well as improve his relationship with his wife at home. The interviewer has had an important lesson in cultural competence with this population. She has also reenacted the same scenario that the client experienced at home. This might be called countertransference, because of the ways in which the interviewer felt compelled to respond like the client's wife, leading to the same type of angry reaction from him. Fortunately, the interviewer was able to recover and seems on a good path with this client, which can also serve as a role model for helping David work with his wife regarding the communication challenges.

OPPRESSION AND DISCRIMINATION

Although many of the areas covered in this chapter fall under the general description of potential oppression and discrimination, this particular case example further highlights the importance of careful, unbiased interviewing in order to help empower clients who are encountering subtle or even overt oppressive circumstances.

A unique situation in Canada lends itself to this discussion. For generations there has been tremendous tension between the English-speaking and French-speaking provinces in Canada. This is a divide of both language and culture that has been at the center of great debate and legal controversy. One particular example of this challenge has been the difficulties that many interviewing professionals from the French-speaking provinces experience in securing employment in the English-speaking areas. The problems are overt, covert, and complex. For example, there are both French and English schools of social work, each with their own common educational principles and values, but also influenced by their respective cultures.

The following case example concerns a social worker from the French-speaking province of Quebec who is employed in Toronto, Ontario, an English-speaking province. The social worker and his colleagues from Ontario have similar education and experience, but he is beginning to experience what he believes to be subtle prejudice and oppressive interactions from his peers and superiors. Talking with friends has not seemed to help, so he has decided to meet with the Human Resources Department (HR) at his agency for advice and support. The HR officer is from Ontario, does not speak French, and has little if any experience with French Canadian culture, except what little training she has received about it.

The social worker, Peter, is thirty-three years old, and is bilingual and bicultural, having lived in both French- and English-speaking provinces for most of his life. The social worker is single and just beginning his professional social work career. The interview takes place in the agency's HR office.

Interviewer: Good morning, Peter. What can I do for you today?

Peter: Well, I've been having a problem at the agency for a while now, but I wasn't sure I should do anything about it or talk to anyone.

Interviewer: What's going on?

Peter: I really like the work, and I've been here for about six months now.

Interviewer: That sounds good, but I take it there's more.

Peter: I really think so. At first I wasn't sure, I thought it was just me, but things keep getting worse.

Interviewer: Obviously something about the job?

Peter: Yeah. You remember from when I was hired as a social worker here that I'm bilingual and bicultural.

Interviewer: Yes, as I recall, you were born and raised in Montreal and got your social work degree there before moving to Toronto about five years or so ago?

Peter: Actually, I've been here about eight years now, just six months at this agency.

Interviewer: I'm sorry, Peter; I had forgotten you were here that long.

Peter: That's OK; time does seem to go by pretty quickly. Anyway, I'm beginning to think that I'm being discriminated against at the agency.

Interviewer: That's a serious statement, Peter. Would you tell me more about it?

Peter: It's not only my colleagues, it's my boss too. I feel like I've been put in this box and I can't get out.

Interviewer: Sounds very frustrating. Can you give me a little more detail about the situation?

Peter: I feel like most people here treat me differently. I think because I came from Montreal and went to a French social work program people think I'm different and treat me that way.

Interviewer: For instance?

Peter: For one thing, I was hired as a regular social worker to work with all of the client populations we serve. Since I've been here, I've only been assigned to French Canadian clients. I know I'm bilingual and have a sense of the French Canadian culture, but I am not limited to that perspective. I know there are a number of other social workers here that speak French and could be assigned to those types of cases, but I seem to be the only one who gets them. On top of that, when I talk to my supervisor about it, he just tells me that I should be happy working with that population because that's my background and experience. I feel singled out. It's kind of like "Give all of the black clients to the black social worker. He'll know what to do." Like I said, don't get me wrong, I love the work, but I feel like I'm being cast into a very narrow position here. I'm not one-dimensional, and neither are the other workers at the agency.

Interviewer: I can see how frustrating this has got to be for you, Peter. Have you talked with any of your other coworkers about this situation?

Peter: Yeah, but they don't seem to understand, and I get the feeling that they'd prefer that I'd be the only social worker that works with the French Canadian clients. I don't think this is fair. In fact I feel marginalized and discriminated against. So that's why I finally came to you.

Interviewer: I'm really glad you did, Peter. I think I can help. I would suggest that the first step is to arrange a meeting with you, me, and your supervisor to talk this out a bit.

Peter: I'm not going to lose my job, am I? It's taken me a long time to get a position in this province. It seems like the English-speaking areas don't want French Canadians. I don't want to lose my position. Maybe I should just let this go.

Interviewer: No Peter, I don't think so. This is an important issue. As a social worker, I know you know that to be true. I will advocate for you in this situation and promise you that this discussion will not lead to your losing your job.

This is a very important point in the interview. First, the interviewer is demonstrating empathy, understanding, support, and advocacy for Peter. She does not know the entire situation, especially the viewpoint of Peter's supervisor, but she does recognize that it is certainly a concern for Peter. She is also beginning to empower Peter in this situation by providing a legitimate format and structure to safely discuss these concerns.

The HR worker arranges an appointment with Peter and his supervisor to discuss this matter. The supervisor (Ronald) has been generally briefed on Peter's concerns, and although initially a little defensive, is open and willing to work on the problem.

Interviewer: I appreciate the two of you agreeing to meet with me today to discuss this issue. Ronald, I have discussed with you the concerns that Peter has shared with me, particularly around feeling, to use my words, marginalized in his work at the agency. You have shared your thoughts about Peter's concerns with me, but would you please review them with him now?

Supervisor: Sure. Peter was hired as a general social worker at the agency. His French Canadian background, including his bilingual and bicultural experience, has been a great asset to the organization. I have tried to best utilize those skills by assigning him to the cases that could most benefit from them.

Interviewer: Was Peter hired to work only with French Canadian clients?

Supervisor: Well, no . . . all of our caseworkers that can speak French and English are typically given a mixed group of clients.

Interviewer: So if I understand you correctly, Peter should also be given a mixed group of clients on his caseload.

Supervisor: That's standard operating procedure.

Interviewer: I've looked through Peter's records and cases, and he has not been a assigned to a single English-speaking, non–French Canadian client. Why is that?

Supervisor: I just assumed he'd want those types of cases because he's come from those areas and that's his background.

Interviewer: But Peter has spent a good deal of time in the English-speaking Canadian areas as well, and appears to be proficient in working with both. Wouldn't it be a good idea to broaden his assignments? After all, aren't there a wide range of clients from both the English- and French-speaking areas?

Supervisor: I guess so.

Interviewer: Actually, Ronald, in looking through the agency's records, it appears that at least 25 percent of the cases are French Canadian clients, and Peter has been assigned to all of them. In addition, he has not been assigned a single English-speaking client or anyone from other than the French provinces.

The interviewer wants to present the actual facts in a nonintimidating manner that will be more conducive to implementing change in this system and advocating for Peter.

Supervisor: That may be true; I wasn't aware of it.

Interviewer: Peter, would you like to share your thoughts on this matter?

Peter: Ronald, I've been here for quite some time now, and I've seen the other workers getting their case assignments. It seems to me that you never give them French Canadians.

I'm the only one. That's really not fair, and in my opinion, it's not the best use of my or the other workers' talent. It also doesn't help me or my coworkers grow, and I also think it limits our impact on the entire agency client base. I went to HR as a last resort because I didn't feel like you were listening to me, or cared. I feel singled out and discriminated against in this situation, even though I don't really think you mean to be doing it. But that's how a lot of prejudice happens. You should know that, you're a social worker like me.

Interviewer: Ronald, what do you think about what Peter has said?

Supervisor: Until this very minute I hadn't realized what I was doing. Peter, maybe you don't believe me, but it's the truth. I think you're a great worker, and I was so excited to finally have a truly bilingual, bicultural worker at the agency that I could utilize effectively. I assumed you'd be happy to work with the population that you came from. I didn't even think about giving you other cases.

Peter: That's the problem, you didn't think about me being anything other than a French Canadian. I don't want to be put in a box. I have many talents and skills, and I want to be treated like all of the workers here.

Supervisor: I'm beginning to see how shortsighted I was in all of this, Peter. I can promise you that I will make things right.

Interviewer: I think this is a good start, Ronald, but I also think we should continue to have some periodic discussions to see how this progresses in the future. Would you both be OK with this?

Peter and his supervisor begin to work on altering not only Peter's workload, but their relationship together and with his colleagues. Although this scenario may seem simplistic, and certainly not all such situations are resolved so quickly or easily, this type of discussion is essential to identify subtle discrimination and oppression and move beyond it in the workplace. Careful and skillfully timed negotiations are crucial to this process.

Peter was being discriminated against and oppressed by his agency and supervisor, though most likely it was unconscious. It took quite some time for him to realize this fact and even more time to find the courage to seek help, finally through HR. The HR interviewer was sensitive, caring, empathic, and skillful in the manner with which she began to help empower Peter in this complex issue. More often than not, issues of oppression and discrimination are subtle, like this one. They are easy to overlook and dismiss. This vignette is a good example of the importance of taking seriously all client concerns surrounding such matters.

SEXUAL ORIENTATION

A white male psychiatric administrator in his early thirties came to see a white male therapist in his forties for problems at work. The client was a very successful supervisor, but felt socially isolated from his coworkers and peers. This was the presenting concern in the initial interviews.

> **Interviewer:** Hello Andrew. It's nice to meet you. I understand that you have been experiencing some difficulties at work.
>
> *Andrew:* Yeah, I've been at this psychiatric facility for several years now. I'm doing quite well and have been promoted to a supervisory position.
>
> **Interviewer:** Sounds like you've been successful.
>
> *Andrew:* That's not really the problem. You see, the longer I'm there, the more awkward I feel.
>
> **Interviewer:** Can you explain to me what you mean, feeling awkward?
>
> *Andrew:* Well, yes and no. I mean, I like everyone that I work with, and I seem to get along well with all of my

coworkers and staff, but I just feel off. I can't put my finger on it.

Interviewer: That's OK; let's talk some more about those vague feelings.

The interviewer is empathically validating the feelings of the client despite the fact that he can't quite understand what they are about in any concrete sense. The interviewer trusts that this is a genuine emotion and believes that further careful and trusted exploration may help uncover or give greater clarity to the emotional state.

Andrew: Good, it's just that I'm usually very good about understanding myself and my instincts. I've been in therapy before, when I was a teenager, so I know the process. I also work in the field, so I really appreciate and respect the process. I know I'm stuck.

Interviewer: That's a good way to put it, I think, Andrew.

Andrew: Thanks.

Interviewer: So you find yourself liking the people at work, but also feeling awkward around them?

Andrew: I've tried socializing with them, but it doesn't feel right. I feel so isolated and lonely, even when I'm in a crowd with the people I know. So I don't socialize with any of them any more.

Interviewer: Do you have any friendships outside of work?

Andrew: No, not really. I don't date, and I work a lot, more than I have to, actually, just to keep busy, I think, and to avoid being alone.

Interviewer: Well, it sounds like a way to cope, but I'm not sure you're comfortable with it, are you?

Andrew: No, I'm really not.

This is how the first few weeks of therapy went with this client. The interviewer empathized and explored the client's feelings, trying to help him uncover what might be contributing to them. He also worked with the client to try to develop a plan to socially connect with others outside of work. Unfortunately nothing seemed to materialize in the sessions, or work outside of them, until several weeks later.

> **Interviewer:** How have things been going this week, Andrew?
>
> *Andrew:* Well, I think I'm beginning to realize something.
>
> **Interviewer:** What's that?
>
> *Andrew:* I really appreciate coming here, and it's helped me trust you and explore a lot of thoughts and emotions. There have been things on my mind that I have wanted to talk about with you, but just haven't been ready. It takes time for me to trust people. But now I think I'd like to talk about some of this with you.
>
> **Interviewer:** I'm glad you feel safe enough here, Andrew, and I certainly understand that trust takes time. So what would you like to talk about?

The interviewing process has obviously been of benefit to this client, and demonstrates the importance of trusting the process and patiently being with the client at his own pace. This client would probably not have even thought about opening up and sharing had this not happened.

> *Andrew:* For some time now, I've been thinking that I'm probably gay.
>
> **Interviewer:** What has led you to think that?
>
> *Andrew:* Well, you know that everybody has sexual fantasies, right?
>
> **Interviewer:** I can't be certain about that, Andrew, but that has been my impression, yes.
>
> *Andrew:* For as long as I can remember, I've fantasized about being with men. I've tried dating women, but it never feels right. I mean, I've dated some very attractive women, and even tried to have sex with them, but it just isn't me. I know these women are beautiful, I just don't really want to be sexual with them.

Interviewer: So how long have you known this about yourself?

Andrew: Oh, for a while now, maybe a couple of years. It's been a passing thought since adolescence, but I've never taken it seriously until recently.

Interviewer: If you don't mind my asking, Andrew, have you dated or been with any men sexually?

Andrew: That's just it, no. I mean, I have in my mind, and I've watched gay porn and been turned on by it, but I've never actually been with a man. But I'm pretty sure I'm gay, I mean almost positive.

Interviewer: Maybe I'm reaching here, Andrew, but do you think your feelings of isolation and awkwardness have anything to do with this?

Andrew: Yeah, I do. Even my talking to you about this today feels relieving. I feel centered and relaxed, in here anyway.

Interviewer: Well, I'm glad to hear that, Andrew. I want this to be a safe place for you.

Andrew [*pauses*]: You know though, it's weird. I was watching TV the other day and there was this gay man on some show who was really flaming, you know what I mean . . . the voice, the feminine gestures, and the whole stereotypic gay deal. Well, I found myself thinking and actually talking to the TV, saying "What a fag!" Then I thought, wait a minute, I'm a fag! That was so weird.

Interviewer: What was weird about that?

Andrew: I guess I just realized that there are all sorts of gay people, just like there are all sorts of straight people. I don't have those affectations like some gay men do. I don't know why I don't, but I don't. I'm also not particularly attracted to gay men who do. I'm just who I am, but I know I'm gay.

Interviewer: I think that's such an important insight about you and people in general, Andrew, whether they are gay, lesbian, bisexual, heterosexual, or whatever. People are different, even within any type of diversity.

Andrew: Yeah, you're right. Anyway, I just thought that was interesting.

From this point on, Andrew began to explore his own sexuality in a different light. He gradually felt more comfortable with his gay identity, and started reaching out to other gay men for friendship and dating. The comfort that Andrew felt about himself also enabled him to build friendships with a lot of his straight colleagues and coworkers. He came out to many of them as he felt more comfortable.

This was a powerful learning experience for both the interviewer and the client. Obviously all people are different, but it took this experience in the interviewing relationship for both of them to truly recognize this important fact. As simple as it may sound, diversity is diverse. People can't be categorized in limited ways. Each person must be understood and appreciated for his or her uniqueness. The culturally competent interviewer must strive for that awareness and continue to use it in every client situation.

AGE

A married couple in their seventies come to see a male therapist in his thirties for couples work.

Interviewer: It's good to meet you, Mr. and Mrs. A. I understand that you are experiencing some marital difficulties? Who would like to tell me a little about this situation?

This intervention allows the couple to decide who will speak first about their concerns.

Mrs. A.: Well, I have been feeling very upset with my husband for quite some time. I thought we were getting along very well. We have been married almost fifty years. However, within the last year he has become obsessed with sex. He wants to do it all the time. He's also started buying me very revealing lingerie and wants me to perform oral sex on him all of the time. I'm not opposed to most of this, but he's become so pushy and aggressive.

Interviewer: OK, Mrs. A., let's see if I understand. You feel that you and your husband have had a good marriage for many years, but within the last year he has become more insistent on having sex with you. He also wants you to wear lingerie that you may not be comfortable with, and insistent on you performing oral sex far more often than you would like it. Am I getting this straight?

Mrs. A.: Yes.

Interviewer: I think it's important as we get started for me to explain some of the ground rules for couples therapy. First of all, I see my role as being an advocate for the relationship. In other words, I don't take sides. I want to help the two of you arrive at solutions that are best for you as a couple, even if that might mean having me help you negotiate a separation. It certainly doesn't sound to me like that's where things are with the two of you, but at least you, Mrs. A., seem clearly upset about how your sexual relationship with your husband has been changing. I also wanted to let both of you know that communication is so crucial in this kind of work. Words are very powerful and can deeply affect each member of the couple. For example, Mrs. A., when you just used the word "always," I wondered if you actually meant all of the time, every time, or if you are feeling very frustrated with how often these uncomfortable things happen. If you actually mean the word "always," that signals to me, and to your husband, that there are never times when these uncomfortable situations do not happen. Please understand that I am not trying to single you out, Mrs. A., but to demonstrate how these kinds of exchanges could become problematic. When I hear them, I will ask either of you that said them to clarify in order to avoid more emotional problems. Does that make sense to both of you?

Mrs. A.: I think so, and I agree. You're right, it's not that he acts this way all of the time, but it does feel that way.

Interviewer: OK, good. Now Mr. A., could I ask you how you are feeling about this situation?

Mr. A.: My wife is right about what I want. I'm a man, and I have needs. I know my sexual appetite, for lack of a better word, has increased a lot this past year. I also agree that I have wanted her to dress in a more sexy way and I want more oral sex.

Interviewer: OK, thank you, Mr. A.

The interviewer is finding himself feeling very strange about this situation. He knows that older adults have sex, but this type of sexual situation feels shocking to him. The interviewer does not share these reactions with the couple, but is aware that he has an obvious bias or prejudice about it. He recognizes that he must keep an open mind as he continues to explore this topic with the couple.

Mr. A.: Well, don't you think she should be more sexually active with me?

Interviewer: Like I mentioned a few minutes ago, Mr. A., I'm really not here to judge or referee between the two of you. Obviously you, Mr. A., don't feel your requests are unreasonable, but you, Mrs. A., seem to be feeling uncomfortable with them.

Mr. A.: I get all of that, but what are we going to do about it if we disagree with each other? We can have that argument at home.

Interviewer: That's a good point, Mr. A., but I think the difference is that I am an objective party here. I am not invested in either of your preferences about handling this issue, except in the ways that understanding both of you might help to bring about a successful resolution. Does that make sense?

Mr. A.: I guess so. So now what?

Interviewer: Mr. A., can you tell me what has happened to alter the way in which you are feeling about having sex with your wife?

Mr. A.: Like she said, about a year ago I started feeling like I really wanted to have more sex with her. My wife is a beautiful woman. I really enjoy being with her, and I think she looks fantastic in that lingerie. I don't understand why she wouldn't want to have more sex.

Interviewer: So Mr. A., you are kind of surprised that your wife is not more interested?

Mr. A.: Yeah, I thought she'd feel flattered and maybe even excited.

Interviewer: Mrs. A., when you hear your husband talk about you this way, how does it make you feel?

Mrs. A.: I don't think I really believe him. I mean, look at me: I'm a seventy-year-old woman. What does he see in me?

Mr. A. [*interrupting*]: I see a gorgeous sexy woman that I want to make love to.

Interviewer: I understand your enthusiasm, Mr. A., but I would like the two of you to not interrupt each other. Mrs. A., anything else you'd like to say about how you are feeling?

Mrs. A.: I'm not opposed to having more sex, but not as much as he wants it. I mean, he wants to be together five days a week. And every time, and I do mean every time, I am supposed to wear this sleazy underwear, and give him oral sex.

Interviewer: So the frequency that your husband wants and the kind of activity and dress is awkward for you?

Mrs. A.: Yes, that's right.

Interviewer: Mr. A., how do feel about what your wife just said?

Mr. A.: I just don't get it. Like I said, she's so sexy and beautiful, and I love her so much. I really want to have sex with her.

Interviewer: So it sounds to me like you both are interested in a sexual relationship together, but disagree on some of the details about frequency, dress, and types of activity. Is that right?

Mr. and Mrs. A. [*together*]: Yes.

Interviewer: Well, at least you can both agree on the difficulty. Mrs. A., how often would you like to have sex with your husband?

Mrs. A.: Oh, I don't know, maybe twice a week.

Interviewer: And how does that sound to you, Mr. A?

Mr. A.: I don't like it. I don't want to be sexually frustrated.

Interviewer: Mrs. A.?

Mrs. A.: Well, I understand, but I can't help it. I also don't want to always wear that lingerie, and to do oral sex.

Interviewer: What bothers you about those things, Mrs. A.?

Mrs. A.: Like I said, I'm an old woman. I really don't feel comfortable wearing the kinds of things he buys me. As far as the oral sex goes, I just don't like it every time. I sort of feel used. I guess I want to have some control in this situation.

Interviewer: That's the first time you've mentioned feeling used and wanting control, Mrs. A. Mr. A., what is your reaction to how your wife is feeling?

Mr. A.: I didn't know she felt that way. I never would want to hurt her. I'm really sorry, honey.

Mrs. A.: Well, we've never really talked about it like this before.

The couple's work continued with this interviewer for several more months as they began to understand each other better and negotiated a common decision about their sexual life. For the interviewer this experience was an extreme eye-opener. He realized how ageist he was being in his view of the sexual lives of older adults. No longer would he hold such a narrow viewpoint or presume to speculate about anyone's sexual life or preferences. This case, although about age, is another powerful example of the inherent blind spots for all interviewers in their ongoing work to become culturally competent workers. Once this interviewer realized his biases, he was much freer to pursue the sessions in a more open-minded and objective manner.

SIZE AND APPEARANCE

Clients' physical appearance can have a dramatic effect on how the interviewer perceives and reacts to them. Many of these reactions are idiosyncratic, but others can be influenced by culture. It is absolutely crucial for successful interviewers to be aware of their positive and negative reactions to clients of all sizes and appearance. The following case example illustrates this dynamic. The client is a young obese woman in her late twenties. She is probably more than 150 pounds overweight. The interviewer is a female social worker of normal weight, but with a history of weight problems dating back to childhood.

Interviewer: Hi Sally. What can I do for you today?

There are obviously many ways to open a session. This more casual intervention is an unassuming approach to connect with the client.

Sally: Well, like I said on the phone, I'm concerned about my weight.

Interviewer: What is it that bothers you about your weight?

Sally [*annoyed*]: Can't you tell, I'm fat!

Interviewer [*feeling defensive*]: I don't mean to sound disrespectful or insensitive, Sally, but I really would like to know what you think about your weight.

Sally: I can't stand it. I've been fat like this for over ten years, and I keep gaining weight despite the fact that I've tried exercise and dieting.

Interviewer: So this has obviously been a long-standing and very frustrating situation for you.

Sally: I'm really at my wit's end. I need help.

Interviewer: Well, I'm glad you came to see me, and I hope we can work together on this situation.

Sally: Me too.

Interviewer: So you mentioned that you've been at this weight for over ten years, and tried to lose weight by dieting and exercise, but it has not helped. Have you seen a doctor about it?

Sally: Yeah, she's says there's nothing wrong with me. I've had all types of tests, and I guess I'm normal.

Interviewer: You say you guess. Are you not sure?

Sally: No, it's just so frustrating. I don't know what to do.

Interviewer: I imagine you have thought about this a great deal. It might help me work with you if I knew a little bit more about that.

Sally: I know what it is . . .

Interviewer: What is it?

Sally: I eat when I'm sad or lonely, or depressed.

Interviewer: When does that tend to happen?

Sally: Most every day. I get home from work, and I try not to eat, I have a good healthy dinner, but as the night goes on, I get lonely, or whatever, and I start eating junk food to feel better.

Interviewer: Does it make you feel better?

Sally: Well, at first, then I start feeling guilty and bad about myself, and then things get worse, and sometimes I eat even more.

Interviewer: Sounds like a vicious cycle.

Sally [*sarcastically*]: Tell me about it.

Interviewer [*again feeling irritated with Sally*]: Are you feeling angry with me about this in some way?

Sally: Not really, I just am irritated in general. I want this to stop. Do you think you can help me?

Interviewer: Well, I will certainly do my best. I think the first thing to do is for us to get to know each other a little bit so I can understand your history, and together we can decide on a plan to help you.

Sally: How long is that going to take?

Interviewer: I'm not sure, but let's try meeting for a couple of times and then reevaluate how things are going. How does that sound?

Sally: OK, I guess.

Sally and the interviewer meet for several sessions and begin to explore her history of eating, loneliness, lack of friends, and nonexistent dating history. Sally talks about how she alienates just about everybody. The interviewer is beginning to feel that way about Sally too. Perhaps this feeling is being stirred up by Sally, but given the interviewer's own history of weight problems, perhaps some of the negativity is a defensive reaction to her own feelings about weight and eating. The interviewer decides that in order to be effective with Sally, she will need to pay close attention to the emotions she is experiencing in the sessions and carefully explore the extent to which they may be coming from the client, her own emotional background, or even a relational combination of both. This is a complex dynamic for the beginning interviewer, but is illustrated here to help alert all professional helpers to the complex relational exchanges from both parties. This process continues in the next session.

Interviewer: Well, Sally, how has the week been?

Sally: The same . . . can't you do anything about this?

The interviewer immediately recognizes this familiar dynamic. Sally seems defensive, and this response generates anger and a distant feeling in the interviewer. The interviewer also realizes that this distant feeling is exactly the way many people feel about Sally, according to her own reports. The interviewer wonders if this kind of exchange helps to prevent positive relationships in the client's life and in effect keeps her isolated and engaged in self-destructive behavior. At the same time, the interviewer recognizes her own fears about eating from a distant past. Part of the interviewer actually wants to stay away from or distant from Sally to protect herself. This silent insight is not necessarily one that the interviewer feels she needs to

share with the client, but it certainly might be helpful in creating a
more helpful process with Sally.

> **Interviewer:** I get the sense you're frustrated with me; are
> you?
> *Sally:* Well, yes. I want to get better.
> **Interviewer:** And I want to help you do that, but it's diffi-
> cult when I get the impression that you are annoyed with
> me.
> *Sally:* I'm not really annoyed with you; I just want to get
> better.
> **Interviewer:** I'm glad to hear that, Sally. And please under-
> stand that it's perfectly OK to be angry with me, I just want
> you to know that sometimes it feels to me a little alienating.
> *Sally:* Well, I do appreciate the work we're doing, and I can
> tell you're trying. I just get impatient, and I'm worried that
> I will never be OK.
> **Interviewer:** I can see how you would feel that way, given
> how long you have been dealing with this issue. Why don't
> we begin to look at some things you might try to help deal
> with these feelings of loneliness and isolation, as well as
> your socialization?
> *Sally:* OK.

This interview demonstrates complexities in how diversity can
affect both the client and interviewer. The client's weight and her way
of dealing with others about it was an unconscious trigger for the interviewer until she could access her own biases and resistance to examining how her past was influencing the process. The client too was
beginning to recognize how her defensive style might be contributing
to the entire situation. Fortunately this case seems to be moving in a
good direction, as a result of this mutual awareness.

RESEARCH IMPLICATIONS AND BASIS OF PRACTICE

Cultural competence is a relatively new emphasis in professional practice, regardless of discipline. The feminist and civil rights movements

helped to bring the idea of diversity to the forefront. From a research standpoint, diversity and cultural competence have certainly moved from intuitive knowledge to practice wisdom, and are beginning to be widely written about from a quasi-theoretical perspective. The validated knowledge is mostly in the exploratory stage, but all helping professions are emphasizing the necessity of cultural competence in all areas of practice (Baldwin, Wampold, & Imel, 2007).

SUMMARY

This chapter demonstrated the almost unlimited facets of the concept of diversity and cultural competence. All clients are diverse and present unique challenges to the interviewer. In addition, all interviewers are similarly diverse. Interviewing with cultural competence is a lifelong learning process for the professional interviewer. The case examples in this chapter barely scratch the surface of the challenges in working with diverse clients in a culturally competent manner. What is important to remember in working with any client is to understand that each is different in many unique ways. Don't presume anything. Careful and competent nonjudgmental exploration is crucial to successful work.

RECOMMENDED READING

Campbell, C. (2003). *Anti-oppressive social work: Promoting equity and social justice.* Halifax, Nova Scotia: Author.

Empowerment and antioppressive practice principles are key elements of interviewing work in both the Canadian and US populations. Campbell's work is a helpful resource in this area.

Lee, J. (2001). *The empowerment approach to social work practice* (2nd ed.). New York: Columbia University Press.

This classic book on empowerment is a must-read for all professional interviewers.

Stampley, C., & Slaght, E. (2004). Cultural competence as a clinical obstacle. *Smith College Studies in Social Work, 74,* 333–47.

This is an important article for any professional interviewer working with any type of population. The article emphasizes the need to utilize cultural competence in all clinical encounters in order to be an effective helper.

Rothman, J. C. (2008). *Cultural competence in process and practice: Building bridges*. Boston: Allyn & Bacon/Pearson.

This is an excellent text for both beginning and advanced professional interviewers. It provides a comprehensive overview of the essential elements and utilization of cultural competence in clinical practice.

MULTIMEDIA SOURCES

Crash. (2004). Paul Haggis (Director). Lionsgate.

This Academy Award–winning film is one of the most powerful depictions of the subtle complexities and challenges in understanding others.

National Center for Cultural Competence, www11.georgetown.edu/ research/gucchd/nccc/index.html.

This site provides comprehensive research and helpful recommendations in the area of cultural competence, especially as it relates to interviewing.

Interviewing in Various Modalities

The preceding chapters have discussed fundamental techniques of interviewing, demonstrating a variety of methods. This chapter examines the modalities in which interviewing takes place, that is, individual, couples, family, and group. It emphasizes how to use theory and specific techniques to help the interviewer recognize and become more proficient in working with these modalities. The use of a specific theory has a direct bearing on the type of interviewing technique and responses used in each client situation. The case examples here dig into the complexities of interviewing in various modalities, without losing sight of the need to develop a trusting relationship with the client.

INDIVIDUALS

As the reader may recall from chapter 2, Linda's first session ended with her appearing to be relatively engaged with the interviewer. She discussed concerns about her troubled marriage, its effect on her children, and her ambivalence about wanting to leave her husband. Linda also spoke a little about her unhappy and lonely childhood and seemed to make a connection between those feelings and what she was experiencing in the present situation with her husband.

There are many theoretical formulations and speculations the interviewer could make about Linda and her situation, even from this first session. One theory is not necessarily better than another in most situations. What is important is to arrive at a differential approach that best serves the process, and is comfortable for the interviewer and client. Most beginning interviewers learn one or a few theoretical approaches, and naturally try to apply them to all of their clients. As interviewers mature and become more experienced, however, they realize that not all clients can be fit into one theoretical box. Over time, successful interviewers develop a wider theoretical template that includes both theories and interviewing techniques. They also develop a more complex and comprehensive working model of self and types of clients. This process is what leads to consistently successful interviewing with most clients. It is a process of informed trial and error that continues to move toward greater expertise as the interviewer matures. This is true in all professions.

The interviewer working with Linda knows only a little bit about her presenting concern and her past. However, what he does know is important and informative. Object relations theory might suggest that Linda did not receive good enough parenting from both her mother and absent father, which could have led to her present insecurity, and perhaps even her unconscious choice of a distant husband. That is a speculation, not a certainty, like all theoretical formulations, but it might be a helpful one. Self psychology theory might hypothesize that Linda is mirror hungry because she did not receive enough positive validation throughout her childhood and in her present situation. If that is the case, the interviewer could focus on providing direct empathic mirroring in order to help Linda build self-confidence. Rogerian therapy would emphasize the use of empathy in much the same way as self psychology, but the interviewer would have a basic belief in the inherent ability of Linda to discover and resolve her own problems with understanding help from the therapist. Other approaches would focus on similar or different aspects of Linda's situation, but all of the interviewers would have the same goal in mind: to understand and help Linda resolve her situation and have a more satisfactory life.

> **Interviewer:** Hi Linda. How have things been going since our last session?
>
> *Linda:* Oh, about the same. Nothing has changed, but at least there haven't been any major blowups since I saw you.
>
> **Interviewer:** I guess that's good. [*Pauses for a few seconds.*] We talked about a lot of things last week, including your present situation with your family, and a little bit about your childhood. Is there any particular thing you'd like to talk about today?

This is an important response from the interviewer. He summarized the last session in order to reengage the client, checked to see if he understood her, and made it clear, by the nature of his open-ended question, that she is in charge of the direction of the therapy. From a theoretical standpoint, this type of client-centered approach is often used in the relationship-oriented therapies such as the psychodynamic models, object relations, and self psychology. Some of the more directive approaches, such as cognitive-behavioral therapy or solution-focused therapy, might begin to suggest a structure or plan for approaching the situation. In other words, the interviewer might work with Linda to develop specific measurable goals in treatment. The present interview continues with the more client-centered approach for now, because it allows the interviewer to gather more information through the client's initiative rather than probing for material that may not be in line with the client's interests or needs.

> *Linda:* There are some other things I didn't tell you about in our last session.
>
> **Interviewer:** [*Silence to let Linda gather her thoughts.*]
>
> *Linda:* Well, you see . . . I've been having an affair with this man for a while.
>
> **Interviewer:** Can you tell me more about it?
>
> *Linda:* I met him at work. We work together in the same office. He was very nice to me when I first met him. He got

me coffee, talked to me a lot about my life, and told me how pretty I was. He made me feel special.

Interviewer: So he really made you feel good about yourself at a time when you were really not feeling that way with your husband?

This is an obvious empathic summary statement, and it is important to recognize that the interviewer shows no judgment; he is demonstrating complete acceptance of the client. This can be difficult sometimes, especially if the interviewer has definite thoughts, feelings, and values that are different from the client's. If that is the case, those feelings need to be silently recognized as part of the working model of the interviewer's self, but not introduced into the interview. That would disrupt the process of understanding, relationship building, and reparative work.

Linda: I guess it's wrong, but I couldn't help it. I felt so alone and unhappy for so long.

Interviewer: So you have some mixed feelings about it?

Linda: Yeah . . .

Both the interviewer and client sit in silence for about twenty seconds.

Linda: We've been seeing each other for about two years now. We meet after work, and sometimes on the weekends.

The client feels safe to proceed because of the interviewer's nonjudgmental approach.

Interviewer: What are things like when you're together?

Again, the interviewer is using open-ended questioning to allow the client to go at her own pace.

Linda: In the beginning it was good, but now it all just seems to be about sex. He just wants to meet for a few minutes, have sex, and then leave.

Interviewer: How does that make you feel?

Linda: Not much better than being with my husband. I try to talk with him about it, but he tells me he has to get home to his family.

Interviewer: So he's married?

Linda: Yeah, with a bunch of kids.

Interviewer: This sounds very complicated, but more importantly it seems like it makes you feel isolated.

This is a direct statement, and perhaps a bit presumptuous, but the interviewer trusts his instincts.

Linda: Exactly.

Interviewer: How have you been handling this issue?

Linda: I just keep seeing him . . . I've told him I'm not happy with our arrangement and that I feel used, but he reassures me that he cares about me and really enjoys seeing me. He says it's just difficult to get away or spend much time with me.

Interviewer: So you've told him you're not happy with the present arrangement, but that doesn't seem to have much of an effect on him?

This is clearly a summarizing statement aimed at being sure the interviewer understands the client and reemphasizing what has been discussed.

Linda: This is such a mess. I'm not happy in my marriage, and I'm not happy with him. What should I do?

Interviewer: I really believe that's a decision that only you can make, Linda. I can understand that you feel very unhappy with both men, and you're not really sure you want to be in either relationship. Have you thought about couples therapy?

The interviewer is communicating to the client that he is not there to tell her what to do, while subtly communicating his belief in her ability to make decisions. The question about couples therapy is a logical one because so much of the situation concerns the marriage. However, the interviewer poses this question in a very open-ended and nondirective manner.

> *Linda:* I've thought about it, and asked my husband to go to therapy with me in the past, but he says we don't have any problems and he would never come to therapy.
> **Interviewer:** So you really feel that's out of the question?
> *Linda:* Yeah, and at this point I really don't want to even try to work on my marriage.
> **Interviewer:** You sound very certain about that.

The interviewer is validating the client's obvious definitive opinion.

> *Linda:* I'm just feeling really stuck.
> **Interviewer** [*wondering where to go next*]: So you've got these two pretty unhappy relationships with distant men in your life?

The interviewer paraphrases the situation in order to help the client reflect on what has been discussed.

> *Linda:* Sort of the story of my life, huh? I grew up pretty alone, and my relationship with my dad was almost nonexistent. I'd see him every few months, kind of unexpected . . . but we'd always do what he wanted to do, you now, go to the fair, carnival, et cetera. We'd never talk . . . Maybe get something to eat, I'd go on a few rides, and he'd take me home. I always felt alone and awkward when I was with him.
> **Interviewer:** I know we've touched on this already, Linda, but there seems to be some kind of similarity in these relationships. I don't mean they are your fault . . . they just seem to have happened.

Although the interviewer does think that there may be some common unconscious elements to these relationships, he does not believe that the client is choosing to put herself in unhappy situations. To say

*something to that effect to Linda would seem blaming and perhaps
even hurtful. He offers an open-ended suggestion to consider.*

> **Linda:** I think about that too sometimes; it is sort of like a
> pattern, isn't it?
> **Interviewer:** Well, it could be, and it could be worth
> exploring.

The session ends with both the interviewer and client moving
into an area of agreement about some of the themes that may be contributing to the problem. This case contains elements that imply that
the client's early history and relationships may have contributed to her
present situation and lack of self-esteem. In this case, psychodynamic
approaches are a helpful way to proceed. This case will be revisited in
chapter 11 to demonstrate how interviewing that uses this theoretical
framework can proceed toward a helpful resolution.

COUPLES

The interviewer's role with individual clients is to focus solely on
them. Of course aspects of their lives are examined and taken into
consideration, such as family, friends, work, and partners, but the primary emphasis is on helping that individual resolve a personal
situation.

Couples work is different. Many beginning, and even veteran,
interviewers make the mistake of taking sides with one of the partners.
That path is fraught with problems. The interviewer working with a
couple should be "the advocate for the relationship," not for either of
the partners. What does it mean, to be an advocate for the relationship?
Simply put, the interviewer does not take sides, suspends judgment,
and works with the couple to arrive at a decision or resolution that in
the couple's opinion is best for them. This could mean a satisfactory
resolution and compromise, and it could also mean a decision to separate or divorce. This interviewing process is not easy, and it demands
great patience and a supportive, nonjudgmental stance on the part of

the interviewer. That stance, however, is tremendously helpful to the couple.

There is a variety of theoretical approaches and understandings of the dynamics of couples interviewing. A combination of interpersonal and intrapsychic concepts seems to be most helpful to the process. Interpersonal approaches are probably best derived from family systems theory and technique. In family systems models, all human beings develop their identities from the roles that they perform within their families. These conscious and unconscious roles permeate an individual's life, especially in the choice of a partner and the way in which they raise a family. Bowen's concepts of differentiation, triangulation, and family of origin help the partners understand the extent to which they have been able to experience themselves as separate people apart from their families. *Triangulation* demonstrates the normal and dysfunctional ways in which partners (or family members in general) involve others (usually family members) in their conflicts as a way of deflecting or buffering emotional conflicts. *Family of origin* is the historical theme that an individual derives from living within the family. All families have their own unique roles, values, communication patterns, and so forth that shape their members. Family therapy concepts are applicable to both couples and family interviewing.

Intrapsychic concepts are also key factors in understanding and interviewing couples. These generally are part of psychodynamic and attachment theories. It is well recognized that partners in coupling situations are drawn to others who are familiar to them. This familiarity can include both positive and negative traits. Object relations and attachment theories, for example, would propose that the types of emotional relationships developed in early life set the stage for the kind of person one will become in adulthood, and more specifically, signal the type of partner an individual may choose. These are not always conscious choices, and they are not always good or emotionally healthy choices, but they are familiar choices. This inner emotional process can contribute to the quality of the couple's relationship. It is important for the interviewer working with couples to understand that these dynamic early developmental processes are an important aspect of any couple's relationship. The following case example demonstrates couples interviewing and the utilization of both family and intrapsychic processes in working with them.

John and Jane Allen came to couples therapy because John had discovered that Jane was having an affair with her boss. The Allens are motivated to resolve this problem in their relationship. John and Jane both work, and live in a modest home with four children ranging in ages from seven to sixteen. John's and Jane's early family histories are important in the interview process, as will become evident as it proceeds.

> **Interviewer:** Hi Jane, John. I understand that you have come to couples counseling because of some recent conflicts in your marriage. I am very interested in helping both of you and want you to know that I see my role as an advocate for your relationship. That means I don't take sides; I work toward helping the two of you resolve issues and problems in your relationship in a mutually satisfactory manner. That's not always easy, I know, but I find that by advocating for the relationship and not either partner exclusively, the therapy is much more effective and helpful. Do you have any questions?

The interviewer wants the couple to know from the very beginning, even before any discussion begins, that she will be objective, impartial, and devoted to their relationship, regardless of the outcome, that is, resolution, separation, divorce, or impasse. This is a crucial emphasis in couples interviewing.

> *John* [*angrily*]: So even though Jane had an affair, you're not going to say that she's wrong?
>
> **Interviewer:** You sound pretty angry, John, and I can certainly understand that, but you're right. I'm not here to referee or pronounce right and wrong. I've found that being open to both partners, and trying to understand and work with both of them in a nonjudgmental manner, is most

effective. On the other hand, I'm not going to pretend that a dishonest affair in any relationship isn't extremely hurtful and damaging. Does that make sense?

John: I guess so [*becoming calmer*]. I'm just so upset.

Jane: [*Remains silent.*]

Interviewer: I want to hear from both of you, and it sounds like you might like to go first, John? Where would you like to start?

The interviewer is wise to start with John, who has the most anxiety and greatest need to talk. She will be sure to involve Jane as the interview proceeds.

John: Well, like I said, Jane had an affair.

Interviewer: Can you tell me a little bit more about this affair? I mean, how did you find out about it, what is the situation, and of course how has it affected you?

The interviewer wants to proceed in an open-ended manner in order to fully understand the situation initially from John's point of view. She also does not want to presume to know what an "affair" means in this particular situation. This type of questioning with couples is a very effective interviewing technique that intuitively flows from the curiosity of the interviewer and her sincere and unbiased interest in helping the couple.

John: An affair is an affair. You know, Jane had sex with her boss!

Interviewer: I can tell you're pretty angry about it. Tell me more . . .

John: What's there to tell? Jane works at a local art store. She's an artist, has been all of her life. Anyway, the store is a pretty small local business. There aren't many employees: just the boss, his wife, a couple of other men and women, and Jane.

Interviewer [*curious*]: So the man Jane had the affair with is married?

John: Yeah, that's even better isn't it?

Interviewer: John, I'm not trying to judge the situation, only to understand what has happened. I can tell this is so hard for you. Are you OK continuing to talk about this?

This is an important and timely empathic response from the interviewer. She wants to understand the entire nature of this couple's situation, but she is also keenly aware of John's pain. She realizes that she must go slowly and sensitively with him.

John: Yeah, I'm sorry . . . I guess I shouldn't be so upset about it.

Interviewer: Now, John, I'm curious as to why you would apologize for feeling upset . . .

John [*interrupting*]: Well, you know, I'm probably at fault here in some way. Maybe Jane should talk for a while.

Interviewer: Well, maybe she could, John, but I don't get the sense that you're really ready to stop. I think you have more to say, and I'd like to hear it. I also think that you are entitled to your feelings. Do you want to go on?

Even though the interview is in the very early stages, the interviewer has already begun to recognize that John's apologetic nature may be an indication of his personality style and a signal about how he functions in life. This is a tentative insight that the interviewer will store away in her working model of John for the future.

John: OK. I had been noticing that Jane was coming home later and later each week. You see, she works evenings a lot. I started to get suspicious and would drive by the store to see if her car was still there. I did this for a while without going in, just to see if Jane was OK. Well, when I would ask her about staying late, she would say that she had a lot of cleaning up to do. I wanted to believe her, but I felt suspicious. Finally, one night about a week ago, I drove by again, and noticed that all the lights were out, but Jane and her boss's cars were parked out front. I decided to go in. There were only a few lights on, and it didn't look like Jane was doing anything but sitting there talking to her boss. I felt kind of embarrassed, apologized, and went home. When Jane came home, I asked her about the situation with her boss, and after a while, she admitted that they were having an affair.

Interviewer: Well, that really helps me get a sense of things. Thanks, John. How did you feel about all of this?

John: You know . . . hurt, angry, betrayed . . .

Interviewer: I can imagine . . . Jane, can you tell me your side of things?

The interviewer has successfully engaged John, and gathered a fairly comprehensive picture of the story and emotions from his point of view. This seems like a natural resting point for John, and time to begin connecting with Jane.

Jane: Well, it's exactly like John said. I was having an affair with my boss . . . but it's over now.

Interviewer: It's over?

Jane: Yeah . . . [*silence*].

John: Yeah, it's over, but you're still working there. What's that all about?

Interviewer: OK, so let me see if I understand. Jane, you admitted that you had an affair with your boss after John confronted you about staying late at work. You've also said that it's over. John, you seem very upset with the fact that Jane continues to work at the same place where her boss is. This sounds very complicated to me.

Now the interviewer feels that she is beginning to gather a more comprehensive picture of the situation, as well as some of the emotional reactions of the couple. She also is curious about the fact that Jane is still working with her boss, and that John is quite upset about it. This makes the situation very emotionally conflicted in the mind of the interviewer, and she feels compelled to explore it further.

Interviewer: So, John, I get the sense that you want Jane to quit her job?

John: Well, wouldn't you? [*Pause.*] Oh, that's right, you're not going to take sides . . .

Interviewer: Well, John, I'm not going to take sides, you're right, but I can certainly see that you are very hurt and upset by this and feel that the right thing for Jane to do is quit her job. If she quit her job, how would that make you feel?

John: At least I'd feel like she was truly sorry and committed to our marriage.

Interviewer: I can understand how Jane's quitting her job could help you feel a little more trust in her.

The interviewer has summarized John's feelings and understands his logic. Now it's time to explore Jane's perspective. Note how the interviewer has not sided with either partner and is working on building a relationship with both of them.

Interviewer: Jane, what is your reaction to John's thoughts and feelings about this situation?

Jane: I can understand how he feels, but that job is my whole world. I love it there. The affair is over.

John: So that's it. The affair is over, and I should just forget about it and be OK with you continuing to work with him.

Interviewer: OK . . . I think I can understand both of your positions. I can also see, Jane, that your continuing to work there is extremely important to you. What do you think about John's point that you continue to work with your boss?

Jane: I can see how that might make him mad, but like I said, it's over.

The interviewer is now beginning to get a sense of Jane's interpersonal makeup. Jane's job seems to be her whole world, and perhaps a major contribution to her self-esteem. The interviewer can also see how Jane's remaining at her job will affect John. Perhaps exploring some options here might be helpful and expand the interviewer's diagnostic impression of this couple.

> **Interviewer:** Jane, I can tell that your work is so important to you, and you don't want to give it up. However, I can also tell that your continuing to work there has John feeling very angry, hurt, and upset. This is a tough situation for both of you. I have a question for both of you. Is the income Jane receives from her job essential to your family budget?
>
> **John:** No. I told her she could quit and find another art store job. I told her she didn't even have to work, that we could make it on my income. But Jane wants to work at that place only. I guess I can understand, it means so much to her. I'm probably the reason she had the affair anyway. Am I wrong to want her to leave that job?

Now the interviewer is getting an even more compelling picture of this couple. Although John is angry, he is also hesitant to assert himself with Jane. This may be a clue to John's low self-esteem, and is a good example of a defense mechanism called turning against the self. It is an unconscious way to avoid confrontation and anger and is often used by individuals who are extremely insecure. Jane's insistence on working at the same job despite John's concerns seems to the interviewer to be a selfish act, and an indication of her own insecure sense of self. These are just initial speculations, but could serve to structure future couples work.

> **Interviewer:** Jane, John, I can see that our time is coming to an end. However, I want to explore with you the idea of continuing couples counseling.
>
> **John:** Do you think there's any hope for us?
>
> **Interviewer:** Yes, John, actually I do. Just the fact that the two of you came here to work on this very complicated problem shows me that you want things to be better. That's a most encouraging point.
>
> **John:** Well, I want to come back. Do you [*meaning Jane*]?
>
> **Jane:** I guess so . . .

Interviewer: I'm not sure I understood you, Jane. Would you like to continue counseling?

Jane: Sure.

Interviewer: OK then. We'll set up another time. In the meantime, I think it might be helpful if the two of you spent some time sharing your feelings about this situation and how it has affected both of you. I can tell there is a lot more to discuss, and we can start with that next time.

John: Will you talk to me about this, Jane?

Jane: Sure.

John: Well, that's a start. We'll see you next week.

Interviewer: It was good meeting you. Good luck, and we'll continue next time.

The interviewer has made a good connection with John and Jane. She has also developed a basic understanding of their presenting problem and some initial intuitions regarding diagnostic impressions of this couple. For example, Jane's affair can certainly be seen from a family therapy perspective as triangulation. Her extramarital relationship with her boss has come between the couple, and is a vehicle through which Jane can and probably has met some of her emotional needs, directing them toward her boss, rather than John. That kind of dynamic is common and very problematic for any couple. The interviewer does not have enough information regarding family-of-origin issues, or the extent of either John or Jane's differentiation from their families. This is just the beginning of the work. Far more information and emotions will surface as the couples interviewing continues. Affairs are typically an indication or symptom of deeper interpersonal issues in the relationship as well as in the partners. Future work will need to include both of these factors.

FAMILIES

Interviewing families is like couples work. Family therapy concepts and intrapsychic themes are useful theoretical and technical tools for the interviewer when working with a family. The family therapists discussed in chapter 1 provide excellent conceptual frameworks for understanding and working with any family. Bowen's family-of-origin, differentiation, and triangulation concepts, used in interviewing couples, are equally valuable and essential when interviewing families. In addition, Minuchin's structural theory emphasizes family roles, subsystems, boundaries, and scapegoat components as crucial for assessing and working with families. These two prominent theorists' ideas will serve as the theoretical foundation for examining the case example below.

The Williams family came to therapy because of the parents' concerns about their sixteen-year-old son, Michael. The parents have discovered that Michael has been drinking with his friends. The drinking problem is quite extensive. Michael engages in this activity every weekend. His parents have just recently discovered this because he came home very drunk one Saturday evening. Michael is an average student, and does not seem to have any other major difficulties. He is the oldest of four siblings, a strong support to them and well liked. He has a very close relationship with his mother. He is a sounding board for his mother, as his father is not emotionally available to his wife. Michael's father holds down a good job and provides well for the family. When he comes home each evening, he usually drinks about a half case of beer and falls asleep, not interacting much, if at all, with his wife or children. Michael and his father do not get along at all. The family comes to the interview focusing on Michael as the problem. Michael and his parents are the only family members at the first interview.

> **Interviewer:** Thanks for coming in tonight. I understood from talking with you, Mrs. Williams, that you and your husband have some concerns about your son Michael? Who would like to talk about this first?

Once again, the interviewer is providing the clients with the opportunity to decide for themselves who will speak, where they will begin, and what will be said. This is a common interviewing technique, especially in family therapy. Often the first one to talk is considered to be the family spokesperson, even if he or she is not one of the parents.

Michael: Well, I don't know what the big deal is, I just got caught drinking.

Mother: Just got caught drinking . . . Michael, this is a very serious situation, and your father and I are very worried about you.

Father: He's just a bad kid. What were you thinking, drinking and driving like that?

Michael: What do you know about it? For your information I never drink and drive, but how would you know?

Interviewer: Michael, I can see that both of your parents are very worried and upset about this recent situation. I can also sense that you don't seem as concerned.

The interviewer is summarizing what he believes the family is feeling.

Michael: I don't think it's such a big deal. Besides, my dad's the one who wanted me to come to therapy. My mom agrees with me, don't you, Mom?

Mother: Well now, Michael, I didn't exactly say that . . . I am concerned and don't think you should be drinking at sixteen.

Father [*to his wife*]: So you told him it wasn't a big deal?

Mother: Now, I didn't say that, I just wanted Michael to know I could understand wanting to drink, but that it wasn't really a good thing to do.

Father: So you took his side as always.

Interviewer: OK, let's pause a minute so that I can see if I understand.

The interviewer has already recognized some of the tension in the family, and uses this opportunity to take a step back and explore some of the different perspectives, thoughts, and feelings of all of the family members. This intervention sets a tone of respect for all family members, as well as communicating the interviewer's genuine interest in understanding the entire family.

Interviewer: I'm getting the feeling that there is some tension between you and your dad, Michael; I'm also sensing,

Dad, that you may be feeling that your wife has not taken this issue as seriously as you. Mom, it seems like you want to understand Michael, but are also worried about his drinking. Am I getting this right?

The interviewer has done an excellent job of summarizing his sense of the family dynamics, without judging any members, while allowing for the discussion to continue. He is also beginning to sense a stronger bond between Michael and his mother, than between the father and mother, and that this may be a source of serious conflict in the family. From a boundary standpoint, the interviewer might silently hypothesize that there may be a strong subsystem between Michael and his mother that shuts out or even triangulates the father in the family system. These are initial thoughts, and it is far too early to confirm them or even pursue them directly with the family. However, they could be very important.

Mother: I'm just trying to be a good parent. Michael is not a bad boy, he's just going through some tough times, I think, and I want to be a support to him.

Interviewer: I can certainly understand that you want to support your son, and it also sounds like you're concerned that if you come down too hard on him you might alienate Michael and make the problem worse?

This is an interpretation by the interviewer. He is not sure the mother is feeling exactly the way he described it; so he poses a question to clarify and seek further information.

Mother: I think that's exactly how I'm feeling.

Father: Like I said, always taking his side, aren't you?

Mother: I'm not meaning to take sides; I'm just trying to be a good mother to Michael. I know this is serious, that's why we're here.

Interviewer: I don't mean to stray too far away from the reason you all came in, and yet I want to be of as much help to the family as possible. Dad, you mentioned that your wife "always" sides with Michael. Would you talk a little more about that?

Father: Well, she just does, that's all. They're always talking together. She confides in him, and he does the same with her. I think she favors him, always has, even over the other kids.

Interviewer: How does that make you feel?

Father: I really don't care what they do, but I don't think it helps.

The interviewer has a sense that the father is in denial about his feelings surrounding this issue and believes that a gentle confrontation may be helpful to both him and the family.

Interviewer: I may be wrong about this, Dad, but I sense that you really do care about the nature of the relationship between Michael and your wife.

Father: I just think she should be firmer with him. He manipulates her, and I don't think he's a good kid.

Interviewer: What makes you think Michael is not a good kid?

Father: He's always getting into trouble. This drinking thing is just the latest and biggest problem.

Interviewer: I want to explore those thoughts further, Dad, and I also want to discuss a little bit about family therapy. I have found that using some words can lead to greater conflict and limit communication. I've noticed you using the word "always" in connection with Michael. I'm wondering if you actually believe that Michael "always" is a certain way or does certain things, or perhaps that's your way of expressing your feelings. Do you really believe that Michael is always bad, for instance, or that your wife always sides with him?

Father: Well, now that you put it that way, I guess I don't really think that either of them are always that way; but sometimes it feels like it.

Interviewer: And how does that affect you?

Father: I feel shut out.

Interviewer: Thanks for that honest comment, Dad. Mom, Michael, what do you think about what Dad just said?

Mother: I don't mean to seem that way. I just feel for Michael, and sometimes it seems like his dad doesn't care about him. Maybe I'm trying to make up for that . . .

Michael: He just doesn't like me.

Interviewer: How do you know that, Michael?

Michael: We just don't seem to get along or spend any time together. I don't have very many good memories of him as a kid either.

Father: Well, if you weren't in trouble so much and now drinking like this, maybe things could have been different.

Michael: You're one to talk about drinking. You come home every night and get drunk and pass out . . . and I mean *every* night!

Father: You watch what you're saying, you stupid brat!

Mother: OH NO! This is exactly how things are at home.

The interviewer now has witnessed a helpful example of the family dynamics. This gives him an opportunity to go even deeper into them in the interview.

Interviewer: Well, let's step back a minute again. I can sense that there is a great deal of tension between Dad and Michael. Clearly the family is in conflict over this, and I think the drinking issue has intensified the problem.

At this point the interviewer continues to explore these issues, and the family decides that continuing therapy is a good idea and a possible way to help improve the relationships among all members. A great deal of information has surfaced about the family in this session. The interviewer's initial speculations about boundaries and triangulation seem to be accurate and an indication of where the family therapy may go in the future. The revelation about the father's drinking is also a profound complication to the family problem and may be a crucial element in future work. Considering the father's extensive drinking, Michael may have been scapegoated by the father, and Michael's drinking behavior could be a symptom of the larger drinking problem in this family. These too are speculations, but speculations derived from the use of strong family theory. The interviewer has his work cut out for him with the parents, son, and family in general.

GROUPS

The final modality covered in this chapter is group work. As an interdisciplinary modality in the helping professions, group work is probably the most diverse. Social workers, psychologists, nurses, probation officers, psychiatrists, addictions workers, and a myriad of other helping professionals use the group modality because of its potentially powerful effect on the group members.

The role of the group interviewer is complex. Not only must he or she develop a relationship with the individual group members, but also with the group itself, in order to be effective in any meaningful way. Therefore, the skills of the group interviewer must incorporate key aspects of the previous three modalities: individuals, couples, and families. The theories and techniques discussed for use in those modalities are also critical elements for the group interviewer. Interviewers must use engagement skills and interventions as in working with individual clients. On the other hand, they must not engage individual group members without keeping an eye on the effect on the entire group. Working models of the interviewer and group members are complex because they include not only individual working models of the interviewer within the group context, but also individual and working models of the group itself. This complexity can make group interviewing a very daunting task. In addition, group interviewers must incorporate concepts from family systems and group work theory in order to understand the group interview dynamic and process, and must intervene using their own theoretical template of group work practice.

There are far too many types of groups to cover here in a reasonable fashion. The recommended reading and multimedia sources at the end of the chapter provide a number of useful adjunct sources to help expand the interviewer's knowledge base.

The group case example focuses on a hypothetical alcoholism recovery group. Alcoholism is a major problem in the United States, in Canada, and across the world. There are many forms of treatment for this chronic problem, and various opinions about what types of treatment are most successful. Regardless of those opinions, the recidivism (return-to-treatment rate) has hovered around 70 percent for decades. Group therapy has been considered a useful intervention if it is combined with other therapeutic modalities, including individual, couples, and family work, at various times in the recovery process. Group work has been considered successful because of the common circumstances experienced by the group members, that is, alcoholism, loss, divorce, medical illness such as cancer, returning from war, and so forth. The unique bond of experience for the group members provides a potentially healing environment that is not as powerful in other modalities.

In this case example, the male interviewer is meeting for the first time with six men who have recently been discharged from an alcoholism in-treatment facility. The group members range from thirty to fifty years old, and they are in various stages of alcoholism.

> **Interviewer:** Good evening all. I'm glad to see you could make it here tonight. The fact that all of you came is a very positive start. Let me explain a little bit about the group process so we are all on the same page. Afterwards, please feel free to ask me any questions about the group.

By this opening statement, the interviewer is recognizing the potential strength of the group and also praising all members for making the commitment to it. He is also setting the stage immediately for the group to join in on the conversation and process.

> **Interviewer:** The purpose of this group is to provide a confidential setting where all of you can feel comfortable in

sharing your thoughts and feelings about your difficulties with alcohol, and how it has affected your life. All of you have come from inpatient treatment and had some type of group work in your respective programs. Those groups have been supportive, educational, and therapeutic to some extent, ultimately leading you to be discharged and referred to this group for follow-up. Over time, I am hoping that we will all get to know each other, and that this group will serve as a way to help each of you continue in your recovery, and help each other through sharing your own experiences and interacting with each other in helpful ways, such as offering advice and self-disclosing about your own thoughts and feelings. This process, I know, will take time, and will probably be a risk for all of you. I'm here to help support all of you in this process. The basic ground rules are simple. Each group member should not interrupt another. Group members should respect each other's experience and try not to judge another. Group members can talk about whatever is important to them, and be able to look to the group for direct and indirect support when necessary. In a general sense, I think that's it for starters. As I'm sure you've already learned, groups evolve in stages, and we are in stage one: getting to know each other. Are there any questions?

Group Member 1: Do we use our real names, or is this like AA?

In Alcoholics Anonymous, members do not use their real names.

Interviewer: That's a great question. As the group leader, I already know all of your real names because you were referred to me along with your in-treatment discharge plans. I am OK with each of you handling that any way you'd like.

Group Member 2: I'm OK with our real names since our leader knows them anyway, as long as we all agree to keep what we talk about confidential.

Group member 2 is risking the first step in this group process. This may be a signal that he is a potential group spokesperson or leader, or perhaps just anxious about getting clarity on this issue.

Group Member 3: I'm OK with that too. How about the rest of you?

In turn, the other group members each agree to use their real names. This may seem like a simple process of agreement, but symbolically it demonstrates a developing norm of trust within this group.

Interviewer: Great. It seems like we're all willing to approach this with a completely open process. To me that is a signal of initial trust, not an easy thing to do with people one has just met.

The interviewer is validating the positive group process and acknowledging the strength of each individual and the entire group in arriving at this decision.

Interviewer: How should we start to get to know each other? [*leaving this up to the group*].

Group Member 2: I think we should just say why we're here and what we want out of this group. I'll start, if that's OK with you guys.

Group as a Whole: [*Silently nods in agreement.*]

Group Member 2: I'm Bill and I'm forty-two. I started drinking when I was a teenager. I used to steal liquor from my parents' house and get drunk with my friends. I started with whatever they had, but eventually decided on vodka. I chose vodka because people couldn't smell it on me. That way I could use anywhere, at school, at work, at home, you name it. I was able to barely finish high school with nobody finding out about my problem. I didn't think it was a problem then. I tried to go to college, but I partied so much that it eventually affected my grades; I didn't go to class and finally dropped out my sophomore year. I started working in a grocery store, but kept drinking almost every day at work. Work is where I met my wife. She's three years younger than me. We started drinking together right away in our twenties. I started drinking more and more, until my behavior started getting really bad at home. I didn't notice it, my wife did. She told me I was treating her really bad and talking to her very mean. I denied it, and kept drinking until things started getting bad with my kids, and I finally almost lost my job because I was so drunk I couldn't perform at work. That's when they sent me to rehab. I'm glad they didn't fire me, and I'm hoping this will work, but I'm scared.

Interviewer: Thanks for sharing so much, Bill. I'm sure that took a lot of courage. Anyone want to comment on what Bill just said?

Here the interviewer responds with a directly empathic response, which again serves two purposes. First, it validates Bill. He did take a big risk, and set the possible tone for the group as a whole. Second, the interviewer's response indicates that speech such as Bill's is appropriate and important in this group. The interviewer implicitly reinforces a group norm, that is, openness and honesty is OK, even good, in this group. This exchange also allows the interviewer to begin to form some tentative diagnostic opinions about Bill, as well as a working model to refer to as the group evolves.

Group Member 3, Steve: Man, that was great! I had a similar kind of situation, except I didn't start drinking until I was in the army.

Interviewer: So your experience was similar to Bill's? Can you tell us in what ways, Steve?

Steve: Sure. Although I didn't start until I was twenty, I found myself steadily increasing my drinking until it started affecting my life. Bill, my drink of choice was whiskey.

Bill: Yeah . . . I never got into it, but I hear it's a great buzz.

Interviewer [*to Bill and Steve and the group*]: So it seems like you and Steve have something in common regarding your drinking. How about the rest of the group? How do you all relate to what Bill and Steve have had to say?

For the rest of the session, each member in turn slowly begins to share in his own way his unique history with drinking, how it has affected his life, and how he arrived in this group. The interviewer's role is to help the process begin and serve as a mediator for the group. One can begin to see the subtle and direct ways in which the interviewer is helping the entire group to begin to form a bond around discussing the members' painful memories regarding the role of alcohol in their lives. It appears that some initial engagement has happened. This will take some time, and will evolve into the subsequent stages of group process.

RESEARCH IMPLICATIONS AND BASIS OF PRACTICE

Individual, family, couple, and group interviewing all originated or have evolved into the intuitive, practice wisdom, and theoretical levels of research knowledge. Methodological challenges within all modalities have always been the biggest difficulty in researching interviewing. Some modalities are further along than others in this regard, particularly individual work as a result of the recent surge of neuroscience research. The high recidivism in many types of group work begs the need for greater and more extensive study in this area. Attachment theory demonstrates some promise in individual, couple, and even family work. In every theoretical orientation or modality, however, the importance and effect of the therapeutic relationship has been validated (Prochaska & Norcross, 2003). Recent evidence-based studies have also validated the efficacy of the therapeutic relationship (O'Hare, 2005). Overall, however, there is still a good deal of research to be done on the effectiveness of the interviewing process in all modalities.

SUMMARY

This chapter examined the nature of interviewing within the four main modalities: individual, family, couples, and group. The case examples and some preliminary theoretical examination have helped to demonstrate the common and distinct features within each of the modalities.

RECOMMENDED READING

O'Hare, T. (2005). *Evidence-based practices for social workers: An interdisciplinary approach.* Chicago: Lyceum Books.

The reader is encouraged to revisit O'Hare's comprehensive work on evidence-based practice within all modalities and problem areas, especially as they relate to interviewing.

Prochaska, J. O., & Norcross, J. C. (2003). *Systems of psychotherapy: A transtheoretical analysis.* Belmont, CA: Brooks/Cole.

Prochaska and Norcross's text is one of the most comprehensive available in examining the wide range of theoretical approaches to interviewing. Their work is also pivotal because of the emphasis on the importance of the relationship in effective practice.

Individuals

Readings on interviewing individuals are thoroughly covered in preceding chapters.

Couples

Gurman, A. S., & Jacobson, N. S. (Eds.). (2002). *Clinical handbook of couple therapy.* New York: Guilford Press.

Siegel, J. (1992). *Repairing intimacy: An object relations approach to couples therapy.* Northvale, NJ: Jason Aronson.

The Gurman and Jacobson book is undoubtedly the most comprehensive couples text. The editors and authors cover a wide range of theoretical and practical application in this modality. Siegel's work is by far the most detailed psychodynamic text on working with couples. Her emphasis on the relationship is especially important for interviewers.

Family

Bowen, M. (1978). *Family therapy in clinical practice.* New York: Aronson.

Minuchin, S. (1974). *Families and family therapy*. Cambridge, MA: Harvard University Press.

Bowen and Minuchin are considered by many to be the key family therapy theorists and practitioners. Reading their classic work is essential to family interviewing.

Group

Rogers, C. (1965). *Client-centered therapy*. Boston: Houghton Mifflin.
Yalom, I. D. (1985). *The theory and practice of group psychotherapy*. New York: Basic Books.

Rogers's work on groups is a classic in interviewing technique. His anecdotal casework is very helpful to the group interviewer. Irvin Yalom's classic book serves as the underlying foundation with which to understand working with groups of all kinds. Although it is recognized that not all groups are psychotherapy groups, Yalom's concepts have been recognized as universally applicable to all group work. His text is practical, theoretical, and extremely comprehensive.

MULTIMEDIA SOURCES

Film has provided some of the best examples of actual interviewing situations (such as those mentioned in previous chapters) as well as of the dynamics and process of specific modalities. The reader is encouraged to revisit those earlier references. The additional sources here are also quite helpful in understanding the process of modalities.

Couples

Annie Hall. (1977). Woody Allen (Director). United Artists.
Who's Afraid of Virginia Woolf? (1966). Mike Nichols (Director). Warner Brothers.
When a Man Loves a Woman. (1994). Louis Mandoki (Director). Touchstone Pictures.

These three classic films provide a broad view of the dynamics of couples and the implications for interviewing.

Family

Ordinary People. (1980). Robert Redford (Director). Paramount
  Pictures.

There is probably no better example of the complexity of family process for interviewing than this Academy Award–winning film. The
interviewing sequences with family members and therapist are invaluable in terms of theory and technique.

Group

The Big Chill. (1983). Lawrence Kasdan (Director). Columbia
  Pictures.
Boyz n the Hood. (1991). John Singleton (Director). Columbia
  Pictures.
The Breakfast Club. (1985). John Hughes (Director). Universal
  Studios.
Girl, Interrupted. (1999). James Mangold (Director). Columbia
  Pictures.
The Usual Suspects. (1995). Bryan Singer (Director). Spelling Films
  International.

These five films are certainly not an exhaustive list of relevant depictions of group dynamics. However, their range, depth, and variety provide the interviewer with tremendous food for thought on the process
with diverse groups.

Interviewing Specific Age Groups

In addition to the variety of approaches necessary for interviewing in different interdisciplinary modalities, the interviewer must also be knowledgeable, adaptive, and creative in working with clients of different ages. This chapter explores this process in depth, examining crucial developmental theories as well as specific techniques necessary to developing successful relationships with people of all ages. Case examples provide the interviewer with detailed approaches and explanations for children, adolescents, and adults.

CHILDREN

Interviewing children is a unique endeavor that is quite different than working with adolescents and adults. The reason is simple: children at different degrees of developmental maturity demand differential interviewing styles and techniques. Most preadolescent children are not verbally as competent as older people. One factor in this difficulty is that children's brains are not as fully developed as adolescents' and adults'. They do not have the ability for abstract thought, and their language skills are limited.

Major theorists and practitioners all agree that the most fundamental developmental process for children is the ability to play and to use play to form a sense of self and master their world (Erikson, 1950; A. Freud, 1936; Piaget & Inhelder, 1969; Vygotsky, 1978; Winnicott, 1971). Play is the symbolic vehicle through which children experiment with life, try on different roles, act out scenarios, and achieve mastery. The interviewer needs to use a combination of play and developmentally appropriate verbal interaction to be successful working with children. Children do not need to work through their problems by talking and gaining intellectual insights as adults might; they can work through complex difficulties symbolically in a carefully constructed play therapy situation with an attuned and insightful interviewer. Working with children (and adolescents) also involves parents or primary caretakers to some extent. Children are usually part of a family. The primary caretakers are more often than not the ones who have brought them to the interview. There are varying degrees of confidentiality in interviewing work with children, and the degree of confidentiality depends on the context of the case. Most often some type of general ongoing communication (whether by phone or in interviews) with the primary caretakers is essential for successful work. The child should be aware of, and to an age-appropriate extent involved in, what type of communication the interviewer will have with the primary caretaker about the process. Most often, the family wants to know how the interviewing is going, to provide useful information to the interviewer, and to be assured that their child is improving.

Tommy, age eight, was brought to the interview by his mother, a thirty-eight-year-old divorced woman. The parents had divorced within the last year. Tommy's older sister seemed to be doing well in adjusting to the divorce, but Tommy was having trouble. At school he had become withdrawn in class and was not playing with the other children as he had before the divorce. The school social worker referred Tommy to the interviewer because of these problems. He also was having trouble getting along with his sister at home. Tommy and his sister used to enjoy time together, but since the divorce seemed to argue and fight about almost everything. Tommy did see his father on occasional visits, but these were few and far between, and the father tended to cancel his time with Tommy abruptly, or just didn't show up to visit him. Prior to the divorce, Tommy and his dad seemed to have a good relationship. Tommy idealized his father. The divorce was a very upsetting event in Tommy's life. The interviewer provided individual therapy to both Tommy and his mother on a regular basis.

The interviewer is new in his field, and does not have much experience working with children. Initially, after talking with Tommy's mother and the school social worker, he tried to engage Tommy in talk therapy, with or without the use of traditional games such as checkers or cards. Tommy did not respond well to this type of interaction and did not seem capable of discussing his thoughts or feelings about his situation. The interviewer knew he must try something else. In this session, Tommy notices a box of toys in the corner of the interviewer's office. Tommy goes over to it to check it out. The box holds a variety of figures, blocks, and other general and nondescript objects. Tommy seems pleased with these things and begins to engage the interviewer in play.

> *Tommy:* Let's play war.
> **Interviewer:** OK, Tommy. How should we do that?

The interviewer recognizes that Tommy has taken the initiative in the session and wants to be supportive and allow him to take this play in a direction that is comfortable for him. The interviewer also realizes that this could be a potential breakthrough.

> *Tommy:* You take these guys and some of the blocks and go build your fort in that corner [*pointing in the direction of the opposite side of the room*]. I'll take my guys and set up my fort here.
> **Interviewer:** Sounds good. Do you want me to build any special type of fort?

Again the interviewer wants to allow Tommy to lead the process.

> *Tommy:* No, you know . . . just build a fort.
> **Interviewer:** All right . . . I'm going to make a really good one.
> *Tommy:* Well, probably not as good as mine . . . you'll see!

The interviewer intuitively realizes that this play is going to be interactive and has some special meaning for Tommy. Tommy has never been this enthusiastic in previous interviews.

> **Interviewer:** Tommy, my fort is built. How about yours?
> *Tommy:* No, I'm still building mine.
> **Interviewer:** OK, tell me when you want me to look at it.
> *Tommy* [*after a few minutes*]: OK, I'm done.
> **Interviewer:** Do you want me to see it?

The interviewer senses that Tommy feels the need to be in complete control of this play situation, and thus respects it. The interviewer recognizes that this is important and meaningful, but doesn't quite understand why yet. However, he trusts his instincts and curiosity in this process.

> *Tommy:* No, just have your guys come over and attack my fort.
> **Interviewer:** OK, we're on our way.

The interviewer heads his odd band of soldiers (various figures of all types, i.e., army men, knights, monsters, animals, etc.) across the room in the direction of Tommy's fort. Before the interviewer can get even halfway across the room, Tommy interrupts.

> *Tommy:* My guys can dig underground, and they just popped up and killed your guys.

He playfully, but aggressively, uses his figures to knock over the interviewer's army and proceeds to move to the interviewer's fort and destroy it.

> *Tommy:* I WON! Your guys are dead and your fort is gone!
> **Interviewer:** Yeah, you really got me. Your guys are good.
> *Tommy:* They're the best.
> **Interviewer:** What do you want to do now?
> *Tommy:* You set up your fort again and tell me when you're ready.
> **Interviewer:** OK . . . [*After a few minutes*] I'm ready, Tommy.

Tommy: OK, attack me.

Interviewer: All right, my guys are coming.

The interviewer again gets about halfway to Tommy's fort, but his army and fort are demolished by Tommy's army.

Tommy: Got you again. Your guys are not very good.

Interviewer: Well, I tried, Tommy, but I think your guys are just better.

Tommy: Like I said, they're the best. Let's do it again.

The reader can probably imagine where this scenario is going. Tommy continues to reenact this fighting scene over many months of therapy. The scenario varies a bit—for example, the interviewer is allowed to travel various distances before Tommy pounces—but Tommy always wins. The interviewer recognizes that this type of play has empowered Tommy. Tommy feels a complete sense of control and confidence. However, the interviewer is becoming frustrated and even a bit angry about being battered so badly and consistently. He decides to try to vary the situation in future interviews.

Tommy: Let's get out the men!

Interviewer: OK . . . same thing?

Tommy: Yeah, build your fort and come after me.

Interviewer: All right, but today I think I might win.

Tommy: No way!

The interviewer finishes his fort and begins his move toward Tommy's fort. Tommy again intercepts the interviewer's army near his fort. This time the interviewer takes a different stance.

Interviewer: Tommy, my guys have a new machine that lets them dig underground. They can come up right inside your fort.

Tommy [*very excited*]: Oh yeah! My guys have a special force field that can stop them.

Interviewer: Oh no . . . I guess I'm done for.

Tommy: Yep, you can't beat me!

As the reader can see, winning is very important to Tommy, at all costs. This type of dynamic continues for quite some time. In the meantime, the interviewer hears from both the school social worker and the mother that Tommy is doing really well in therapy and that "Whatever you're doing with him . . . keep it up!" The interviewer comes to recognize that Tommy's play has enabled him to symbolically gain control of his world (the fort, his men, etc.) and to feel a sense of mastery and confidence. The unconditionally empathic and supportive relationship with the interviewer has successfully enabled this process. In other words, what Tommy could not control in his real world (visits and relationship with his dad) he can symbolically accomplish in the interviews. Over time Tommy begins to engage in more mutual play with the interviewer and even occasionally allows him to win. The interviewer never talks much directly with Tommy about his dad, family, or school, but recognizes the importance and success of this sustained play therapy.

This is a very typical example of interviewing with children. Understanding the power and importance of play in development and therapeutic work is crucial to successful work with children.

ADOLESCENTS

Most adolescents are involuntary clients, unlike most adults. As a result, they require a certain type of interviewing approach and understanding. The primary caretakers also need to be involved in the process to some extent, in order to ensure a coordinated effort. This involvement could take the form of family therapy, individual or couple sessions with the primary caretakers, or occasional phone conversations regarding general progress. Sometimes it is also helpful to coordinate efforts with other collaterals, such as probation officers, school social workers, and so forth.

Adolescent developmental theory is extremely helpful in understanding and intervening with adolescents in session. Some key concepts that the interviewer must be aware of include adolescent developmental level and the separation-individuation process in general, the capacity for abstract thought, the careful and clinically informed use of self-disclosure by the interviewer in building trust, the importance of the peer group, and the ways in which teenagers communicate about their world through the use of (manifest and latent) symbols. Like children, many adolescents are hesitant to speak as directly as adults about their thoughts and feelings, especially about their families. They are more comfortable talking about friends, interests, hobbies, teachers, school (to some extent), and other less emotionally threatening topics. All of these are grist for the mill, and the skillful interviewer can learn a great deal about adolescent clients, as well as help them negotiate difficult problems in life, without a great deal of direct focus on their families. After all, adolescents are developmentally moving away from the family and using other relationships to form mature identifications that will help them in adulthood. These can consist of their primary peer group or idealized figures, usually adults who can serve the same type of emotional function in identity development that parents did in childhood.

Peter Blos has written about adolescence as a time of the "second separation-individuation," like the first one that happens around eighteen months to three years in life. Adolescents, according to Blos and others, fluctuate in their dependency needs with the family, moving toward and away from them much like toddlers do in negotiating their first sense of independence. Adolescents' use of this process is much more mature and symbolic because of their capacity for abstract thought in this negotiation process, but it is a separation-individuation process nonetheless (Blos, 1979; Erikson, 1968; Lucente, 2012).

The reader may remember John from chapter 3. He was an involuntary referral to the interviewer. He had been arrested for vandalism. The first interview demonstrated that John was beginning to engage in the process, but was hesitant and cautious in his conversation with the interviewer.

Interviewer: Hi John. I'm glad to see you're back. How are things going?

Obviously the interviewer wants to continue a tone that communicates John is free to talk about whatever he wants. This technique is used, not to avoid John's presenting concerns or the interests of the court, but to create an atmosphere where he will feel free to talk about topics that are important to him. The interviewer believes that in that process, meaningful content for discussion will emerge.

> **John:** OK, I guess.
> **Interviewer:** Anything in particular that you want to talk about?
> **John:** No.
> **Interviewer:** Well, I'd like to get to know you better. Can we talk about your family?
> **John:** What's there to talk about?
> **Interviewer:** Well, I really don't know much about them. How many people are in your family?
> **John:** There's my mom and dad, and I've got a couple of older sisters, but they don't live at home.
> **Interviewer:** How do you get along with your family?
> **John:** I really don't see them much at all. My sisters have their lives, and both my parents work and don't get home until about seven or eight at night.
> **Interviewer:** Sounds like you're alone a lot.
> **John:** I don't care . . . it doesn't bother me . . . I can take care of myself.

The interviewer can sense that this may be a touchy subject for John. John seems a little defensive and wants to make it clear that he is OK being alone frequently, but the interviewer also believes that John may have some other feelings about this, just by the way he talks about it. This information will be stored away in the interviewer's working model of John for a later time, but it could signal some issues around dependency and separation-individuation for the client.

> **Interviewer:** I'm sure you can take care of yourself, John. I apologize if I insulted you. It's just I can imagine some people might not like having all that time alone.
> **John:** Well, I'm OK with it.

Interviewer: That's good to hear. So what do you do with your time?

John: I hang out with my friends, go the drop-in center, you know.

Interviewer: The drop-in center, I've heard of that. What's it like?

John: It's OK. There's pool tables, foosball, music, and some pretty cool kids that hang out there.

Interviewer: Aren't there also counselors there?

John: I don't think they're really counselors, just adults to talk to and hang out with . . . they're OK.

The interviewer is getting the sense that John does have some type of supportive social network. Perhaps that should be explored more.

Interviewer: So how do you get along with the people at the drop-in center?

John: Some of the kids are OK, but some of them are kind of stuck up.

Interviewer: What do you mean, stuck up?

John: You know . . . they think they're too cool for everyone. They wear the cool clothes; think their music is the best. They're real tight and don't talk to anybody except their own.

Interviewer: How's that?

John: I don't care . . . they're jerks!

Interviewer: Really doesn't sound like you think too much of them.

John: Like I said, they're jerks.

Interviewer: What do you and your friends do together?

John: Well, most of them live pretty far away, and I don't see them very often.

Interviewer: So you're kind of on your own a lot?

John: Yeah, but I'm fine . . . I've got lots of things to do.

The interviewer is getting a clearer picture that John may be much more lonely than he lets on. His family is not around, he doesn't seem to fit in with some of the kids at the drop-in center, and the friends he does seem to have are not close enough to see on a regular basis. The interviewer's working model of John is expanding and beginning to paint a picture of an isolated adolescent who perhaps is needy and maybe a little angry about his empty world. This awareness comes from exploration of the client's everyday life with peers, not a deep intrusion into his family situation and some of the obvious contributions that may have led him to act out. It may be pure speculation, but perhaps the vandalism incident was a way of acting out some of John's anger, and even a cry for help of sorts. It certainly got him some attention, and now he's "forced" to be connected with an interviewer to talk about his life.

ADULTS

This section explores interviewing adults of different ages, with varying problems. The possible adult situations are endless. The case examples here represent a typical cross section of adult clients in order to give the interviewer a sense of the approaches necessary in working with them. Tommy's mother, introduced earlier in this chapter, is presented. Other examples are a young professional struggling with relationship issues and an older adult approaching retirement.

A Parent

Tommy's case, discussed earlier, is a rich example of the kind of work that can help children resolve challenges in life and put them back on track. The interviewer continually worked with Tommy's mother (Mrs. T.) to learn how Tommy was performing in school and getting along at home and with his friends. Tommy was not interested (or perhaps even capable) in talking about these issues, yet this information was crucial to the interviewer's ability to understand Tommy's life. To work successfully with any child or adolescent, the interviewer must be in some sort of ongoing communication with the primary caretakers to ensure continuity and have a complete picture of the client's life outside of the interview.

The interview that follows shows an adult who is in the midst of raising a child. Child rearing is one of the crucial stages of life. Erikson's life stage theory defines the task as "generativity vs. stagnation." In other words, this is the time in life when many people are drawn to give back to the world, through family (children) or career. This stage is the logical next step after forming the capacity for intimacy with another (Erikson, 1950). Mrs. T. is struggling not only with Tommy's difficulties, but also with her own sense of competence and self at this time in life.

> **Interviewer:** Hi Mrs. T. Thanks for coming in today. We spoke on the phone, and I understand that you are concerned about your son, Tommy?

This call was the first contact with Tommy's mother, prior to the session discussed above.

> *Mrs. T.:* Yeah, like I said on the phone, Tommy has been having some problems in school and at home.
> **Interviewer:** Can you tell me a little more about that?
> *Mrs. T.:* His grades have been slipping, he's distant with his friends, and his teacher says that he is just withdrawn in general.
> **Interviewer:** I'm assuming that's not his normal behavior or performance?
> *Mrs. T.:* Oh no, up until a few months ago Tommy was doing fine.
> **Interviewer:** What do you think might have changed things?
> *Mrs. T.:* Well, my husband and I recently divorced. Things had been bad for a while, but he was living in our home until about a month ago. Since he left, Tommy seems to have really changed.
> **Interviewer:** I don't want to pry, Mrs. T., but could you tell me a little bit about the nature of the divorce in order to better understand how it might have affected Tommy?

The interviewer is careful to respect Mrs. T.'s privacy, but also realizes that this information may be crucial to understanding Tommy's behavior and helping him in therapy.

> **Mrs. T.:** Oh, I'm fine talking about it. You see, Tommy's dad was having an affair with a woman from work. I found out about it recently. We had been in therapy for about a year, but nothing changed. He just moved out and is living with her.
>
> **Interviewer:** How were things prior to this affair?

The interviewer feels the need to explore the circumstances a bit further in order to understand the family and couple dynamics that certainly affected Tommy in some way.

> **Mrs. T.:** He had been pretty distant for several years. I don't know, he's in his forties, maybe it was a midlife thing? Anyway, he was never a very affectionate man, or very interested in talking. He went to work, came home, and sat on the couch, watching TV and drinking.
>
> **Interviewer:** Do you think he had a drinking problem?
>
> **Mrs. T.:** I don't know. He didn't seem to drink very much; he just wasn't interested in me.
>
> **Interviewer:** How about his relationship with the kids?
>
> **Mrs. T.:** Well . . . that's really why I'm here.
>
> **Interviewer:** You mean Tommy?
>
> **Mrs. T.:** Yeah . . . Tommy and his dad used to be very close. Even though his dad didn't seem to care about me or his daughter very much, he did spend a good deal of time with Tommy, especially on the weekends.
>
> **Interviewer:** What kinds of things did they do together?
>
> **Mrs. T.:** Oh, you know, father and son things. They would play sports, build Legos, those kinds of things. Tommy really loved being with his dad. He really seemed to look up to him.
>
> **Interviewer:** And now that the two of you are divorced, how has that changed Tommy's relationship with his dad? Does his dad have visitation rights?

Mrs. T.: Oh yes! The thing is, his dad rarely sees Tommy. I think he's too preoccupied with his new life, you know, his girlfriend.

Interviewer: How often does he see Tommy?

Mrs. T.: Well, that depends. He's supposed to see him every Wednesday evening, and every other weekend.

Interviewer: And does he follow through on this arrangement?

Mrs. T.: That's the problem. He is *so* inconsistent with Tommy. I never know if he is going to show up, and he seems to call and cancel at the last minute a lot. Tommy is devastated by it . . . I can tell.

Interviewer: How can you tell?

The interviewer does not want to jump to any conclusions, and wants to be sure he understands Mrs. T.'s perceptions.

Mrs. T.: Well, Tommy doesn't say anything, but he withdraws. He goes to his room and just plays alone with his toys. I try to talk with him or get him and his sister involved in some type of game or TV show, but Tommy just wants to be alone. It's really heartbreaking!

Interviewer: It does sound really sad, and especially hard on you.

Mrs. T.: Oh, I'm not worried about me. I'm used to it and I can take it. In fact I just got into therapy myself, and it's really helping. But I'm so worried about Tommy. I talked to the school social worker about him, and she recommended that he come to see you.

Interviewer: I'm more than happy to help. Mrs. T., can you tell me a little bit more about how Tommy is doing in school and with his friends?

The interviewer now has a fairly good sense of Tommy's family life, at least from his mother's perspective, and now needs to know more about other crucial areas of Tommy's world in order to prepare to see him.

Mrs. T.: Like I think I told you on the phone. They say he's distant.

Interviewer: Excuse me, Mrs. T., who are they?

Mrs. T.: Oh, I'm sorry, his teachers and the school social worker.

Interviewer: Can you give me some more examples of how Tommy is distant at school?

Mrs. T.: Well, he used to really look forward to going to school and seemed to do well and get along with his friends. Now he keeps to himself, doesn't do well in his school work, and is just a very quiet and withdrawn boy. That's not like my Tommy. He used to be so happy.

Interviewer: I know this may sound so obvious, Mrs. T., but do you think it's the divorce and time away from his dad?

Mrs. T.: Absolutely! I've tried to talk with him about it, and so has the school social worker, but he won't talk at all . . . I mean he won't discuss anything about the divorce or his dad.

Interviewer: In order for me to try and help Tommy, can you tell me what kinds of things he likes to do?

Mrs. T.: Sure, like I said, he's a typical boy. He likes to play . . . all sorts of things.

The interviewer feels that he has a good sense that Tommy is withdrawn and perhaps a little depressed regarding the loss of his dad. He also senses that this loss has affected almost all areas of Tommy's life. Therapy seems in order. Now is the time to explain to Tommy's mother the interviewing process and the need to coordinate efforts with her, the school, and perhaps Tommy's father.

Interviewer: Thanks, Mrs. T. Well, from what you've told me [*all the interviewer has to go on*], it certainly seems like Tommy is struggling, and I think it's safe to say that it probably has a great deal to do with the divorce, especially since there do not seem to be any other major factors involved in

Tommy's life. I think it might be helpful if I saw Tommy in individual therapy. I certainly want to stay in touch with you about how he is doing. We can do that by phone or in person. Therapy is confidential, but Tommy is eight, and technically his therapy is not bound by any confidentiality laws. However, I will let Tommy know that we'll be talking occasionally about how he's doing, so he doesn't feel like we're talking behind his back. I will also get a release of information to talk with his school social worker, if that's OK with you?

Mrs. T.: Of course, whatever you think.

Interviewer: I really think this needs to be a comprehensive effort, Mrs. T. Tommy is not going to get better unless I can work with him, you, and the school. By the way, do you think his dad would be willing to talk with me about Tommy?

Mrs. T.: I really don't know. I'll give you his number. I can tell you that he'll probably be pretty inconsistent, like he is with Tommy.

Interviewer: Well, I'll do my best. I think that given the way you've described Tommy's previous relationship with his father, it could be very important to have him involved. Well, I think that's about it for today. Is there anything else you'd like to tell me or need to know before we end?

Mrs. T.: I don't think so . . . You came highly recommended. Have you worked with children a lot? How does the therapy usually go?

Interviewer: Yes I have, and that's a good question. I've found that children Tommy's age may not be as able or willing to discuss their problems as adults are. For one thing they don't have the verbal skills, and their brains are not as developed as adults' for more advanced discussion. Children do, however, have an amazing ability to communicate and work out their problems through play. Their play can be symbolic of the emotions in their life. I will try to get a sense of what Tommy is into, and I think the therapy will flow naturally from there. I will stay in touch with you so we can monitor how he's doing on a regular basis. Also, please let me know if there are any things going on in his life that might help me work with him . . . say for instance a missed visitation with Dad, or a particularly good or bad day in school. That will help.

Mrs. T.: Thanks, that helps a lot. So I guess we should set up an appointment? Should I sit in on the first meeting?

Interviewer: Let's play that by ear. Tommy may feel like just meeting with me alone right away, or he may want you in the room for a while. We'll see . . .

Mrs. T.: Sounds good.

This is a good example of how to conduct an initial interview with a parent interested in bringing a child to therapy. The interviewer was careful to explore the situation as thoroughly as possible in order to have a comprehensive sense of the entire circumstances surrounding the child. The interviewer also thoroughly explained the therapy process, described collaboration with important individuals, and gave the parent the opportunity to ask any questions about the nature of working with children. Of course this is just the beginning, and much more important information will probably emerge as the interviews proceed.

A Young Adult

Maria is a thirty-two-year-old, single, professional Hispanic woman coming to the interview with concerns about her relationship with a new man in her life. One of the main features of young adulthood is what Erikson called "intimacy vs. isolation." Many young adults are drawn to form permanent relationships and are beginning to think about their future in terms of these relationships and perhaps living together, marriage, and even having children (Erikson, 1950). This is the case with Maria. She has been dating for quite some time but until now had not been able to find a suitable man in her life. Maria comes to the female interviewer because of some major conflicts in the developing relationship with this man.

> **Interviewer:** Thanks for coming in, Maria. I understand from our phone conversation that you are concerned about a new relationship in your life?
>
> *Maria:* Yes, I have been dating for quite some time, and been in a couple of relationships, but none has been very serious until I met Juan. He's very different from any other man I have ever dated. I can really talk to him. He really seems to care about me, and we seem to have the same interests.
>
> **Interviewer:** Sounds like a good guy. How did you meet him?

This is a very natural part of getting to know any client. Open-ended questions allow the client to direct the interview while providing the interviewer with a beginning sense of the working model for future use in the process.

> *Maria:* I used to go to bars to meet friends, or sometimes get set up through blind dates from friends, but those just didn't ever seem to work out. I've been using online dating services for a couple of years now. I'm very careful. I take my time. I usually take several months communicating online before I even talk by phone. Then I spend awhile interacting on the phone before I finally agree to meet in person. Even then, I always ask for his number. I don't give mine out right away, and we meet at a public restaurant.
>
> **Interviewer:** I can tell that you are very thorough and careful about all of this.
>
> *Maria:* Well, I'm a professional woman, and I don't want to jump into anything lightly.
>
> **Interviewer:** This process is very important to you.
>
> *Maria:* Yes it is.

Interviewer: So I sensed from your phone call that things may not be going so well with Juan. Can you tell me about it?

Maria: This is very embarrassing. I mean, everything we talk about is confidential isn't it?

Obviously this is a very serious and private matter for Maria. The interviewer needs to assure her that the therapy relationship will be secure.

Interviewer: Absolutely, Maria. Everything discussed in here stays in here unless you want me to talk to anyone, or you are suicidal or a threat to yourself or another.

Maria: Good, I understand all of that, and it's reassuring.

Interviewer: Well, about Juan?

Maria: We have been sexually intimate for several months now. Juan told me he had had a vasectomy, so we haven't used birth control. Just this month, I found out that I'm seven weeks pregnant.

Interviewer: How are you feeling about that?

Although perhaps obvious, it is extremely important that the interviewer is nonjudgmental, understanding, and accepting with any client in this situation. These types of challenges are filled with many complex thoughts and emotions, as well as value judgments. The interviewer needs to proceed carefully with Maria.

Maria: I don't know.

Interviewer: I'm not sure I understand, Maria, when you say "I don't know."

Again, the interviewer does not jump to conclusions, but continues to provide a safe environment in which to continue to explore the situation.

Maria: Part of me is excited about being pregnant, and part of me feels betrayed by Juan. He says he really thought he was "fixed." I'm not so sure I believe him.

Interviewer: Why don't you believe him?

Maria: Well, there's this other thing . . . [*Silence.*]

Interviewer: Yes.

Maria: I just found out that he's married, with two kids.

Interviewer: That's a lot to take in, I'll bet.

Maria: I trusted him so much, and I think I really love him. I don't know what to do.

Interviewer: Have you been thinking about some options?

Maria: Sure . . . The rational part of me says I should just dump him, but he says he's in the process of getting a divorce from his wife and wants to be with me. I don't know if I can trust him, since he never told me about the possible divorce until now, and the whole vasectomy thing.

Interviewer: This is a very complicated situation, Maria. You obviously have very strong and mixed feelings about Juan.

Maria: I'm also embarrassed to tell my family and friends. I don't want them to think less of me. I've always been so responsible, through school, my profession, and with my family. I'm afraid I'm going to seem like a failure if I stay with Juan. I don't believe in abortion, and I really want to keep this baby; but I also don't want to be seen as an irresponsible single mother.

Interviewer: What makes you think you would be seen as an irresponsible mother?

Maria: I think sometimes there are stereotypes about Hispanic woman getting pregnant out of wedlock . . . you know.

Interviewer: I think I can understand.

This intervention is also crucial because the interviewer can't "really" understand what Maria is feeling; she can only imagine. However, she wants to convey an empathic statement that is supportive and encouraging.

Maria: Also, there's my family.

Interviewer: What about your family?

Maria: All my life my father has had affairs, and I think children resulted from these relationships. My mother has known about them and been devastated. I can't let her down.

Interviewer: So there are some deeply personal and family issues involved in all of this as well?

Maria: Yeah, it's really a mess isn't it? I'm a mess.

The interviewer's working model of Maria has become much more expanded even in this first session. She has learned about Maria's important sense of self, her insecurities, and the complex emotions regarding Juan. This is not unusual, but creates a unique challenge for the interviewer.

Interviewer: Based on what we've talked about, I can see how you might feel that way, Maria. However, it sounds to me like so much of this dilemma was out of your control. As you said, you were so careful in deciding to even date Juan, and had no reason not to trust him after such a long time getting to know him. I'm not sure you could have seen this coming.

Maria: Well, maybe not, but I think I should have.

The interviewer is not trying to make excuses or cover up for the client's feelings, and wants to provide an objective "reality check" from her perspective on Maria's typically thorough and good choices (at least that's how it appears thus far).

Interviewer: Well, you certainly have a variety of concerns, and there is also the issue with Juan. I think there's value in our continuing to work on how you might proceed with these challenges, but I was also thinking that maybe some couples counseling with Juan might help. It's certainly up to you.

The interviewer is making an informed recommendation of sorts based upon all of the information she has received. She does not insist, however; she merely makes some suggestions.

Maria: Well, I was thinking I'd like to do both . . . I'd like to see you weekly for a while, and Juan has agreed to come in to talk about all of these other issues with his family, the pregnancy, and the divorce. What do you think?

Interviewer: I think that's a very good plan. Why don't we set up some additional appointments?

This case presents the interviewer with a complicated situation. The combination of individual and couples work can be difficult, but also constructive, especially in this type of tangled problem. The interviewer does a nice job of sorting through Maria's situation, beginning to form a good sense of her working model of self, and has set a good direction for further work.

An Older Adult

Phil is a sixty-five-year-old retired computer programmer who is coming to the female interviewer with a myriad of personal and family concerns. Phil is depressed about his recent "forced" retirement, his unhappy marriage, and the fact that he has two adult children living at home. He has always been a somewhat anxious and withdrawn man, but his pressing concerns have prompted him to seek help.

Interviewer: Hi Phil. Thanks for coming in today. I remember from our phone call that you are concerned about a number of things, including your retirement, your marriage, and your family situation. Can you tell me a little bit more about all of this?

Phil: Well, where should I start?

Interviewer: Anywhere you like.

Phil: OK. I just retired, even though I really didn't want to.

Interviewer: I'm sorry, Phil, you didn't want to retire?

Phil: Yeah, they kind of pushed me out . . . you know, I'm too old to do my job.

Interviewer: Was that a company policy?

Phil: Not really, but they were making things difficult for me and the time just felt right. They gave me an OK severance package.

Interviewer: But it doesn't sound like you really wanted to leave. How does that make you feel?

The interviewer is already picking up on Phil's ambivalence and possible anger about this situation.

Phil: Oh, it's OK, I guess, but I really miss working. I loved that job.

Interviewer: I'm sorry, Phil, what did you do?

Phil: A computer programmer.

Interviewer: Since you like the work so much, have you thought about looking for work at a different company?

Phil: Yeah, I have, but I'm too old and nobody will hire me.

Interviewer: Sounds like you've tried.

Phil: Yeah, a bunch of places.

Interviewer: That sounds tough.

Phil: I'm getting used to it.

Interviewer: Now, you mentioned your wife and family. Do you want to talk about that?

Phil: My wife is sixty-two; we've been together for a long time. We're not very close. We haven't been together for probably five years.

Interviewer: You mean sexually?

Phil: Yeah . . . she's just not interested. I also don't feel very close to her. She's very critical of just about everything I do. I've thought about divorce for years, but stayed because of the kids; and now I think I'm just too old.

Interviewer: You mentioned the kids.

Phil: They're another story altogether.

Interviewer: What do you mean?

Phil: Well, they're both grown up, twenty-six and thirty-two, and have never left home, even to go to college. They've got degrees, but want to stay at home, I think to be around their mother. And another thing, they're all fat, I mean really fat. I try to get them to exercise, cook good meals, you know; but they just sit around.

Interviewer: So your wife and kids don't work?

Phil: Nope.

Interviewer: I can tell by the tone in your voice that upsets you.

Phil: Well, wouldn't it upset you?

Interviewer: I can see how it could be upsetting to anyone, Phil. This also sounds a little depressing. Do you feel that way sometimes?

Phil: That's why I came here. My wife suggested it. She said I needed to get out of the house and go see someone because I had the problem.

Interviewer: The problem?

Phil: Yeah, apparently there's nothing wrong with them, it's all me.

Interviewer: Would you like to bring them in for therapy?

Phil: No, that's not going to do any good, and besides, I tried and they all refused.

Interviewer: But you came in on your own.

Phil: I thought it might help. I feel pretty lonely right now.

Interviewer: I can see where you might feel that way. I know we've only been talking for a short while, Phil, but how does it feel talking here today?

Phil: Actually pretty good. I don't feel anxious, and you certainly don't yell at me like my wife.

Interviewer: Well, I'm glad to hear that.

Phil: Well, what now?

Interviewer: How would you feel about coming back for another session?

Phil: I think that would be OK. You're not a bad-looking woman either.

Interviewer: Well thanks, Phil, I'll take that as a compliment. So how about we set up another time?

Phil: Sounds good to me.

It seems clear that Phil is struggling with a variety of personal and family issues. The interviewer has been able to engage him and to begin to gather important information for a working model of Phil's self. At this point it appears that perhaps some individual work might be helpful, as the interviewer gathers more information for her ongoing assessment. Phil's depression might merit medication, and ongoing therapy might also help him transition into his retirement, as well as looking toward new endeavors.

RESEARCH IMPLICATIONS AND BASIS OF PRACTICE

Relationship interviewing with clients of varying ages has been developed from research at all knowledge levels: intuitive knowledge, practice wisdom, theoretical knowledge, and validated studies. This is especially true in regard to establishing the relationship as the key factor in successful interviewing (O'Hare, 2005; Prochaska & Norcross, 2003). The case examples in this chapter demonstrate the crucial technique and relational dialogue necessary to form a solid connection with the clients, and to begin the careful and important process of assessment and the development of working models of interviewer and client that are an essential element in successful work.

SUMMARY

Interviewers must adjust their approach to the developmental level of each client they see. The chapter provides compelling examples of interviewing drawn from that perspective. Interviewing with children, adolescents, and adults of varying ages requires a solid knowledge of development and technique. The case examples in this chapter are a good representation of the situations interviewers will find themselves in throughout their careers.

RECOMMENDED READING

Children

Axline, V. M. (1947). *Play therapy*. New York: Ballantine Books.

Axline's book on play therapy is a step-by-step gem for any interviewer working with children.

Cozolino, L. (2002). *The neuroscience of psychotherapy: Building and rebuilding the human brain*. New York: W. W. Norton.

Cozolino's work provides important neuroscience information for working with clients of all ages. Knowledge of the developing brain at different stages of life, as well as what specific areas may be more critical than others depending on the age of the client, is invaluable to the interviewer.

Erikson, E. (1950). *Childhood and society*. New York: W. W. Norton.

Erikson's analysis of life stages is essential information for interviewing clients of all ages.

Freud, A. (1936). *The ego and the mechanisms of defence*. New York: International Universities Press.

Anna Freud's writings are rich with theory and technique as they relate to interviewing children.

Mahler, M. S., Pine, F., & Bergman, A. (1975). *The psychological birth of the human infant*. New York: Basic Books.

Mahler's pivotal infant and childhood research is a strong developmental resource for working with children, and one of only a few works of validated knowledge.

Stern, D. (2000). *The interpersonal world of the human infant: A view from psychoanalysis and developmental psychology*. New York: Basic Books.

Stern's work, combined with Erikson, Mahler, and Cozolino, provides the interviewer with a comprehensive picture of child development.

Piaget, J., & Inhelder, B. (1969). *The psychology of the child*. New York: Basic Books.

Vygotsky, L. S. (1978). *Mind in society*. Cambridge, MA: Harvard University Press.

Piaget and Vygotsky are excellent sources for understanding child development, especially in the area of learning.

Winnicott, D. W. (1971). *Playing and reality*. New York: Routledge.

Winnicott is the quintessential expert on both developmental theory and play therapy technique in interviewing children.

Adolescents

Blos, P. (1979). *The adolescent passage: Developmental issues.* New York: International Universities Press.

Blos's writings are universally accepted as a breakthrough for understanding the developmental process of the second separation-individuation process and its implication for interviewing adolescents.

Erikson, E. (1968). *Identity: Youth and crisis.* New York: W. W. Norton.

This key Erikson text focuses exclusively on the adolescent process. It is an essential source for interviewers working with teens.

McKenzie, F. (2008). *Theory and practice with adolescents: An applied approach.* Chicago: Lyceum Books.

This book provides a comprehensive overview of theory, technique, and relationship building with adolescents.

Adults

The interviewing material on adults has been covered in chapters 2–5.

MULTIMEDIA SOURCES

A number of poignant films can help the interviewer understand and appreciate the knowledge needed to work with children, adolescents, and adults. Sources for adults have been covered in previous chapters; references for children and adolescents are below.

Children

Harold and the Purple Crayon, www.sonypictures.com/tv/kids/harold andthepurplecrayon/.

Based upon the classic book of the same name, this website and HBO show is a wonderful example of the importance and developmental power of play for children. It is essential viewing for any interviewer working with children.

E.T.: The Extra-Terrestrial. (1982). Steven Spielberg (Director). Amblin Entertainment.

This classic Steven Spielberg film captures the essence of the necessary emotional relationship in child development. E.T.'s symbiotic relationship with Elliot replicates the parent-child interactions that are so crucial for healthy development.

Peter Pan. (1953). Clyde Geronimi, Wilfred Jackson, & Hamilton
    Luske (Directors). RKO Radio Pictures.

There have been many versions of this classic film; this Disney original is poignant and meaningful. Peter Pan's and Wendy's characters and relationship captures the fundamental essence of the wish to be forever young and at the same time grow up.

Adolescents

The Breakfast Club. (1985). John Hughes (Director). Universal
    Studios.

This film is without a doubt the most representative depiction of adolescent development to date. Although filmed in the 1980s, it has withstood the test of time.

Ordinary People. (1980). Robert Redford (Director). Paramount
    Pictures.

Some may see this film as a family resource, and it is. It also holds a tremendous amount of information regarding adolescents, especially how they interact with their families.

CHAPTER SEVEN

Differential Interviewing

Interviewing is a complex process that includes key elements and ongoing contributions from the interviewer and the clients. The practice template, working models of self and other, and the clinical validation method are essential and invaluable aspects of successful relational interviewing.

As interviewers begin to develop in their respective fields, they all internalize a practice template. The practice template is the ongoing sum total of the knowledge and skills necessary to become a successful interviewer. This template starts out small, typically with one or two theories and their related skills, but builds with the interviewer's professional experience. From a neuroscience standpoint, one can understand this process as the development and formation of neural networks that contain the entirety of this knowledge and experience. Initially, interviewers hold this knowledge and skill in the forefront of their minds (more explicit than implicit memory). Over time, however, this growing body of knowledge and experience probably settles more into the implicit areas of the brain, and can be accessed as needed during the interviewing process. One analogy for this process is learning to drive. The beginning driver must pay close attention to all of the essential aspects of driving, but as she becomes more proficient, the mechanics of driving are relegated to the implicit areas of brain memory, and driving becomes an automatic process. The same is true for the interviewing practice template. All elements of knowledge and skill can be consciously accessed if necessary, but tend with experience to operate more automatically (McKenzie, 2011).

The same is true of the working models of the interviewer and the client. All human beings have an internalized sense of self that includes all aspects of our history. This consists of thoughts, emotions, feelings, experience, knowledge, skills, and so forth. It is an ever-expanding realm of the brain. One part of that knowledge is the interviewer's working model of his or her professional self. That working model includes the practice template, professional and personal experience, and many elements that are far too numerous to mention. Suffice it to say, experienced interviewers should have a good sense of who they are as professionals, and how their experiences influence what they think and do with clients.

The interviewer also develops a working model of the client. Although certainly not as extensive as the interviewer's own working model of self, the working model of the client develops over time through the interviewing relationship. This knowledge helps the interviewer understand, assess, and work successfully with the client. It is the essential element in helping the client.

The clinical validation method is derived from the interviewer's use of the working models of self and client in the context of the interviewing relationship. The clinical validation method is used primarily under circumstances in which the interviewer is immobilized by emotional entanglements with the client that derive from the interplay of the working models of both the interviewer and client. In traditional language, this would be called the transference-countertransference dilemma. The clinical validation method, however, is a more expansive, relational process of managing interviewing challenges. It goes beyond the limitations of traditional transference and countertransference concepts, enabling the interviewer to help the client through the entire intersubjective realm of the relationship.

The following case examples illustrate how to use the self in relational interviewing.

SELF-DISCLOSURE

Mr. Brown's twenty-year-old son, Joe, has been seeing a male psychologist for several months, following a brief psychiatric hospitalization for anxiety and depression due to the breakup of a long-standing relationship. Mr. Brown has also had occasional sessions with the psychologist regarding his concerns about Joe's well-being. Mr. Brown is divorced. His son is living with Mr. Brown's ex-wife. Mr. Brown and his ex-wife do not communicate, and the divorce was highly conflictual. Despite that, Mr. Brown has maintained a positive attitude regarding his ex-wife in front of his son. The literature on divorce indicates that it is detrimental for parents to berate or criticize their ex-spouses in front of the children. Recent events have prompted Mr. Brown to call the psychologist for a phone interview.

> **Interviewer:** Hello.
>
> *Mr. Brown:* Hi, this is Mr. Brown. I'm calling about my son, Joe. You said you might have a few minutes to talk with me about him today? Of course I'll pay for the session.
>
> **Interviewer:** Oh hi, Mr. Brown. Yes, this is a good time. What seems to be the problem?
>
> *Mr. Brown:* Well, it's about Joe and his mom.
>
> **Interviewer:** OK . . . [*Brief silence.*] You know I can't talk about anything Joe discusses in therapy, but I certainly can talk with you about your concerns about Joe.

This is an important distinction that must be made to parents about adult children. By law, there is strict confidentiality for adults eighteen and over.

> *Mr. Brown:* I know . . . it's really more about me.
>
> **Interviewer:** What's going on?
>
> *Mr. Brown:* Well . . . lately Joe has been talking to me a lot about his relationship with his mother. He tells me that he feels very bad about himself when he is around her.

Interviewer: What do you mean, feels bad about himself?

Mr. Brown: He says that she is mean to him, criticizes him a lot, and just generally makes him feel bad. You know how Joe is, he isn't always real talkative, but this worried me.

Interviewer: What else did he say?

Mr. Brown: Well . . . this is what really bothered me. Joe said that the only time he feels bad about himself is when he is at home with his mom. He said he feels fine with his friends and when he's out. He also said that he thinks there must be something wrong with him because of how he feels around his mom. He wonders if he is a bad son. He doesn't know what to do, and he's looking to me for help.

Interviewer: How are you feeling about all of this?

Mr. Brown: You know I try to be very positive about his mom, but Joe's recent emotional situations have me very worried about him, and I want to help him any way I can.

Interviewer: Sounds like you're there for him.

Mr. Brown: I try to be, but these recent feelings about himself in relation to his mom really bother me.

Interviewer: In what way?

Mr. Brown: Well, you know we've talked about the divorce, and the way Joe tells me he is feeling about himself seems exactly the way I felt when I was married to his mom. Eventually that's why I left, you know . . .

Interviewer: So you're sensing some of the same things may be going on with Joe?

Notice that the interviewer uses the word "sensing" as a tentative way of acknowledging Mr. Brown's feelings without confirming the absolute validity of them: that is, they are Mr. Brown's feelings.

Mr. Brown: Yeah, maybe it's just me, but when Joe talks this way, it all feels so familiar. Part of me wants to tell Joe that's exactly how I felt when I was married to his mom, but I guess I think it would be wrong to be critical of her. You know, a parent shouldn't criticize his ex in front of the kids. But Joe is really troubled and isolated. I think if he knew he wasn't the only one who felt this way, it might make him not feel so alone or sad.

Interviewer [*a long pause*]: You know, Mr. Brown, when I was a kid, I wish my mother's friends would have told me what kind of person she was . . .

This phone session went on for some time. The important point is that the interviewer intervened with a sensitive and carefully timed, tactful self-disclosure. He didn't actually tell Mr. Brown it was OK to share thoughts and feelings about his ex with Joe, but he implicitly gave him permission through his indirect use of self-disclosure.

In general, self-disclosure is discouraged because of the dangers of imposing the interviewer's personal thoughts and emotions on the client. In this situation, however, the interviewer felt that doing so was therapeutic. As it turned out, it was helpful for Mr. Brown and especially for Joe. The interviewer decided to share this indirect piece of information only after careful self-examination of the working models of self, Mr. Brown, and Joe. It was a difficult, yet productive, process.

THE INFERIOR MAN

Mr. D., a forty-four-year-old sales executive, came to the interviewer with feelings of mild depression and a sense of apathy about his entire life. This case example focuses on the intersubjective realm, working models, and clinical validation method. It begins after Mr. D. had been in therapy for several months.

Mr. D.: Well, here we are again. Are you going to fix me today [*jokingly*]?

Interviewer: I'm not sure I know what that's supposed to mean, but I'll do my best.

Mr. D. [*again in a somewhat sarcastic manner*]: I've been coming here for a while, making you rich, and I'm still not better.

Interviewer: Well, let's talk about that. What do you really want to have happen by coming here?

Even though Mr. D. is a pleasant man, and his joking is his usual way of engaging, his dialogue with the interviewer does generate a degree of anxiety and leaves the interviewer feeling a bit awkward and inept. The interviewer has been feeling this off and on for some time, although the interviews seem to have helped Mr. D. The interviewer struggles with why these feelings are so prevalent and where they might be coming from, that is, Mr. D. himself, or the relationship between the two of them. The interviewer has been silently engaged in examining and processing the working models of himself and Mr. D., but has thus far not been able to arrive at any insight on this uncomfortable impasse. The interviewer senses from his experience that this is important, but feels stuck.

Mr. D. [*again jokingly*]: Well, I want you to fix me. That's why I pay you. You should have the answers by now.

Interviewer: Well, why don't we talk about how you have been feeling lately?

Mr. D.: I really can't stand my job, and I'd like to leave, but I just don't know what I'd do. We've talked about my starting my own business, and I think I could manage that financially, but I'm just not sure if that's what I want either.

Interviewer: I know this is an ongoing dilemma. When you think about starting your business, what thoughts do you have about that?

Mr. D.: I want to feel successful and good about myself. I know I'm successful in my job, but as you know that's not what I really wanted to do, I sort of felt pushed into the field by my folks, especially my dad. I guess you could say I've been a success, but I don't really feel that way.

Interviewer: So from a certain perspective, many people might say you've been a very successful businessman, but you don't feel that way.

Mr. D.: No, I guess not.

Interviewer: What do you feel are your greatest strengths and limitations?

Mr. D.: Well, despite all of my business success, I've always felt kind of inferior and inept, even in childhood. It's like I don't feel I could be good at anything.

The interviewer began to feel a tremendous sense of insight and relief at this statement. It resonated with his own feelings of ineptness and awkwardness with Mr. D., and seemed to explain why the interviewer continually felt stuck with the client. The interviewer realized that this new information about the working model of Mr. D. was the key to unlocking the emotional impasse in their relationship. The interviewer no longer felt inept, but understood that he was carrying and experiencing Mr. D.'s feelings. One might call this a projective identification; in other words, the interviewer was living out the emotional entanglements of Mr. D., and in so doing became unable to help him. The process of examination and the insight that brought emotional relief and the ability to reengage with the client is a wonderful example of the clinical validation method (McKenzie, 2011). This new insight shifted the entire focus of the interviewing process, enabling Mr. D. to examine these lifelong feelings and modify his life.

Of course, changes of this sort take time. The example above highlights a key time in the interviewing process that dramatically changed the nature of the work. This process could only have happened through the careful examination and use of the elements of the intersubjective realm in this relationship. The interviewer needed to take time and examine not only the manifest (surface content) of the interviews, but also the latent (unaware) material in order to uncover the emotional impasses and help Mr. D. to improve.

THE "BEAUTIFUL" WOMAN

This case example of Susan is taken from McKenzie, 2011, pp. 34–35. The male interviewer had been working with the client for over a year prior to the interview below. Susan came to therapy because of a variety of concerns, especially her marriage, but the interviews soon centered on her poor self-image. The interviewer did not find Susan to be an unattractive woman, and felt that her continual focus on a perceived unattractiveness was obsessive and obviously related to early development. In exploring Susan's childhood, the interviewer discovered that indeed she did not have a very positive relationship with her parents, and experienced them, for the most part, as critical and distant. This history certainly contributed to Susan's poor self-esteem and self-image. As the interviewer became better acquainted with Susan and her history and present circumstances, he began to feel strangely attracted to her. It is not unusual for interviewers to feel attracted to their clients, but these feelings were unusually strong for this interviewer (Searles, 1959). In fact, for the first time in his career, the interviewer found himself thinking that this client was perhaps the most beautiful woman he had ever seen in therapy. These feelings were not present at the start of therapy, but suddenly emerged as the interviewer began to learn more about Susan's history and present circumstances. The interviewer knew this was some form of countertransference, because of its unusual nature and the fact that his perceptions were not accurate and were interfering in his ability to stay present and engaged in the process. The interviewer used the clinical validation method to examine the working models of himself and the client in order to ascertain any emotional issues that could help explain this impasse, but initially was unable to arrive at any insight. The following case example provides a clear and important example of the resolution of these types of complex interviewing issues.

> **Interviewer:** Hi Susan. How are you today?
> *Susan:* Oh, you know, not so well. I've been feeling really down on myself again, especially my looks. I'm just so ugly. I know I am.
> **Interviewer:** How do you know that?
> *Susan:* Come on . . . just look at me. I'm never going to look good.
> **Interviewer:** Doesn't anyone ever tell you that you look nice or attractive?

The interviewer is very aware of his own sense of attraction to the client but has always kept this to himself, feeling that it would complicate the process, especially since he was not sure of the origin of the emotions. Exploring Susan's sense of herself further might shed important light on this dilemma.

> **Susan:** Well, people at work and my husband tell me I look nice, but I know they're just saying that.
> **Interviewer:** How do you know that?
> **Susan:** I just know, that's all. I mean, I just have to look in the mirror. I'm ugly.

This discussion continues for quite some time in the interview, with Susan perseverating about her ugliness.

> **Interviewer:** Did you always feel this way?
> **Susan:** Well, when I was a little girl, my father and I were very close. He used to play with me a lot, and tell me how pretty I was. He would give me baths . . . nothing inappropriate, mind you . . . I was probably around four or five. I really think I was the apple of his eye, and I felt pretty then. I actually think my mom was a little jealous of us.
> **Interviewer:** That sounds like such a wonderful time in your life. Did things change?
> **Susan:** Yeah, when I started to enter puberty, even a little before that time. My dad just cut me off. I didn't know why. I felt so hurt and alone. I eventually thought it must be because he thought I was ugly. After he became distant, he never told me I was pretty again.
> **Interviewer:** And those feelings have stayed with you ever since.
> **Susan:** Yeah, I know they must be true.

This exchange brought about a flood of insight for the interviewer. For the first time he realized why he felt the way he did about Susan. He was experiencing the same feelings of attractiveness that Susan's father had for her as a small child. The interviewer also knew that Susan needed to recapture her sense of self. This insight brought emotional relief to the interviewer and enabled him to reengage in the therapy with a new recognition and understanding of Susan. Although he never shared his thoughts, emotions, and reactions to Susan, this insight enabled him to help Susan recognize that it was her father's discomfort with her budding sexuality in puberty that prompted him to abruptly turn away from her; it did not have anything to do with Susan's being ugly. In fact it was probably the contrary. As Susan was able to take in, recognize, and discuss these issues, she began to gain a much better sense of self, including her body image. The counter-transference reactions of the interviewer enabled this process to develop and succeed.

These are very complex relational dynamics that must be handled extremely delicately in order to provide help. It takes many years of self-awareness and understanding, even therapy, in order for an interviewer to be able to work well with such complicated concepts.

THE ABUSED WOMAN

Tammy, a thirty-nine-year-old woman, came to see the interviewer because of issues related to a history of chronic childhood sexual abuse by her father. This horrible history had drastically shaped Tammy's entire life and contributed to some very bad relationship choices, including her present marriage. The following case example illustrates the importance of timely self-disclosure in certain circumstances in order to help the client come to a key insight and recognition of their thoughts, emotions, and behavior.

Tammy had been seeing the interviewer twice a week in therapy for about a year prior to this interview. During that time, the interviews focused intensely on Tammy's history of abuse and how it permeated her present life. One week, the interviewer had to reschedule one of Tammy's two weekly appointments because of an unavoidable conflict. The interviewer made special arrangements to see Tammy at another time that week, knowing how important it was to her to see him and have consistency in the therapy. However, the interviewer also had a very bad headache that day. It did not keep him from coming to the appointment, but he was not his usual self. Because of his headache, he was not as engaging as usual, although he tried his best to be there for the client. The interviewer recognized his distance, but did not want to burden Tammy with any explanation, since he knew she would be sensitive and apologetic about the extra appointment. Several weeks later the following exchange occurred.

> **Interviewer:** Hi Tammy. It's nice to see you. How have things been going?
> *Tammy:* [*Silence.*]
> **Interviewer:** Is something the matter?
> *Tammy:* No, I'm OK.
> **Interviewer:** You seem quiet, or maybe even a little upset.

The interviewer is trying to carefully allow Tammy the opportunity to discuss what he senses is some problem, but wants her to feel the freedom to go at her own pace.

> *Tammy:* No, I'm just kind of in a bad mood today.
> **Interviewer:** Do you want to talk about it?
> *Tammy* [*sounding unsure*]: I don't know.
> **Interviewer:** I'm getting the sense that maybe you do have something on your mind, Tammy. I really am interested and want to help if I can.

The interviewer is letting Tammy know that he does have an empathic sense about her feelings (he's known her for quite some time), and wants to provide her the opportunity to talk about whatever might be troubling her.

> *Tammy:* Well, OK. Remember that extra session we had a few weeks ago? You know, when you had to cancel, but then rescheduled later in the week?
> **Interviewer:** Yes, I do. Is there something that is bothering you about that session?
> *Tammy:* This is difficult for me to talk about . . .

Interviewer: OK, take your time, Tammy. I want to be there for you.

Tammy: Well, I know you were aroused in that session. It made me feel very uncomfortable and frightened.

Interviewer: What made you think I was aroused?

Tammy: I could just tell, that's all. You seemed distant, and I could tell it was because you were aroused.

Interviewer: Tammy, I think it is extremely important for you to know that I definitely was *not* aroused in that session. You mentioned that I seemed distant. As a matter of fact, I had a terrible migraine headache that day, but decided to see you anyway because I did not want to miss the session. I know how important they are to you. I was distant because I was in a great deal of pain. I probably should have told you about the migraine, but I didn't want to interfere in your session with my issues. In hindsight, perhaps I should have told you about it, since my distance in the session clearly affected you.

Tammy: But I was sure you were aroused.

Interviewer: I can understand you felt that way, Tammy, but I am telling you that I was absolutely *not* aroused. On the other hand, you clearly experienced me that way. Something must have been happening that contributed to those feelings. You mentioned my distance. It's true that I was distant that day, but it had to do with my migraine. Was there something about my distance that may have influenced your sense that I was aroused?

This is a crucial point in the therapy. Tammy has clearly distorted and projected her perceptions of reality onto the interviewer. Normally the interviewer would have taken time to gradually explore these thoughts and feelings, but in this situation felt that it was imperative to inform the client that he was not experiencing any sexual feelings (quite the contrary, given the extreme pain he was suffering from the migraine). This was especially important, given Tammy's history of sexual abuse. The interviewer suspects that for some reason related to the session,

Tammy has projected and distorted her perceptions of the interviewer. The interviewer realizes that this is an important opportunity to carefully, gently, and empathically explore the basis of this distortion.

> **Tammy:** Well, now that you mention it, do you remember how I've talked about my father sexually abusing me when I was a child?
> **Interviewer:** Of course. Do you think there may have been some connection to this session?
> **Tammy:** Maybe . . . You are always so connected to me, and I have never felt those kinds of feelings coming from you before, so it was very weird and scary.
> **Interviewer:** So what do you make of that?

It is absolutely crucial for the interviewer to allow the client to go at her own pace and not assume or put forth any of his own speculations about why Tammy might have been feeling the way she did in that session.

> **Tammy:** I've never told you this before, but at the times my father would sexually abuse me, we were usually alone. He would get very distant and quiet. He would just stare at me for a long time, and then he would start abusing me. I think that's how I felt in our session. I felt like you were going to abuse me.
> **Interviewer:** That's a really important and valuable insight, Tammy. As I said, I was not feeling aroused or interested in abusing you, but I can understand how my uncharacteristic manner that day contributed to your feelings and perceptions. I apologize for the confusion. I think I should have let you know immediately how I was feeling. That might have kept you from those reactions.

The interviewer is clarifying the situation, acknowledging the client's important insight, as well as his unintentional contribution to the distortions that occurred in that session. This relational style of interviewing was extremely helpful for the client and the therapeutic relationship in the future. It set a tone for an even greater level of trust and exploration. From that session on, the work with Tammy and the interviewer moved at an even greater pace. Over time, Tammy recognized her capacity to distort her world in and outside of the interviews. This helped her function better in all of her relationships, and ultimately led to the conclusion of a successful therapy. The success did not come from this one interaction: it was the culmination of years of concentrated work around these themes that had originated in the client's background and were being lived out in all areas of her life.

This case example is a wonderful illustration of the relational aspects of the client's transference distortions of the interviewer, stimulated by his unintentional distance. The sensitive and relational manner in which this important and delicate situation was handled was the key to Tammy's progress.

THE YOUNG COUNSELOR

The final case example illustrates the importance of timely and diplomatic self-disclosure in providing key therapeutic empathy with a sensitive, anxious, and somewhat insecure young adult. Josh was a twenty-five-year-old counselor who came to the interviewer to begin his own therapy as a way of improving his professional skills through self-awareness, and to work on some important issues from his childhood to the present. The interviewer was a thirty-year-old psychologist, who was relatively new as a professional interviewer.

The client came from a large family with alcoholic parents. He was the oldest of eight children. Josh always had a close and special relationship with his mother, who used him as an emotional confidant in place of his father. This dynamic put a terrible strain on Josh's parents, as well as the relationship Josh had with his father. Josh's father physically, emotionally, and verbally abused all of the children, but Josh received the brunt of it and intentionally put himself in the position of protecting his younger siblings from his father as best he could. Partly as a result of this caretaking role with both his siblings and his mother, Josh inevitably became a professional counselor.

Josh had some unresolved emotional issues related to his mother that became the focus of a good deal of his therapy. He always felt, but was never told by his mother, that he was her favorite. In many ways Josh saw himself as his mother's spouse, especially in the sense of his caretaking role. This confusion was played out in the relationship with the interviewer in the form of a transference relationship. Josh idealized the interviewer, was very attracted to her, and sensed that she might also be attracted to him. This dynamic was important to Josh because of the confusion he experienced with his mother. Josh felt a tremendous need to know the interviewer's feelings about him for this reason. In other words, that knowledge would validate his experience and intuition. The following case example illustrates this transference and the tactful, empathic, and sensitive way in which the interviewer handled it. At this point in time, Josh had been in therapy for nearly three years.

Interviewer: Hi Josh. How are you doing?

Josh: Good . . . you look pretty today.

Interviewer: Thank you. What would you like to talk about today?

Josh: I've been feeling kind of down about work lately.

Interviewer: What's going on?

Josh: I just got my annual evaluation from my director and it really upset me . . . I even cried in front of him . . . sort of embarrassing . . .

Interviewer: Sounds very upsetting and surprising. From our discussions, it seemed like you were doing really well, getting along with him, and were expecting a positive evaluation. What did he say?

Josh: Well, it wasn't really all that terrible; it just wasn't all that positive either. He just seemed to be focusing on minor things, not the way I worked, or the programs I've developed. You know, I've told you all of the things I've done this year. I've never worked so hard in my life, and the staff seem to really appreciate it. I think he was getting back at me for criticizing Kathy.

Interviewer: Kathy your coworker?

Josh: Yeah, I'm sure they're having an affair, and he's always so protective of her. But Kathy's always late, and he has the rest of us do a lot of her work. She gets away with a lot.

Interviewer: So you think maybe he was picking on you?

Josh: Yeah . . . it was stupid to cry.

Interviewer: Why do you think it was stupid?

Josh: I shouldn't have shown my vulnerability. I think he reminded me of my father that day.

Interviewer: How so?

Josh: You know, always critical, never satisfied with anything I did. I wouldn't cry in front of him, but would always go to my mom and talk . . . and sometimes cry.

Josh is a very sensitive and introspective client. The interviewer does not have to work hard to engage with him to help him use the interview. She does, however, provide an empathic and caring environment and relationship in which to work.

Interviewer: You really felt this was unfair, just like your relationship with your dad.

Josh: Yeah . . . but it always helps to come and see you. You're so perfect. You know me so well. I love seeing you.

Interviewer: Well thanks, Josh, I enjoy our time together too.

The interviewer felt it was important to reciprocate these positive feelings, especially in light of the length of treatment and the presenting concern of the day.

Josh: You know I'm so attracted to you. I always have been.

Interviewer: Yes, you talk about that a lot.

Josh: Sometimes I think I imagine it, but at other times I definitely know that you're attracted to me too. Are you?

Interviewer: Well Josh, if I was attracted to you, how would that make you feel?

Josh: Great, fantastic! I know nothing would happen . . . I mean, you're my therapist and all.

Interviewer: You're right; we've talked about the boundaries in here.

Josh: And I'm not trying to change that . . . it's just that I think if you told me if you're attracted to me, it would help me know if my instincts were accurate. I really sense that you are attracted to me, and it would be helpful to know if I'm right or just imagining it. Don't you see?

Interviewer: I do see, Josh, but I don't understand what stops you from trusting your own instincts without feedback from me.

Josh: Oh OK . . . don't tell me. But I think I'm right, and I wish you would verify it.

This discussion continued off and on for several sessions. The interviewer was troubled by it because she did find Josh attractive, and thought it might help him to know his instincts were correct. However, she also felt that disclosing this to Josh might complicate the interviewing process. The interviewer consulted with her agency psychiatrist, who suggested that instead of self-disclosing this information to Josh, she give him a copy of an article about interviewers' feelings about clients. The article was a 1959 classic by Harold Searles titled "Oedipal Love in the Countertransference." Basically, Searles's premise was that it was natural and often essential for interviewers to find their clients attractive because it provided them a sorely needed sense of validation that was missing in their lives. To know that the interviewer found him attractive could help bolster and repair the lack of self-esteem Josh had experienced most of his life. In fact, one might say that Josh was reenacting this need or dynamic in the relationship with the interviewer.

The interviewer never did directly share with Josh that she was attracted to him, but she gave him the article, which was more than enough to convince Josh that his instincts were correct. This is a wonderful example of the carefully timed use of indirect self-disclosure in a transference-countertransference situation. The interviewer was sensitive to Josh's needs, but handled them in a very professional manner. This case, like the preceding ones, demonstrates not only the complexity of interviewing, but also the value and necessity of ongoing supervision. All beginning interviewers need this kind of support. Most experienced ones also do from time to time. Just as interviewing between client and therapist helps, so does interviewing between a therapist and supervisor. If in doubt, hold off sharing about countertransference or self-disclosure until you have thought it out or had a consultation.

RESEARCH IMPLICATIONS AND BASIS OF PRACTICE

Since interviewing in the helping professions began, there has been a keen interest in examining not only the basic process itself, but the more complex and essential emotional elements of the relationship between the client and the interviewer and the ways in which those interactions and dynamics affect the course of therapeutic work, regardless of the discipline. From a research standpoint, intuitive knowledge has driven the examination of these intricate processes since professionals began to practice interviewing. Practice wisdom, developed from anecdotal material, further solidified the intuitive basis. The comprehensive and rigorous structure of the case study, as early as Freud's era, has been for generations the operationalized basis of theoretical knowledge in the interviewing realm.

With the onset of attachment theory, infant research, and neuroscience, particularly such contributions as Bowlby's attachment styles, Stern's RIGs and evoked companions, and neuroscience's mirror neurons, the research knowledge regarding interviewing issues such as self-disclosure, silence, transference and countertransference, and the intersubjective realm are reaching the level of validated knowledge (Bowlby, 1969; Stern, 2000; Cozolino, 2010).

SUMMARY

This chapter broadened the discussion of interviewing by examining the intricate, complex, and essential elements of self-disclosure, transference and countertransference, and the intersubjective realm, among others. The relationship between the interviewer and client is undoubtedly the most important and crucial component of a successful interviewing situation, regardless of the professional discipline. The case examples display not only a variety of delicate and complex situations, but illustrate the ways in which they must be understood and managed in an empathic relational manner. Interviewing is challenging. Becoming a successful interviewer in any profession demands self-awareness and the ability to use that awareness appropriately to help the client. This chapter has provided a foundation for that work.

RECOMMENDED READING

Bowlby, J. (1969). *Attachment and loss:* Vol. 1, *Attachment.* New York: Basic Books.

This volume of Bowlby's work, as well as others he wrote, provides an important framework for understanding the importance of early attachment and its implication for the relationship in the interviewing process.

Cozolino, L. (2010). *The neuroscience of psychotherapy: Healing the social brain.* New York: W. W. Norton.

This Cozolino book cannot be recommended highly enough for the material on mirror neurons and the innate empathic capabilities of human beings early in life. Especially important is the validated research knowledge in the areas covered in this chapter.

Freud, S. (1940). *An outline of psychoanalysis.* New York: W. W. Norton.

Freud's work is essential reading to help interviewers understand the early development of the interviewing process, the therapeutic relationship, and its implications for contemporary work.

McKenzie, F. (2011). *Understanding and managing the therapeutic relationship.* Chicago: Lyceum Books.

This text provides a comprehensive understanding of transference and countertransference in the intersubjective realm as well as specific approaches to it in the interviewing process, such as the working models of the interviewer and client and the clinical validation method.

O'Hare, T. (2005). *Evidence-based practices for social workers: An interdisciplinary approach.* Chicago: Lyceum Books.

O'Hare's work is cited again because of his study of the research methods that have been used to operationalize the aspects of the interviewing process presented in this chapter.

Prochaska, J. O., & Norcross, J. C. (2003). *Systems of psychotherapy: A transtheoretical analysis.* Belmont, CA: Brooks/Cole.

These authors present a very helpful examination of the meta-analysis of clinical research surrounding the interviewing relationship.

Searles, H. F. (1959). Oedipal love in the countertransference. *International Journal of Psychoanalysis, 40*, 180–90.

This article by Searles is a classic work on countertransference and its crucial importance and careful use in interviewing.

Stern, D. (2000). *The interpersonal world of the human infant: A view from psychoanalysis and developmental psychology.* New York: Basic Books.

Stern's writing on infant research and the notion of RIGs, as well as the evoked companion in infancy, will help the interviewer understand and better use the self while interviewing.

MULTIMEDIA SOURCES

Equus. (1977). Sydney Lumet (Director). United Artists.

This film, based on the highly successful play by Peter Shaffer, is a powerful example of countertransference and the use of self in the interviewing process. Richard Burton, who plays the psychiatrist working with an adolescent who has blinded six horses with a metal spike, was nominated for an Academy Award for his performance.

A Dangerous Method. (2011). David Cronenberg (Director). Sony Pictures Classics.

This recent film is recommended because of its powerful depiction of the careful and delicate process involved in managing the relationship within the interviewing process.

Huff. (2004–6). Showtime.
In Treatment. (2008–11). HBO.

The reader is encouraged to watch these series with an eye toward the concepts covered in this chapter. The characters Hank Azaria (*Huff*) and Gabriel Byrne (*In Treatment*) provide excellent examples of the delicate, sensitive, and challenging trials of being a professional interviewer in terms of the use of self.

CHAPTER EIGHT

Interviewing in General Mental Health Cases

Interviewing can take on a variety of different forms, depending on the modality, age of the client, presenting problem, and theoretical orientation of the interviewer. Interviewing may also look different depending on who provides it: nurse, social worker, psychologist, probation officer, or psychiatrist. The preceding chapters have examined many of those factors while demonstrating the common thread so necessary in forming a relationship between the interviewer and client. Although the professional disciplines may be different, the interviewing process is essentially the same in terms of how the relationship is established and maintained in order to come to a successful conclusion.

Chapter 7 examined some of the more complex and sophisticated elements that can occur and influence the interviewing relationship. Those processes are usually present to some extent in all interviewing relationships. However, complicated transference and countertransference relationship dynamics are more common in so-called severe mental health cases, such as psychotic, extreme bipolar, and full-blown personality disorders. Those types of situations are covered in chapter 9. This chapter deals with more general mental health cases, such as anxiety, depression, milder bipolar situations, and adjustment disorders. Interviewing style and development of a working relationship are still the most important elements in working with both types of cases. It is the complexity and challenges in the interviewing relationship that are different.

THE DYING MAN

Al is a seventy-two-year-old man in the late stages of cancer; his doctor says Al has only months to live. Al is being provided hospice services in his home. Those services include being visited several days a week by a psychiatric nurse. The nurse has been trained in mental health services and is an excellent interviewer. She meets individually with Al, and occasionally with other family members, to help them cope with and prepare for Al's approaching death. In this case example, Al has been seeing the nurse for approximately three months. She has gotten to know Al and his family, and has gathered extensive information about Al's life in the process of building a trusting and caring relationship with him. Al has decided that he wants to explore the issues in his life that he feels are unresolved, in order to come to peace with himself and his family before he dies. The nurse has begun to work with Al in the interviewing process to help him accomplish this task.

> **Interviewer:** Hi Al. How are you feeling today?
> *Al:* Oh, OK . . . I've got some pain, as usual, but I'm kind of used to it by now.
> **Interviewer:** Have the medical nurses and your doctor been helping you with that?
> *Al:* Oh yeah, they've all been great.

Even though the interviewer is herself a nurse, her role in this situation is to provide mental health services. However, it is also her responsibility to inquire about the other services being provided by the hospice team. Any helping professional working with Al should explore this issue. It is part of being an empathic interviewer.

> **Interviewer:** Good, I'm glad to hear that. I remember when I was here a couple of days ago, Al, that you wanted to begin talking about your relationships with your family and concerns that have been on your mind for some time now.
>
> *Al:* Yeah, but I'm not sure where to start.
>
> **Interviewer:** Well, maybe I can help. What thoughts and feelings seem to be most on your mind regarding your family?

This typical open-ended question allows Al to feel free to begin where he is comfortable.

> *Al:* I think I should talk about my relationship with my kids?
>
> **Interviewer:** Now Al, I've known you for a while, so I know it won't come as a surprise when I confront you a bit on this . . . I think I heard you say, "I think I should talk about my kids" . . . What do you really want to talk about?

This is a gentle but direct confrontation that is quite natural in interviewing relationships that have established a trusting base. However, the tentativeness in Al's comment might prompt an interviewer at any point to challenge or clarify the statement.

> *Al:* No, you're right; I do want to talk about them.
>
> **Interviewer:** OK, where do you want to start?
>
> *Al:* I don't think I've been a good father.
>
> **Interviewer:** Do you have some thoughts or examples of what you mean by not being a good father?
>
> *Al:* I don't think I've ever really been there for them.
>
> **Interviewer:** You don't think that you have ever been there for them? Not once?

The interviewer is trying to help Al clarify his all-or-nothing thinking. Words like never, always, *and other absolute phrases cut off the conversation and do not allow exploration of the situation. It is helpful to the client to explore these absolutes in order to open up a discussion that can be meaningful. It is also important, however, to make a mental note of the client's thoughts and feelings surrounding these absolutes.*

> *Al:* Well, I guess I wouldn't say ever. I think there have been times that I've been a good dad.
>
> **Interviewer:** Do you remember any times in particular?
>
> *Al:* When the kids were younger, especially my first two sons, I remember taking them to an occasional baseball game. We all seemed to have fun. Sometimes we went fishing when we were on vacation. Those were good times, I think.
>
> **Interviewer:** Sounds like they were fun for you.
>
> *Al:* Yeah, I think they were.
>
> **Interviewer:** So what makes you think you weren't a good dad, Al?

The interviewer is trying to gently help the client open up about his negative feelings. It seems as if this is difficult for Al, yet he also seems to feel the pressing need to talk about them.

> *Al:* Well, you know, I mentioned that I was, or maybe I should say am, an alcoholic. I've been in recovery for a long time.
>
> **Interviewer:** I know you've mentioned that, and we've talked about it a bit. You started drinking in the navy, right? Then your drinking continued to escalate until you were in your fifties. How did this affect your relationship with your family?
>
> *Al:* I know it did. You know I worked sales, and it was very stressful. I didn't have a college degree, but still did very well. But I'd come home every night, and I do mean every night, with a twelve-pack of beer. I wouldn't pay much attention to the kids, just watch sports on TV and drink all twelve of those beers and more every night. If I ran out of beer, I'd start drinking the hard stuff; you know, whiskey. I would usually pass out on the couch and eventually make it

to bed. My kids tell me that I was pretty abusive and scary. I wouldn't let them watch any of their shows, and I tended to criticize and belittle them a lot . . . at least that's what they tell me.

Interviewer: So you don't really remember much of this, except what your kids have told you?

The interviewer wants to probe a bit here to explore the extent to which the client recollects these times in his life.

Al: Oh, a little bit here and there. My wife remembers a lot of it and has told me that the kids are right. I've never really been much of a father to them, you see. I don't know if I really knew how, and to tell you the truth . . . I feel bad about this . . . I'm not sure I really wanted to have kids. My wife loves them to death, and they are her whole life. I have to admit that I have been jealous of them and her relationship with them.

Interviewer: That's a very honest statement, Al. Is it hard to talk about?

The interviewer feels it necessary to validate the client's risk taking here. Al is beginning to really open up and share his vulnerability and guilt.

Al: Yeah, but I really want to get this out and try to make things better with my whole family.

Interviewer: You mentioned that you weren't sure you really wanted kids, and that you didn't know how to be a dad. That makes me wonder about your own childhood and how it might have affected you. Could you tell me about it?

This is a logical next step in the interviewer's exploration of Al's problem. All of the literature and research points to the fact that one's childhood experiences shape one's course of life, particularly in terms of coupling and parenthood. Perhaps this exploration will yield some important insights.

Al: I was the middle son of three boys. My dad was also an alcoholic and pretty abusive. He was physically and emotionally abusive. I have to say that, I may have been verbally and emotionally abusive to my kids, but I rarely hit them.

Interviewer: So you weren't as bad as your dad?

Al: Nowhere close to how he treated me and my brothers.

Interviewer: How about your mom?

Al: I always felt close to her, but she couldn't really protect us from Dad.

Interviewer: Does it seem like there is any similarity between how you were raised and your relationship with your kids?

Al: I have thought about that a lot. I do think I was sort of the same way. I never felt close to my dad. He didn't seem to care, and was always critical of me. I think that's what my kids say about me. You see, I am a bad parent.

Interviewer: Well, Al, it does sound like you recognize that perhaps some of the ways in which you treated your children have not been the best, and that you also see how this type of behavior may have been learned from your experiences in your own family.

This is very good paraphrasing by the interviewer. She is helping the client make the connections without judging or criticizing him.

Al: I don't want to blame my dad. Even if he did treat me and my brothers badly, that's no excuse for how I was with my kids, I'm still responsible.

Interviewer: I think that's an important insight, Al. I agree that we all are responsible for our behaviors, and yet our behaviors are influenced by our past relationships, especially our family.

This intervention by the interviewer might be considered an interpretation in the most general sense. She is acknowledging the client's thoughts and emotions, but also providing insight into the larger picture and possible contributions to the situation. An intervention of this type must be done in a timely fashion, that is, when the client is ready to hear it. Al appeared to be ready.

> **Al:** I hope you're right. I don't think I really meant to treat my kids so badly, it just sort of happened. I wish I could take it all back.
>
> **Interviewer:** What would you do differently?
>
> **Al:** I would have stopped drinking, for one thing, and I would have tried to interact more with my kids. But that's all too late now.
>
> **Interviewer:** Well, you can't change the past, Al, that's true, but you can try to have a new relationship with your kids now.
>
> **Al:** How would I do that? They all seem to hate me.
>
> **Interviewer:** Do you really think that?

The interviewer is sensing that the client is frightened and under-standably hesitant to embark on a journey to reconcile with his kids. Al's statement implies that the situation is hopeless. The interviewer is intuitively challenging that idea.

> **Al:** I guess not, but it seems so impossible.
>
> **Interviewer:** Well, I think when you look at the whole picture it probably does seem overwhelming. But maybe we could talk about working things out with your children one at a time.
>
> **Al:** That's a possibility, but I wouldn't know what to say.
>
> **Interviewer:** Well, how about starting with some of the things we talked about today. You could share your regrets, hear what they have to say, and tell them you really want to have a better relationship with them now.
>
> **Al:** It all sounds so easy when you say it.
>
> **Interviewer:** Maybe it does, Al, I'm sorry . . . I think it sounds easier than it will probably be, you're right. It will probably take time, and patience. Your kids might not come around right away.

Al: Maybe never . . .

Interviewer: You're right, maybe never. How would you feel about that?

These are very tough questions, but honest ones and a discussion that the interviewer must have with the client if this process is to move ahead.

Al: I really don't know yet, but I want to do something rather than sit with these awful feelings the rest of my life.

Interviewer: I can tell this is very important to you, Al.

This is an excellent example of the kind of working through that happens in the interviewing process in general mental health cases. Al is not a deeply disturbed client, but he does have some emotional difficulties that have deeply affected him and his family. The interviewer has begun to help him explore, open up, and plan for ways in which he can begin to resolve and come to some closure with this complex situation. The responses are similar to many other situations, but the level and intensity of the process is emotionally deeper, requiring greater patience, introspection, empathy, and insight on the part of the interviewer in order to further the relationship.

FRANK REVISITED

In chapter 3 Frank's case was used to demonstrate a suicide crisis intervention, subsequent intake interview, and follow-up psychiatric visit. The reader may recall that Frank came to treatment initially because of his concern about losing his job and the difficulties he had been having with his boss. The scenario ended with Frank agreeing to go on antidepressant medication and seek out therapy. The interview below is Frank's first counseling session with a female social worker.

Interviewer: Hi Frank. It's nice to meet you. I read the information that I received from your psychiatrist, but wanted to get your impressions about why you're here.

This type of opening intervention is a standard interviewing process. Although the interviewer obviously has written information and perhaps has spoken with referring parties, it is important to hear the client's story. The interviewer should consider that information from and conversations with third parties may not give the same perspective as the client's. Hearing directly from the client helps the interviewer get a more complete and personal client history, as well as setting a tone of respect, caring, and genuine concern for the client's view.

> *Frank:* Well, like you have probably read or heard, I recently lost my job and I was extremely depressed and kind of suicidal.
> **Interviewer:** Yes, I read that. Could you tell me what you mean by kind of suicidal?
> *Frank:* I didn't really want to kill myself, but I was feeling like I didn't really want to live either. I just wanted everything to go away. Does that make sense?
> **Interviewer:** I think so . . . sounds like things were so bad you just wanted to get away from the feelings and not have to be in your situation. Am I getting it right?
> *Frank:* Yeah.

It's important in any interview for the interviewer to continually check in with the client to be sure she understands things from the client's point of view. Beginning, and even veteran, interviewers often make the mistake of presuming to know where the client is, which can take the process down a path that is not only inaccurate but unhelpful. This type of empathic clarification is essential in all interviewing.

> **Interviewer:** Good. How have you been doing lately?
> *Frank:* I'm still looking for work, but I've got a few leads and the medication has really helped me feel less down. I'm also not getting up at night and worrying so much.
> **Interviewer:** That sounds like things have improved a bit?

Again, the interviewer asks a question and does not simply make a statement of fact.

Frank: A bit . . .

Interviewer: Well, Frank, as we get started, I think I'd like to talk a little bit about how this works: in other words, how I do therapy.

Frank: OK . . . good.

Interviewer: This is your time. Everything we talk about is confidential, except, of course, if you are planning to hurt yourself or someone else. Together we'll work toward helping you feel better and function better in your life. Sometimes simply talking about things helps. Other times we might come up with a more specific type of plan where you could work on certain tasks or journal your thoughts and feelings to keep track of any pattern, or there are other kinds of approaches. I think as we get to know each other, we'll come to a way of working that seems best for you. I'm not here to tell you what to do or direct you in a way you don't want to go. However, I may have some ideas and suggestions that could be helpful and that we could explore from time to time. I know this may sound kind of general, but that's basically how I do therapy. Do you have any questions?

This intervention or statement from the interviewer should also be an important part of every interviewing process. The client needs and has a right to know what the process is going to look like, and what he can expect. This interviewer is also letting the client know that she is flexible and has a variety of ways in which she can work with him. In plain language, she is talking about theoretical and clinical approaches. It is not so important for the client to know exactly what those are from a technical standpoint, but he should be able to understand the process and how it may proceed. It's also important to allow the client the opportunity to ask questions and clarify any confusion that may be in his mind about the process.

Frank: Thanks, I think I get it.

Interviewer: Good. If you ever have any questions about the therapy, please don't hesitate to ask me. I want this to be an open and honest process for both of us.

The phrase "for both of us" obviously signals that the interviewer sees this as a relationship between interviewer and client. It sets an important tone for future work.

Frank: Me too.

Interviewer: So is there anything that is particularly on your mind today?

Frank: Well, I've been thinking a lot about the recent stuff with work, and how the interactions with my boss reminded me so much of my relationship with my father.

Interviewer: How so?

Frank: This may sound weird, but I never got the feeling that she liked me, even though I was really probably one of the best workers in the company.

Interviewer: How was that like your relationship with your father?

The interviewer's questions flow naturally from the client's process. She is genuinely curious and wants to know more. This does not have to be or feel contrived.

Frank: All my life, even as a little kid, I never felt like he liked me. He didn't play with me, he didn't seem to care about what I liked, and he was always putting me down.

Interviewer: Now when you say "always," Frank, do you really mean always? I mean, were there never any good times?

Frank: Not that I can really remember. I used to hate it when he came home. I'd go outside or go hide in my room.

Interviewer: You really wanted to stay away from him.

This is a simple, empathic, and important caring intervention to stay in tune with the client.

Frank: Yeah, he really scared me.

Interviewer: In what way did he scare you?

Frank: He was so unpredictable. He could come home smiling and whistling one minute and then without warning he would start yelling at me or calling me names, or worse yet, even become violent sometimes. Mostly it was his constant verbal and emotional abuse though.

Interviewer: For example?

Now that Frank is opening up about this painful topic, the interviewer carefully and empathically helps him tell his story. She is genuinely interested and caring in the relationship with the client.

Frank: Sometimes it started out innocent, but escalated. He used to like to "teach" us how to fight. I guess he was a big fighter when he was a kid and teenager, and nobody could beat him. He would push us, mostly me, to try and hit him. We never could. He was too good, and we were too little. I'd try and try and try to get one punch in, but he would always slap me away. Then he started really slapping me in the face while we fought . . . never his fists . . . always an open hand. But it hurt, and he kept slapping me harder and harder until I cried. My mom would try to stop it, but he just kept it up. He would laugh and laugh . . . I think he really enjoyed it.

Interviewer: That sounds very humiliating.

Frank: Yeah . . . in a weird sort of way, I wanted to please him. I wanted to show him I could be strong and a good fighter, but he would always win, and never let me get a punch in. I thought that was mean and wrong. I guess he thought he was making us stronger, but it felt more like he was showing off . . . at his little kid's expense.

Interviewer: I can see why you might not want to be around him too much.

Frank: Dinner was the worst—in fact, all meals with him. Just before I was a teenager, you know, around ten or eleven, I was a little overweight. I think that's normal, you know, all kids tend to have a little extra weight as they grow into adolescents.

Interviewer: Uh, huh . . .

Frank: It probably wasn't, but it feels like every time we had a meal, he would eventually end up calling me a "fat pig" or a "fat slob," or something related to being fat. This usually happened if I wanted a second helping, but sometimes he'd just say it for nothing. The thing is, he would dish out such small portions, and there would be lots of food left over, sitting on the plates. I was hungry, I don't know . . . maybe I was fat, but even if I was, I don't think calling me names was the right thing to do. To this day, no matter how much I try to feel good about my body, even when I intellectually know I look OK, there is always a part of me that hears that voice "fat pig," and I feel like I am.

Interviewer: So this criticism from you father went on for a long time, huh?

Frank: Seemed like it went on forever. He was always picking on me.

Interviewer: This does sound similar to the way you describe your boss's feelings about you.

Frank: It does, doesn't it? I'm not crazy, am I?

Interviewer: It doesn't seem that way to me, Frank.

These interventions are crucial to help validate and empathize with the client's experience. The client is beginning to piece together important parts of his experience that seems to have a direct bearing on the recent events of his life.

Frank: Well, it gets better. As it turns out, I married someone just like my father. Not my present wife, my ex.

Interviewer: How was she like your father?

Frank: We were married for almost twenty years. At first things seemed good, but as time went on, she began to criticize me like my dad. Oh, she didn't call me fat or anything like that, but she never seemed to be satisfied with how much I made, my work around the house, the kind of lover I was, almost everything.

Interviewer: How did you handle that?

Frank: Well, for years I tried to talk with her, but she always brushed it off, telling me it was my "father" stuff, and that I was distorting things. I don't think I was, though.

Interviewer: Why not?

Frank: Well, here's a really good example. Some years into our marriage, I applied for a pretty good job. It was a step up. I went through a bunch of intense interviews and finally got it. The money was much more than I was making, but not as much as I had hoped I'd get. The night I came home, I was really proud and happy about getting the job. When I told my ex, she exploded about the money and started yelling at me. She even went to her dressing table and threw everything onto the floor. I mean she literally lost it. She berated me for not being good enough and failing in this job situation. It felt just like my father. We didn't last much longer.

Interviewer: That kind of behavior does sound like your father.

This simple empathic line is meaningful to the client. It helps him feel validated and less isolated.

Frank: I don't know . . . sometimes I continue to doubt myself. But you know, my present marriage is wonderful. We've been married for over ten years, and I've never been so much in love and felt so much love for anyone. So I know it's possible to feel good and be treated well. I don't think it's me . . . I mean, of course I contribute to negative situations like everyone does, but I don't think I'm all bad anymore. But when this situation at work happened, it all came flooding back. Those feelings are still there, somewhere in the back of my mind.

Interviewer: I see what you mean, Frank. This recent situation stirred it all up again, didn't it?

Frank: Yeah, and I guess I was afraid I'd never get away from those feelings again.

Interviewer: And now?

Frank: Well, with the meds and some therapy, I think maybe I can work some of this through.

Interviewer: I think so too, Frank. You're obviously very insightful already, and are a sensitive and insightful person. I think we could work on some of these things if you'd like.

Frank: I think it would really help. I feel good just getting to some of this stuff today.

This client is not severely disturbed. He falls under the category of general mental health cases. Frank has some self-esteem issues, based upon his early upbringing, that have shaped who he is and affected his personal and professional life. Yet he does not appear to distort reality, and his issues of self-esteem do not appear to interfere in his ability to succeed in his profession or establish a happy marriage. Frank has lingering issues of insecurity that could be helped by therapy. Some type of relational therapy would probably be effective, such as Rogerian client-centered, object relations, self psychology, or other psychodynamic approaches that focus on building a therapeutic relationship that can provide a corrective emotional experience with the interviewer. This case example demonstrates how that is already beginning to happen.

MARIA REVISITED

Chapter 6 discussed Maria's case. Maria is a Hispanic professional woman who became pregnant in a relationship with Juan, a Hispanic man who was keeping his marriage a secret from Maria. To complicate things further, Maria was under the impression that Juan had had a vasectomy, only to find out that that is either untrue or the procedure (according to Juan) did not work. Maria discussed her very mixed emotions about this complex situation and how it relates to her family history and image of herself as a professional Hispanic woman. Maria has connected with the interviewer and is involved in both individual and couples work to deal with this overwhelming problem. This case is not a severe mental health problem, but is filled with a myriad of complex dynamics and implications for the client's self-image and life circumstances. The following interview picks up some time after the interview in chapter 6.

> **Interviewer:** Hi Maria. How have things been going?
>
> *Maria:* I'm doing OK, but I've been having a lot of morning sickness and am pretty tired most of the time.
>
> **Interviewer:** So you're really starting to feel some of the physical effects of the pregnancy.
>
> *Maria:* Yeah, it's no picnic.
>
> **Interviewer:** So I've heard.
>
> *Maria:* Juan says he's getting a divorce . . . but . . . I don't know, I just don't trust him.
>
> **Interviewer:** Well, given what we've already discussed, that seems like a natural feeling.
>
> *Maria:* Is it? I hope so. Sometimes I worry that I should be more trusting.
>
> **Interviewer:** Maybe it's just me, Maria, but from what you've told me, it would seem very natural for most people to have some suspicion around this situation.

It is important for the interviewer to be empathic to, and validate, the client's emotions here. Maria is confused but also is looking for some genuine reassurance from the interviewer. Adding the phrase "maybe it's just me" tempers the comments and allows for Maria's own judgment to come forth, one way or another.

> *Maria:* Thank you; that is a relief. It really helps to sort this out with you.
>
> **Interviewer:** I'm glad.
>
> *Maria:* I wanted to get your thoughts on another matter about Juan.
>
> **Interviewer:** What's that?

The interviewer does not say that she will give advice, or opinions, but is certainly communicating an openness to listen and explore this issue.

> **Maria:** He keeps telling me that he has filed for divorce, but given the dishonesty I've already experienced from him, I'm not even sure if that's true. I asked him to see a copy of the divorce papers. He seems defensive and insulted that I don't trust him. Am I wrong?
>
> **Interviewer:** I don't know if it's a matter of right or wrong, Maria, but as you have just said, you have already been lied to by Juan a number of times about some very important issues, especially the fact that he may not have even had a vasectomy. In light of those things, it doesn't sound unreasonable for you to feel the way you do and want to have some physical proof that Juan is being honest with you.
>
> **Maria:** Well, that's what I thought too . . . I mean, how difficult is it to produce those papers?

Notice that the interviewer is validating the client's experience in order to help Maria decide what she would like to do. The interviewer is not telling Maria that she is right or wrong. She is conveying an understanding and genuine empathy for why the client might need this type of information. This is a very important demonstration of how the interviewer explores and expresses concern for the client, but does not direct her. It enables the client to truly decide for herself, which is an empowering and confidence-building experience. This is one of the many ways professional interviewing is different than friendship or advice giving. The relationship becomes the vehicle to help the client grow and develop greater capacities.

> **Interviewer:** What if Juan doesn't show you the papers?
>
> **Maria:** I don't know . . . it's going to make it awfully difficult to trust him and stay with him.
>
> **Interviewer:** Are the two of you living together?
>
> **Maria:** No, and that's another thing. He told me he is not going to leave his home until he knows his family is settled.

He also doesn't want to be away from his kids. I don't think we should move in together, at least not for a while, but I think he's dragging his feet and sending a mixed message to his wife and children. I don't even know if he's telling me the truth about any of this.

Interviewer: This is really difficult for you.

This is an empathic statement and furthering intervention by the interviewer. It is all that is needed, as Maria is deep in the process of this discussion.

Maria: Yeah, I know. He seems to really care about me. Does that come across in our couples therapy?

Interviewer: I get that sense.

Maria: Whatever way this goes though, I'm determined to keep this baby. Abortion or adoption is not an option as far as I'm concerned. I don't believe in it, and my family would be extremely upset with me.

Interviewer: You certainly sound very clear about that, and you've mentioned your family before. Their opinion about this and you is crucial, isn't it?

Maria: Yes, especially with my mom, considering all she had to handle with my father's affairs. I think if I gave this baby up, she would be very upset with me.

Interviewer: I can understand that, Maria, but is keeping the baby something you want to do regardless of how your family feels about it?

The interviewer is gently confronting Maria because she isn't quite sure if her decision is entirely hers or based upon her worries about her family's opinion. This is important to know as things move forward.

Maria: Oh, absolutely.

Interviewer: Have you begun to think about how you will manage things once the baby comes?

Maria: Yes. I will be able to take some maternity leave, and I make enough money to support myself and the baby. I know it's going to be rough, and at this point I am not counting on Juan . . . I don't think I can.

Interviewer: This hasn't come up in our couples work, but have you discussed this with him?

Maria: Oh yeah. He says he wants to be there for me, and will help me financially, but he also has to be there for his family. Like I've already said though, I don't trust him, so I'm not counting on anything.

Interviewer: This sounds like a very lonely proposition to me.

The interviewer is expressing the genuine sense of frustration and isolation that the client may be feeling. This is a somewhat leading intervention, but necessary to ascertain what Maria is feeling.

Maria: I am a little scared . . .

Interviewer: I think that would be a normal reaction for anyone in your situation, Maria. However, I also sense your determination.

Maria [*tentatively*]: I guess so . . . I hadn't thought about it quite that way.

Interviewer: Well, maybe it's just me, but there certainly seems like there is a very confident and determined Maria when it comes to the future of this baby.

The interviewer is expressing her very real sense of the client's character as it has been expressed in the interviews thus far. This statement is encouraging and validating.

Maria: Thank you, that means a lot to me. I am really trying, and sometimes I do feel strong about all of this.

Interviewer: I think that's very important.

Maria: I know my family will be there for me. That's a big relief. I'm just not sure how to proceed with Juan.

Interviewer: I think the fact that both of you are in couples therapy is a good sign. I also think we should probably tackle this trust issue and your concerns about the truth of these many issues. I'm sure Juan has a lot to say about it too.

Maria: I hope so . . .

Interviewer: Well, Maria, I think we've really covered a lot today. Our time is about up. I'll see you guys in a couple of days.

Maria is beginning to delve deeper into her present life concerns through the helpful relationship with the interviewer. This case example and the preceding ones of Al and Frank are described as general mental health cases because the issues for all of these clients do not significantly impair their everyday functioning. Yet all of them present difficult and complex dynamics that are challenging to the interviewer.

Although Al is dying, he is still capable and invested in exploring and working through his troubling emotions, which are based upon unresolved conflicts with his family. This is a very promising and optimistic process as Al moves toward a resolution that could give him peace as he ends his life. Many clients would not risk this type of exploration, but it seems that for Al, it is a part of life.

Frank, as well, is able to function in his life, but has begun to explore in greater depth and detail the ways in which his early life has affected his view of himself and the ways in which this understanding may help him in the future. He has been resilient and demonstrates that fact by his ongoing interest in improving his self-concept and approach to life in general.

Maria is confronted with an unfortunate life circumstance that resonates with her past family history, her self-concept as a Hispanic professional woman, and the difficult choices she feels she must make in the future. She seems clearly able to manage her day-to-day life, as well as her plans for the future, but is extremely troubled by the situation of mistrust with the man in her life. The work with the interviewer is aimed at helping her understand and manage the challenging emotions and threats to her self-concept and confidence that affect her life ahead.

RESEARCH IMPLICATIONS AND BASIS OF PRACTICE

Since the onset of professional interviewing, intuition has guided the process of engaging with and helping clients. It is human nature to feel drawn to empathic interactions with others. As interviewing has evolved into a more rigorous and structured format, practice wisdom has informed the ways in which intuitive processes have become formalized within professional disciplines. Theoretical knowledge has helped to predict and understand the nature of the interviewing phenomena, as well as to inform a deeper understanding of the human condition and the curative effects of the relationship interactions in the process. Finally, recent infant and neuroscience empirical research as well as evidence-based studies have provided validated knowledge that gives further proof of the effectiveness of the interviewing process (O'Hare, 2005; *Psychodynamic Diagnostic Manual*, 2006; American Psychiatric Association, 2000).

From a research perspective, then, interviewing has reached the level of validated knowledge. Part 3 of the *Psychodynamic Diagnostic Manual* (2006, p. 381) focuses on the "conceptual and research foundations for a psychodynamically based classification system for mental disorders." Unlike the DSM IV-TR, a primarily behavioral categorization of psychiatric disorders, the PDM is informed by recent infant and neuroscience research and other contemporary studies that indicate the validity, importance, and effectiveness of the relationship in interviewing and psychotherapeutic processes.

Chief among these are the contributions from neuroscience, which indicate that human beings are born with mirror neurons. Mirror neurons enable the individual to anticipate the emotions, behaviors, and intentions of others as early as infancy. This innate empathic process is the core of what drives the relational aspect of interviewing. Furthermore, recent knowledge about developing neural networks and the importance of emotional, behavioral, and cognitive interactions that are healthy and positive indicates the necessity of longer-term relational interviewing for positive and effective outcomes (PDM, 2006).

SUMMARY

General mental health cases are much more the rule than the exception in interviewing work. They require patient understanding and careful exploration in order to form a relationship with the client that can help him or her not only resolve the presenting circumstances, but also uncover the meaningful thoughts, emotions, and experiences that have shaped and in many circumstances interfered in the ability to successfully manage the problem.

The interviewer is continually forming a working model of the client in order to understand the key past and present circumstances that are hindering the process. Many interviewers might be tempted to give advice or direction in these types of situations, and that could be useful. Doing so, however, deprives clients of the opportunity to come to their own decision. Arriving at one's own decision increases one's confidence, competence, and sense of self-esteem in approaching life. Many theoretical approaches can be used in helping the interviewer understand the client and develop an approach to the process. However, it is the interviewing relationship that is the vehicle through which change occurs in general mental health cases.

RECOMMENDED READING

Psychodynamic Diagnostic Manual. (2006). Silver Spring, MD: Alliance of Psychoanalytic Organizations.

This publication is an excellent guide to understanding and assessing the client from a theoretical and empirically based perspective. Derived from infant, neuroscience, and evidence-based research, it is essential reading for any interviewer.

Yalom, I. D. (2002). *The gift of therapy.* New York: Harper.

Yalom is undoubtedly one of the most influential writers, theorists, and psychotherapists in the history of psychotherapy. This wonderful book provides vivid and compelling examples of his clinical work as well as advice to anyone in an interviewing profession.

MULTIMEDIA SOURCES

In Treatment. (2008–11). HBO.

Revisiting this powerful series with an eye on the interviewing process in these general mental health interviews provides rich examples of the pleasures and pitfalls of the relational process.

CHAPTER NINE

Interviewing in Severe Mental Health Cases

The difference between general and severe mental health cases, in large part, has to do with the extent to which clients can function adequately in their respective worlds, as well as their ability to understand and perceive reality and use that perception to interact successfully with others. This is a broad continuum of functioning. Historically, it was best described as patients who were diagnosed as either neurotic or psychotic. Neurotic patients were generally able to function well in their everyday lives, but did experience emotional and behavioral setbacks that might temporarily interfere in this ability. These could be traced back to problems in childhood, which, when uncovered and understood, helped the patient return to an adequate level of living. Phobias, panic attacks, and depression are good examples of these problems. The psychotic, borderline, and other personality-disordered clients were much more debilitated and out of touch with reality, which led to extended periods of inability to function in the world, often leading to extended treatment and hospitalization.

As an example, the term *borderline* was developed to describe patients whose ability to perceive reality and operate in the real world was on the border between psychosis and neurosis.

The DSM-IV-TR helped classify the diagnostic continuum of mental health, and the PDM has broadened that perspective considerably through the incorporation of validated knowledge from infant research, neuroscience, and evidence-based practices. All of this important information has a direct bearing on the way in which interviewers understand the client, as well as their decisions about how to approach the interview.

This chapter illustrates the ways in which interviewers work with clients with severe mental health problems. The basic approach and technique is similar to work with general mental health cases; however, the severity and difficulty that the client has in reality testing and interpersonal experience can often necessitate different types of interventions to help the client become emotionally healthier and able to adapt to the world. These types of clients are the most challenging and difficult to interview. The key to success with them is, as in any interviewing situation, the formation and utilization of the professional relationship. The following case examples demonstrate that delicate and rewarding process.

THE PSYCHOTIC YOUNG MAN

Mark voluntarily came to see the social work interviewer because of problems he was experiencing in his social life. Mark was eighteen when he started therapy and was in treatment for about a year. During that time Mark gradually deteriorated into a psychotic state. The onset of schizophrenia is typically late adolescence or early adulthood. Symptoms can be subtle or dramatic and appear gradually or suddenly. Mark's case was a sad one, with a slow onset of schizophrenia, and presented the interviewer with difficult challenges because of Mark's age. When a client is eighteen or older, all information between therapist and client is confidential unless the client is a threat to himself or others. In these types of situations, the interviewer may share information with others, including family, only with the client's consent, except in special circumstances.

Interviewer: Hi Mark. It's nice to meet you. I know we talked on the phone a bit. If I understood correctly, it sounds like you've been concerned about some of your relationships with friends. How would you like to start?

This is a typical way to convey an initial understanding of the client's presenting concern, while giving him complete freedom to talk about whatever is on his mind. It is also the beginning of a diagnostic process, as the interviewer listens and pays attention to the client's interactions, expression of thoughts and emotions, and general demeanor.

Mark: Yeah, my parents thought I should see someone. I really want to be in a relationship with a girl, but I don't know how to meet them. Can you help me with that?

Interviewer: Well, Mark, can you tell me a little bit more about what you mean when you say you want to be in a relationship with a girl?

The client's question seems a little odd to the interviewer, and he feels a need to know more about the nature of the client's question rather than assuming anything.

Mark: You know . . . I want a girlfriend. Can you help me figure out how to get one?

Interviewer: We can certainly talk about that and perhaps find ways that you can begin to establish some connections with girls that might lead to a relationship.

Mark: Good. How do I do that?

Interviewer: I think that I might be able to help you better with this situation, Mark, if I knew a little bit more about you and the kinds of relationships you've had with women in the past. Would that be OK with you?

The interviewer realizes that the client seems to be approaching this situation in a rather simplistic way, but does not want to judge him as such. Instead, getting to know more about Mark may help the interviewer understand what he means and wants in this request. Again, the interventions flow from a natural curiosity and caring about the client.

> *Mark:* I guess so . . . what do you want to know?
>
> **Interviewer:** Well, tell me a little bit about your family. You said they suggested you come here.
>
> *Mark:* It's just me and my mom and dad. I live at home with them. I just graduated high school, and I got a job in this office.
>
> **Interviewer:** How do you get along with your parents?
>
> *Mark:* They're OK, I guess. I don't spend much time with them. I mostly hang out in my room.
>
> **Interviewer:** What kinds of things do you like to do?
>
> *Mark:* I read, listen to music, go to the library.
>
> **Interviewer:** And you work?
>
> *Mark:* Yeah, but I really don't have any friends there.
>
> **Interviewer:** Why is that, do you think?

The interviewer is purposely trying not to sound critical, and has a genuine curiosity about the environment of the client's workplace and how conducive it might be to friendships.

> *Mark:* Well, I don't think anybody likes me. I try to talk to people, but no one really talks back to me much.
>
> **Interviewer:** So you feel kind of isolated at work?
>
> *Mark:* Yeah, a little.
>
> **Interviewer:** Are there many people at work around your age?
>
> *Mark:* Yeah, there are a lot of them. We just don't seem to get along. Can you help me find a girlfriend?
>
> **Interviewer:** Are there many girls at work?
>
> *Mark:* There are a few of them, and one I really like.
>
> **Interviewer:** Have you talked with her?
>
> *Mark:* No . . . I don't know what to say . . . that's why I came to see you.
>
> **Interviewer:** So I could help you learn how to find a girlfriend?

Mark: Yeah . . . can you?

Interviewer: Well, Mark, we can certainly talk about ways in which you might approach this girl you like, for instance, and perhaps that could lead to some kind of friendship.

Mark: I don't want a friendship, I want a girlfriend.

Interviewer: I think I understand, Mark, and in my experience, it takes a while for a friendship to develop into something more. Do you know what I mean?

Mark: Not exactly. I just want to have a girlfriend.

Interviewer: OK . . . well, Mark, let's talk about what you mean by a girlfriend. What would that relationship be like for you?

Mark: You know . . . like a boyfriend/girlfriend relationship.

Interviewer: Well actually, Mark, I really don't know what you mean. I mean, I have some ideas of what relationships might look like, but I also think that everyone's relationships are different. If I'm going to help you with this, I think I need to know what you mean by a boyfriend/girlfriend relationship.

Mark: OK . . . I mean a girl I can hang out with and have sex.

Interviewer: So someone you can spend time with and also be involved in a sexual relationship?

Mark: You got it.

Interviewer: Did you date any girls in high school?

Mark: No.

Interviewer: So you have never really had a girlfriend?

Mark: That's what I told you. Can you help me get one?

The interviewer is getting the sense that Mark is at the very least inexperienced in social relationships. The client also appears to have a rather concrete and simplistic notion of what a relationship is and how to go about developing one. The interviewer does not get the impression that Mark is mentally deficient, but he certainly seems awkward and a bit odd in his interactions in the interview. This silent hypothesis will help the interviewer in subsequent work, especially as it relates to the way in which he will further engage and talk with Mark.

> **Interviewer:** This may sound like a really simple question, Mark, but why do you want a girlfriend?
> *Mark:* Well, doesn't everybody have them? And I want to have sex.
> **Interviewer:** So is sex a big part of why you want a girlfriend?
> *Mark:* Not just sex . . . but it's important, don't you think?
> **Interviewer:** I think sex is probably a very important part of most people's life; at least in my experience, it seems to be.
> *Mark:* So, I'm not being weird?
> **Interviewer:** No, Mark, I think wanting to have a girlfriend and a sexual relationship is a very normal part of life.

Even though Mark's logic seems to the interviewer to be a little odd, he feels compelled to acknowledge the genuine feelings Mark has about wanting to connect with another. The interviewer is also beginning to recognize that Mark seems to have had some ongoing difficulties in this area and friendships in general. This session ends with Mark deciding that he would like to come back to work some more on finding a girlfriend.

The next case example takes place about two months later, as Mark and the interviewer have been continuing to brainstorm about the girlfriend issue, Mark's family, and socialization in general. Mark has made little progress in his attempt to form any type of connection with the girl at work.

> **Interviewer:** Well, Mark, how have things been going this past week?
> *Mark:* Same as last week. I still can't get her to talk to me. I think she likes another guy.
> **Interviewer:** What makes you think that?

Mark: They're always together . . . and they give me weird looks. I think they talk about me.

Interviewer: Have they said anything directly to you?

Mark: No, but it's the way they look at me, you know, kind of like they're making fun of me.

Interviewer: How are you handling that?

Mark: I try to ignore them, but I know they just think I'm weird or stupid.

Interviewer: I'm sorry, Mark, but how do you know that for sure?

Mark: I just know, that's all. You've been talking to her, haven't you?

Interviewer: The girl you like?

Mark: Yeah . . . you've been talking to her about me haven't you?

This is a very alarming statement for the interviewer. He does not even know the woman Mark has been discussing in sessions, and this accusation leads the interviewer to suspect, at the very least, that Mark is having some paranoid thoughts and difficulty with reality testing. This is a delicate situation that calls for extreme sensitivity and tact in interacting with Mark.

Interviewer: Mark, I have never met this woman, and even if I had, I wouldn't talk to anyone about you, unless you wanted me to and I had your permission. Our relationship is confidential, remember?

Mark: Yeah, I know you said that, but I think you've been talking to her about me. That's why she doesn't like me.

The interviewer is realizing that this is some sort of paranoid delusion of the client's. The interviewer has challenged and clarified it, but Mark seems intent on holding on to it.

Interviewer: Mark, I can assure you that I have not talked to this woman and don't even know her, but obviously you feel that I have. Why would I do such a thing?

Mark: I think you're like my mom.

Interviewer: In what way?

Mark: I think she's trying to poison me.

Interviewer: Really? What makes you think that?

Mark: Oh, I don't know . . . just the way she seems around the house. I can tell that she looks at me kind of funny.

Interviewer: So you're having some of the same kind of mistrustful feelings about me too?

Mark: Well, I guess I believe you, but I have my doubts.

The interviewer is recognizing that Mark may be having trouble negotiating his sense of reality. This requires a more directive approach. Exploring Mark's feelings and encouraging deeper intervention is likely to exacerbate the client's suspicion and paranoia.

Interviewer: I can assure you, Mark, that I would never talk to anyone without your permission unless, like I've said before, I thought you were going to hurt yourself or someone else. I don't think that is the case.

Mark: Yeah, I know. I guess maybe I'm confused.

Interviewer: I know you've been going through some tough times lately.

Mark: Yeah . . . [*Silence.*]

Interviewer: Mark, you mentioned your concerns about your mom. Do you think it might help to have her come into our sessions so we could discuss some of them?

Remember that Mark is over eighteen and legally has a right to complete confidentiality. Inviting the client's mother into the session is totally up to Mark. However, the interviewer believes it could shed some important light on what appear to be Mark's more severe mental health issues.

Mark: No, I don't think that would help. Besides, I don't trust her.

The session ends with Mark insisting that he does not want either of his parents in the interviews. The interviewer is becoming increasingly concerned about Mark's grasp on reality, but is also bound by confidentiality. For now, the interviewer will have to be content with gathering more information and perhaps tactfully suggesting a psychiatric referral to assess the need for possible medication. This will be challenging, however, given Mark's paranoid demeanor.

The final interview happened several weeks later. Mark continued to move in and out of quasi-delusional states, but still seemed able to function at work and home. At this point, the interviewer still did not believe that Mark was a threat to himself or others, but was ambivalent in his decision to involve Mark's family.

> **Interviewer:** Hi Mark. How are things?
> *Mark:* Great!
> **Interviewer:** Wow, you seem so excited. What's going on?
> *Mark:* I'm going to get a job in Washington, DC.
> **Interviewer:** Really? Tell me more about it.
> *Mark:* Well, I've got this connection in DC. He is going to set me up with an interview. I will be working with the president's staff.
> **Interviewer:** How did this happen?
> *Mark:* Well, I've been planning it for a while, and it finally came through.
> **Interviewer:** What kind of work will you be doing?
> *Mark:* It's confidential, you know . . . I really can't talk about it. But I'll be leaving soon for DC.
> **Interviewer:** This is really news to me, Mark.
> *Mark:* Yeah, I really couldn't tell you. I'll be meeting with the president. He and I are going to be working very closely together. Like I said, it's very secret.

The interviewer now completely realizes that Mark is in the middle of a psychotic episode. He knows he will have to intervene, but worries that if he confronts Mark it may agitate him. The interviewer silently plans to contact Mark's family ASAP to recommend an involuntary psychiatric assessment.

Later that day, the interviewer does reach Mark's family and informs them about his concerns regarding Mark's mental health. By this time, however, Mark has left his parents' home, and they are unable to find him. A week or so goes by, and Mark's parents receive word from the police in Florida that they have picked Mark up, wandering the streets and talking about his mission with the White House. Mark is brought back home and enters a psychiatric facility.

Mark stays in the facility for several months and is put on antipsychotic medication. Over time he returns to a relatively stable lifestyle, with occasional psychotic symptoms. He sees the interviewer off and on over the next few months, and finally ends treatment. Over the next few years, the interviewer receives several random voice mails from Mark that express paranoid delusions. Mark never returns to treatment.

This is a classic case example of a young adult who is beginning to suffer from schizophrenia. Sometimes, as in Mark's case, the symptoms evolve slowly and subtly, and are not easily identified by even the most skilled interviewer of any professional discipline. Initially, Mark seems odd and perhaps even a little socially delayed, but over time, the interviewer is able to piece together that the client is, in fact, having some difficulty in functioning, especially as it relates to reality perception and testing. This also appears to affect his judgment, particularly near the end of the interviews when Mark abruptly leaves his family to pursue a delusional career in Washington, DC, only to end up aimlessly wandering the streets in a Florida town.

Could or should the interviewer have handled this situation differently? Perhaps, but given the slow and subtle development of Mark's symptoms, and the fact that he was over eighteen years old, the interviewer was limited in his legal options. Instead, the interviewer did his best to try to understand and assess Mark through careful confrontation and exploration aimed at developing a competent diagnosis. Once this was achieved, the interviewer attempted to involve Mark's family, but by that time it was too late to stop Mark from leaving. Mark eventually got the help he needed, but suffered quite a bit in the process.

This case example is used not to demonstrate the most proficient way to work with clients' severe mental health issues, but to help any interviewer understand the subtle and complex challenges inherent in this type of work. The next case provides a very different type of severe mental health scenario that is often encountered in professional interviews.

THE SEXUAL-ABUSE SURVIVOR

Sandy is a thirty-year-old single mother who has come to the interviewer, a male psychologist, with a presenting concern about her teenage daughter's school problems. The interviewer works with Sandy and her daughter, both individually and in family therapy. In a short time, perhaps two months or so, Sandy's daughter seems to be doing better in school. Sandy, however, continues in individual sessions with the interviewer to work on her panic attacks. She wants to be in therapy, but has a difficult time identifying and communicating her emotional states to the interviewer. She is a challenging client because of this dynamic. The case example begins after Sandy has been in individual therapy about a month.

> **Interviewer:** Hi Sandy. How are you doing today?
> *Sandy:* Oh, OK I guess . . .

From the tone and hesitation in Sandy's voice, the interviewer senses that she is not doing well. This natural empathic intuition prompts the interviewer to gently pursue this hunch.

> **Interviewer:** I get the sense that things might not be going so well?
> *Sandy:* Well, I've been having a lot of panic attacks lately.
> **Interviewer:** Help me understand, Sandy. By a lot, you mean what?

This open-ended question demonstrates the fact that the interviewer does not judge or presume Sandy's situation. He wants to allow her the room to discuss this delicate issue at her own pace.

Sandy: At least a couple of times a week.

Interviewer: Are there any particular situations that influence these panic attacks?

Sandy: No, they just happen . . . you know . . . my heart starts racing, I get sweaty, I have trouble breathing . . . I feel like I'm going to die. I know I won't. We've discussed panic attacks, and I'm taking the medication that the psychiatrist you referred me to prescribed, but I don't know if it's helping.

Interviewer: Sounds very upsetting.

All that the interviewer feels he needs to do here is respond with an empathic statement to help Sandy know he thinks he understands and is with her in the session.

Sandy: I'm OK . . . I just don't know when it's going to happen.

Interviewer: Well, maybe it would help to talk a little bit about how things are going in your life right now. We might be able to make some connections to things that could be contributing to these panic attacks?

The interviewer recognizes that the client is not sure where to go from here but feels a sense that exploring some of her more general life issues might lead to a meaningful connection.

Sandy: I've been thinking a lot about the abuse when I was little . . . you know . . . we started talking about it last time?

Interviewer: Yes, I remember. Do you feel comfortable getting into that some more?

Abuse of any kind is a delicate subject, and it is important for the interviewer, male or female, to allow the client to have control over what and how she discusses it.

Sandy: I'm beginning to remember more.

Interviewer: Like what?

Sandy: My mom and dad divorced when I was probably around six or seven. I actually don't know if they divorced,

I just know he wasn't around anymore. Anyway, my mom wasn't around very much either. She went to work, then to the bars. She would come home with a lot of different men.

Interviewer: Do you remember if this is related to the abuse?

Sandy: I think so . . . but I can't really remember . . . It's all kind of blurry.

Interviewer: Blurry?

Sandy: Yeah, you know . . . I can only remember bits and pieces.

Interviewer: What do you remember?

Sandy: Eventually my mom hooked up with this guy, and he moved into our house. I really didn't like him.

Interviewer: What didn't you like about him?

Sandy: I don't know . . .

She seems to be either resistant, or truly can't verbalize or perhaps even recognize what she is feeling.

Interviewer: Sounds like it was uncomfortable though?

Sandy [*in almost an adolescent tone*]: Yeah, he was creepy.

Interviewer: Can you describe what you mean by creepy?

Sandy: He was always looking at me, you know, like he wanted sex.

Interviewer: So you were very young, weren't you, Sandy? Now, I believe you, but how did you know he wanted sex?

Sandy: Maybe I didn't know it was sex at the time, but it felt wrong.

Interviewer: Did this man abuse you?

This may sound like a bit of a leading question, but Sandy appears to be headed in this direction.

Sandy: He used to take me to the store with him. I didn't want to go, but my mom said I had to go with him. I remember it always seemed to be at night. He would park in the grocery store parking lot and molest me. He would touch me in my private areas, and wouldn't stop, even though I told him I didn't like it.

Interviewer: Do you remember how you felt?

Sandy: I think I might have been scared, but I don't really remember. I just didn't want to be there. I think I spaced out and just let him touch me so it would get over quickly.

Interviewer: Did this happen a lot?

Sandy: Seems like it happened all the time, but I really can't remember.

Interviewer: Sounds like you really don't have very clear memories or feelings about this time in your life.

This empathic statement/question is aimed at validating and normalizing Sandy's emotional experiences with abuse. Memories, thoughts, and experiences can be blocked or put out of awareness (called dissociation) to protect the self in times of trauma.

Sandy: Yeah, I guess not.

Interviewer: Do you remember anything else?

Sandy: I remember that he said he was going to bring me to bed with my mother. That really scared me, but I was kind of relieved because I didn't think she would ever allow it, and then maybe he would stop doing this stuff to me.

Interviewer: How old do you think you might have been?

Sandy: I'm not sure, maybe ten or so.

Interviewer: Did he take you to bed with your mom?

Sandy: Yeah . . . [*Silence.*]

Interviewer: Are you comfortable talking about it?

Sandy: Not today . . . maybe later.

Interviewer: Well, you really shared a lot, Sandy. How are you feeling?

Sandy: I don't know.

Again, the interviewer can't tell whether Sandy is resistant or having trouble identifying and expressing her emotions.

Interviewer: That's OK. I can tell this is a difficult thing for you.

The interviewer wants Sandy to know that he is completely supportive of her thoughts and emotions as well as the pace at which she can handle them in the sessions.

Sandy: We're done for today?

Interviewer: Yes, I think the time's up. See you next time?

Sandy: Do you think I could see you more often?

Interviewer: What do you mean?

Sandy: Well, you know, maybe a couple of times a week? Once a week seems like so long a time to wait to talk.

Interviewer: It does seem like there is so much on your mind and you are beginning to get into some very difficult issues. How about we meet twice a week for a while?

Sandy [*relieved*]: That would be great. Are you sure you don't mind?

Interviewer: Absolutely not, I think it's a good idea.

Sandy: Good . . . there's one more thing . . . If I get really anxious or need to talk to you between our meetings, could I call you?

Interviewer: If things get really bad, you can call my office and let the answering service know that it is an emergency. They will reach me, and I'll call you back.

Sandy: I probably won't do that . . . I mean . . . I'll try not to, but it really helps to know you're there if I need you.

Interviewer: Well, let's see how it goes. I'll see you in a few days, OK?

Sandy: OK.

This client is beginning to open up about what appears to be a very serious sexual abuse situation from her childhood. She seems to feel compelled to talk about it, and it may be directly related to the panic attacks. Yet she also seems to have gaps in her memory, which may be a sign of some type of dissociative disorder, so common in trauma and abuse. The client's request for extra sessions and to have the interviewer available in emergencies is also very common in these types of more severe emotional cases. The interview that follows is the next session.

> **Interviewer:** How have things been going these last couple of days?
> *Sandy:* Not so good.
> **Interviewer:** How so?
> *Sandy:* Well, I've been thinking more about the abuse and really want to tell you more.
> **Interviewer:** OK, like what?
> *Sandy:* You know how I told you my mom's boyfriend told me he was going to bring me into bed with my mom?
> **Interviewer:** Yes.
> *Sandy:* Well, he did . . .
> **Interviewer:** What was that like for you?

Again, it is extremely important for the interviewer to not make any assumptions or try to express emotions that may not be what the client is feeling. This is a delicate time for Sandy, and she seems eager to talk it out with the interviewer.

> *Sandy:* I don't know.

Again Sandy seems unable or unwilling to express emotions.

> **Interviewer:** Do you think you can talk about it?

The interviewer purposely uses the word "think" instead of "feel," because of the client's apparent inability to express emotions.

> *Sandy:* I really thought my mom would get mad at him and not let him bring me to their bed, but he came and got me after my brothers were asleep.
> **Interviewer:** What happened?
> *Sandy:* I don't remember all of it . . . at least I don't think I can.
> **Interviewer:** You seem to have trouble with these memories.

Another empathic statement that is validating, furthering, and encouraging.

Sandy: Yeah, I'm so weird, aren't I?

Interviewer: I don't think you're weird, Sandy, I just think this is a difficult situation for you to fully recall. Go on . . .

Sandy: I think he had sex with me, I mean intercourse. He wanted my mom to watch. Then I think he made my mom have sex with me while he watched. I don't remember feeling anything. It was almost like a dream . . .

Interviewer: What do you mean, like a dream?

Sandy: Well, I couldn't feel anything, not even my body. Now this is crazy, I know, but I also could see myself on their bed from the ceiling, like I was floating above all of this. That's crazy, right?

Interviewer: I don't think so, Sandy. I think maybe it was your way of protecting yourself. Sounds like you were kind of removing yourself from those terribly scary and uncomfortable things. That can happen a lot in abuse and trauma.

Sandy: Really . . . seemed weird to me.

This intervention is both empathic and educational. The client is questioning her sanity, and it is important for the interviewer to help her realize that although her reactions may not be common in everyday functioning, in trauma and abuse they can be adaptive. This can help the client feel less anxiety and less alone with these strange events.

Interviewer: What else do you remember?

Sandy: I don't know for sure, it all sort of runs together. It seems like he came and got me every night, but I can't be sure. My memory is very blurry. I do remember when he started having my mom have sex with me while he watched.

Interviewer: Do you remember how that was for you?

Sandy: Not really . . . I know it happened, but I can't remember any feelings. It's like watching a movie or something.

Interviewer: It sounds like a horrible situation, Sandy, and one in which most people would probably be afraid. But it also sounds like you were able to somehow shut off your feelings. That's called dissociation.

Sandy: Yeah, I've heard of that . . . I guess that was a good thing, but sometimes I wish I could remember the feelings. I have a lot of trouble remembering feelings, or even feeling them.

Interviewer: You mean every day?

Sandy: Yeah, most of the time.

Interviewer: But not when you're having panic attacks.

Sandy: No, those I feel, and they're horrible.

Interviewer: I wonder if the panic attacks are connected to the sexual abuse in some way.

The interviewer can't be sure, but from a trauma and psychodynamic perspective, it's a safe assumption that the panic attacks could be tied to Sandy's unconscious memories. Neuroscience theory and research would probably trace these unconscious experiences and feelings to implicit memories and a chronically traumatized amygdala and limbic system in the brain, cutting off the experience from conscious awareness.

Several more sessions go by when Sandy talks about another memory of her abuse.

Interviewer: Hi Sandy. You look a little nervous to me today.

The interviewer has begun to recognize that although Sandy has difficulty naming and even discussing her feelings, she does communicate through what might be called microexpressions. The interviewer has begun commenting on these subtle emotional expressions in order to empathically connect with the client. Notice, however, that the interviewer always qualifies the intervention with a disclaimer, that is, "to me," so as not to presume or impose feelings or explanations on Sandy.

Sandy: Yeah . . . I guess I am . . .

Interviewer: Do you want to talk about it?

Sandy: I remembered a time when I was little and my mom was in the hospital. I was alone for a while with my mom's boyfriend. He still had sex with me, but it was different.

Interviewer: How was it different?

Sandy: I decided to take control.

Interviewer: I'm not sure I understand, take control.

Sandy: I mean that I initiated everything. I really got into it. I made him climax and I climaxed on top of him. It felt good and powerful, but I also felt like I was very bad.

Interviewer: This sounds like it was a very different experience for you.

Sandy: Yeah . . . I just knew I had to be in control. He liked it.

Interviewer: And you?

Sandy: I think I was just surviving.

Interviewer: I think that's a very important insight, Sandy.

Sandy: I don't know . . . I guess so.

Interviewer: How long did this abuse go on?

Sandy: Until DCFS took me away.

Interviewer: How did that happen, and when was it?

Sandy: I guess I was around thirteen or so. My mom's boyfriend told my mom that when I was old enough, he was going to marry me.

Interviewer: How did your mom react to that?

Sandy: She freaked out and called DCFS. She told them that her daughter was having sex with her boyfriend. They came to our house and interviewed everyone, and finally took me away and placed me in a group home for abused girls. Best thing that could have happened.

At the time of Sandy's sexual abuse, there were no child reporting laws, and DCFS handled the situation by removing Sandy.

Interviewer: It must have seemed like you were rescued.

Sandy: Yeah, except at the time I thought I was bad and that they were going to put me in jail. I was so relieved to find out that I was going to live at the group home and never have to go back to that house.

Interviewer: And you never did?

Sandy: Nope, never had to see those assholes again!

Interviewer: What a tremendous ordeal you had to go through.

Sandy: It wasn't such a big deal. There are probably a lot of other people who have been though much worse.

Interviewer: I guess you're right, but your story is a very horrible one, and I don't think or know of many people who have been through something so terrible.

Sandy: You think so? It's over now . . .

Interviewer: Yes it is, Sandy, but it sounds like the memories are still very much with you.

Sandy: Maybe . . .

Sandy spends the next few weeks discussing her marriage and children. She describes her marriage as a good one, but also talks about many one-night stands that she continues to have.

Interviewer: I can't tell by the look on your face how you're doing today, Sandy.

Sandy: I'm OK . . .

Interviewer: What's on your mind?

Sandy: I had another panic attack last night.

Interviewer: What happened?

Sandy: Same as always . . . sex with my husband.

Interviewer: What do you mean, sex with your husband?

Sandy: Well, every time we have sex, or I should say every time I climax when we have sex, I have this horrible panic attack and want to kill myself.

Sandy says this in a very matter-of-fact way with no emotion.

Interviewer: Do you remember how you felt?

Sandy: Well, if I let myself get really into sex with my husband, I start feeling numb, but I still climax. Then immediately I go into a panic attack. They usually last about an hour and then I'm OK. I don't know why I do it.

Interviewer: Have sex?

Sandy: No, let myself climax. I know I'm going to have a panic attack, but I don't want to just have sex with him and not climax. Every once in a while I climax, but when I do, I know that I'm going to feel horrible.

Interviewer: That's got to be difficult.

Sandy: It is what it is . . .

The interviewer is attempting to tie some emotion to Sandy's cutoff feeling state.

Interviewer: So every time you climax you have a panic attack?

Sandy: Oh no . . . just with my husband.

Interviewer: So you have other sexual partners?

Sandy: Only men. Even though my mom would have sex with me, I never got into women.

Interviewer: Is there any particular man you're seeing right now?

Sandy: No, it's not like that . . . I don't have relationships with other men, I just pick 'em up and have sex.

Interviewer: Where do you usually do this?

Sandy: At bars mostly. I can get any man if I put my mind to it.

Interviewer: You sound very confident about that.

Sandy: Well, it's true.

Interviewer: How long has this been going on?

Sandy: Oh, maybe a few years now.

Interviewer: Now Sandy, please help me understand. I thought you said that you have a good relationship with your husband. I'm confused about the sex with these other men.

Sandy: Well, I am too, a little. You see, I get these urges.

Interviewer: Urges?

Sandy: Yeah, they're sexual, I think. They build up and build up, and I feel like I have to go fuck some guy, any guy.

Interviewer: And these urges can't be satisfied by having sex with your husband?

Sandy: It's not the same thing with him. I love him, sex is different. And besides, I don't have panic attacks with these other guys.

Interviewer: You don't?

Sandy: Yeah, weird huh?

Interviewer: What do you make of that?

Sandy: I'm not sure. I don't really want to be with them; I mean, I don't want to know them, or see them again after sex, I just feel a tremendous urge to fuck them.

The interviewer is beginning to realize that the client has a tremendous struggle with her emotions, or lack of them. He also understands that Sandy's behavior has a compulsive quality to it and that her urges are important and can only be quieted by having sex with men she doesn't know. Although by most standards these behaviors would be considered immoral and wrong, the interviewer knows they are essential to Sandy's emotional survival and seem to be connected to her sexual abuse history. It is important not to judge the client, but help her unravel this complex dynamic.

Interviewer: Can you give me an example of how this happens, to help me better understand?

Sandy: Sure. I try to fight these urges. They don't really feel sexual, I guess, but I know I need to have sex to get rid of them. I go to a bar, find a guy, any guy actually, and come on to him. I told you I can seduce any guy. I have never failed. They all want sex, and I know how to give it to them. Well, we talk for a bit, then go somewhere and have sex. I really get into it, much more than with my husband. I can usually climax pretty quick. But these climaxes feel different than with my husband. They're like energy releases . . . it's hard to explain. Anyway, the urges go away, I leave the guy as quick as I can and go back to my life until the next time.

Interviewer: Well, that does help me understand things better. Thanks, Sandy.

Sandy: No problem.

Interviewer: What do you think is the difference between the sex you have with your husband and the sex you have with these other men?

Sandy: I don't know for sure, but you're right, they are different. When I'm with my husband, I feel love, and I let myself really feel vulnerable, you know, give myself to him. When I'm with the other guys, it's just sex, maybe not even that. I just need to be totally in control. It's really powerful and weird, huh?

Interviewer: Well, it seems clear that these two types of experiences serve two very different purposes. With your husband, it sounds like intimacy, and with the other men, it's a form of power or control for you.

Sandy: Yeah, that sounds right.

This interpretation from the interviewer has helped Sandy begin to understand the connection between her urges with these strangers and a need to feel in control. He is also acknowledging for the client that the two types of sex are very different, but also necessary for Sandy right now.

Interviewer: Well, we've really covered a lot today.

Sandy: Yeah, I'm really crazy, right?

Interviewer: No, Sandy, I really don't think so. I think these experiences with the men are an important outlet for you and fill a need to be in control, unlike the helplessness you experienced as a child in the sexual abuse with your mother and her boyfriend.

Sandy: I think you're right, but I really don't want to do these types of things any more; I just can't seem to stop. Can you help me?

Interviewer: We can certainly work on that together. We have to stop for today, but we can talk about this more next time, OK?

Sandy: Sure, see you then.

Sandy is not psychotic like Mark. Her emotional difficulties stem from horrendous childhood sexual abuse. Those experiences have dramatically shaped her life and sense of self. In order to become more emotionally healthy, so to speak, this client is working through her past and present with the interviewer. This is reparative work. It can be described as a psychodynamic approach, in that the interviewer is trying to help Sandy repair and strengthen her fragile self through a positive, caring, and trusting relationship with the interviewer. This will take time. Neuroscience indicates that before Sandy can become emotionally healthier, she will need to develop new neural networks of thought, emotion, and experience in both the work with the interviewer and in her life outside of treatment. This takes time, but can be successful.

RESEARCH IMPLICATIONS AND BASIS OF PRACTICE

Until recently, perhaps in the last twenty-five years, research in the area of severe mental health cases had reached only the levels of intuition, practice wisdom, and theoretical knowledge. Advances in neuroscience theory and empirical research now have elevated the knowledge base of working with more severe mental health cases to the validated level. An informed interviewer can now work with clients through the lens of both theory and empirical neuroscience knowledge to construct and carry out much more helpful, validated forms of treatment.

SUMMARY

The cases in this chapter demonstrate the unique challenges faced by the interviewer in working with clients suffering from more severe mental health issues. Key to this process as illustrated through the vignettes is the client's tendency to distort reality based upon an organic psychiatric disorder such as schizophrenia or developmental trauma as in childhood sexual abuse. These vignettes demonstrate the careful way in which the interviewer must build a helping relationship while managing these challenging issues.

RECOMMENDED READING

Psychodynamic Diagnostic Manual. (2006). Silver Spring, MD: Alliance of Psychoanalytic Organizations.

Part 3 of this text, "Conceptual and Research Foundations for a Psychodynamically Based Classification System for Mental Health Disorders," reports the recent empirical research on all types of psychotherapy and clinical practice. Interviewers of all professional disciplines will find it an invaluable aid in understanding the nuances of effective clinical treatment.

MULTIMEDIA SOURCES

Equus. (1977). Sydney Lumet (Director). United Artists.
A Beautiful Mind. (2001). Ron Howard (Director). Universal Pictures.

These two excellent films not only wonderfully capture the essence of severe mental health problems, but also provide compelling examples of interviewing and treatment approaches.

Interviewing Clients with Addictions and Dual-Diagnosis Problems

Interviewing clients suffering from mental health problems is a challenging endeavor. Often, clients with these difficulties are also dealing with some sort of substance abuse or addiction problem. This comorbidity complicates any type of professional interviewing because of the multiple factors and coping mechanisms inherent in the process. Clients with mental health issues usually are having some type of difficulty managing their emotions. The various theoretical models may describe this as the inability to self-soothe, or problems with object constancy, or simply managing anxiety. In many of these situations, clients turn to legal or illegal substances to fill those needs. Sometimes clients also resort to destructive behaviors for the same result, such as cutting, burning, or sexual acting out.

The case examples in this chapter demonstrate how an interviewer can successfully work with a client who is suffering from both a mental health disorder and addiction problems. This is considered dual diagnosis. The interviewer faces a delicate balance of surface- and depth-oriented interventions. In other words, the mental health issues may require deeper exploration, interpretation, and confrontation, but these intrapsychic interventions can stir up troubling emotional responses from clients that lead them to rely on their addiction for self-soothing. This client behavior can interrupt the depth-oriented interviewing process and require the interviewer to remain more surface focused in order to help manage the addiction. Once the addiction is sufficiently under control, the interviewer can resume the necessary emotional work, but always with an eye toward the addictive coping mechanisms of the client. This is a very daunting challenge for any interviewer.

CHRONIC MENTAL HEALTH AND SUBSTANCE ABUSE ISSUES

Mary is a thirty-year-old single woman on disability. She lives alone in subsidized housing, barely making ends meet with the small amount of money she receives each month. Mary has a history of mental health issues, including severe depression and anxiety stemming from childhood abuse. She has few, if any, friends and spends most of her time alone in her apartment, reading and surfing the Web. Mary has started seeing a male social worker to help her manage the depression and anxiety and to deal with the repercussions of her abuse. Mary is on medication for her symptoms, but also uses a number of legal and illegal substances for self-medication and recreational stimulation. She would be considered addicted to some of these substances by most mental health professionals. Mary also cuts herself from time to time in order to help her cope with the chronic emotional pain. The case example picks up after Mary has been in treatment for a month or so.

Interviewer: Well, Mary, how have things been going this week?

Mary: You know, the usual . . .

Interviewer: Do you want to talk about it?

Mary: What's there to talk about? It's always the same.

Interviewer: So I'm not sure I understand, Mary. Are you feeling like you want to talk about things today?

Mary: I guess so . . . I was cutting again last night.

Interviewer: Did something happen that made you feel like cutting?

Mary: Yeah, it was what we talked about last session.

Interviewer: If I remember correctly, we talked about a number of things. Can you help me understand what in particular contributed to this cutting?

Mary: We started talking more about my mom abusing me. I started to space out in the session, but when I got home, the memories came back more clearly and the only way I could stop them was by cutting . . . oh yeah, and drinking . . . drinking a lot!

Interviewer: So experiencing the memories made you feel compelled to cut and drink to help you deal with them?

Mary: That's how it always is.

Interviewer: I guess we may have gone too deep in our discussions about the abuse.

Mary: Well, I don't know. It seems to help when I'm here, and then when I'm alone, I can't handle the feelings.

The interviewer is beginning to recognize that there is a delicate balance between helping the client work through her abuse, and the subsequent need to self-soothe in a variety of ways. Mary obviously has a very limited capacity to manage these emotional states except through quasi-addictive measures. This is a challenging problem in treatment.

Interviewer: You mentioned that you started to space out in the session. Can you tell me about that?

Mary: Yeah. It happens all of the time. I want to talk about these things, I think, but my mind goes somewhere else.

Interviewer: When that happens, Mary, do you think you could tell me?

Mary: Well, I'd like to, but I can't always control it, and once I'm in it, I'm too scared to tell you.

Interviewer: Would it help if I was a little more attuned to you about this spacing out?

Mary: What do you mean, attuned?

Interviewer: I'm sorry, I'm not being clear. I guess I mean, if I start to sense that our discussions might be leading you to, as you say it, space out, maybe I can try to talk about it a bit to help identify it and keep it from causing so much trouble.

The interviewer has recognized the dynamic, and is now brainstorming with the client to find a way to better deal with this difficult dilemma.

Mary: Well, maybe. I don't think I'll be able to tell you, though.

Interviewer: I get that sense too, Mary, but maybe I can focus more of my attention on you to see if I can sense when you're beginning to distance.

This is not some type of magical or special ability by the interviewer. It is grounded in neuroscience and microexpressions that are communicated by all human beings. The mirror neurons in the human brain help all individuals cue in on the emotions and intentions of others. Now that the interviewer knows that Mary has a tendency to distance from intense emotions generated in the sessions, perhaps he can begin to pick up on more of the subtle cues and intervene in more helpful ways.

Mary: I guess so . . . it's worth a try.

Interviewer: I think if I can be helpful that way, it might keep you from using substances or cutting, at least when difficult emotions are coming up in the session.

Mary: I'm open to anything that will help stop that.

The interviewer is realizing that if he can recognize the emotional triggers for the client's dissociation, or spacing out as Mary calls it, he can shift the focus of the session from emotional and depth-oriented material to safer surface discussion.

Interviewer: Well, why don't we give that a try in the future? How have things been going otherwise?

Mary: I've pretty much been staying in my apartment. I don't go anywhere. I just read and listen to music. I also get stoned all the time.

Interviewer: How is that for you?

Mary: Well, it's like I just exist. I don't want things to be this way, but I don't seem to be able to change.

Mary is clearly stuck or immobilized by her situation. However, the interviewer realizes that exploring other options is at least a start.

Interviewer: Have you thought about what you would really like to do?

Mary: Yeah. I'd like to get off of disability and get a job. I'd like to have a real life. I feel like I'm just in limbo. I'm stuck.

Interviewer: Like your life is in a rut?

Mary: Exactly.

Interviewer: How often do you get out of your place?

Mary: Well, I come to see you, and I get groceries about once a month.

Interviewer: That's a start.

Mary: I guess so.

Interviewer: Do you think about going out?

Mary: Yeah, but when I do, I usually start to get anxious and then I use.

Interviewer: Use what?

Mary: Well, it depends how I'm feeling. I almost always take something to calm me down or put me out. Typically some type of antianxiety meds and alcohol. That usually does the trick.

Interviewer: So it sounds to me like you're really feeling emotionally handcuffed?

Mary: That's it in a nutshell.

Interviewer: Well, I think the fact that you made the effort to contact me and then have been coming to therapy is a very strong start. It means you're trying to change things, at least by physically coming here and talking about possibilities.

Mary: I just wish I could get out of this rut.

Interviewer: It sounds to me like your emotions get the best of you and then you're completely immobilized.

The interviewer is stating the obvious, but also trying to help the client recognize that her efforts so far are a step in the right direction. This is validating and encouraging.

Mary: Yeah, I know it's the drugs . . . you know . . . the using.

Interviewer: That keeps you from moving ahead?

Mary: Yeah. I need to stop, or at least cut back, but it's so hard.

Interviewer: Have you tried to do that?

Mary: Sure, but I go through withdrawal and get sick and eventually just start using again.

Interviewer: Have you thought about going to a treatment center?

Mary: I've done that a bunch of times and have had some pretty horrible experiences with doctors and staff. I'm not ever going back to a hospital!

Interviewer: Sounds like those were pretty bad times.

Mary: You can't imagine . . .

Interviewer: I know I can't, Mary, and I can understand why that isn't an option for you.

Mary: Good, because I wouldn't go even if you wanted me to.

Interviewer: I certainly wouldn't push you into something unless I thought you were a threat to yourself.

Mary: Well, if I was, I wouldn't tell you because you'd put me in the hospital.

Interviewer: You certainly don't have to talk about anything you don't want to in here.

Mary: I know . . . that's why I like coming here. But I want to get better. How do I do that?

Interviewer: At this point it does feel like we're stuck a bit, doesn't it?

Mary: Yeah, but I do feel better when I'm here.

Interviewer: How do you feel when you're here?

Mary: I feel safe most of the time, except when we get too into feelings, then I space and things get worse.

Interviewer: Would it be better if we didn't talk about the past or emotions?

Mary: No, I think it helps, but it also hurts and scares me.

Interviewer: Kind of a double bind, I guess.

Mary: Yeah.

Interviewer: It sounds to me like we kind of move a little ahead and then a little back. The discussions about your past and how things are in the present seem to help a little, but then if we go too far, you get triggered to use to help you manage the emotions.

This statement again is obvious, but a needed interpretation to help move ahead in the process.

Mary: Well . . . where do we go from here?

Interviewer: You said that sometimes it feels good when you're here. Maybe we can build on that.

Mary: I only feel that way when I'm here, in session. The minute I leave, it's like this doesn't exist. I get home and try to keep busy, but eventually the bad feelings start up and I go into my routine of using.

Interviewer: But when you're here, it's often OK, or even good?

Mary: Yeah, a lot of the time.

Interviewer: Well, I wonder if we might try to find a way to help you sustain some of those feelings in here when you're gone.

Mary: How would we do that?

Interviewer: Well, I was thinking . . . you've mentioned that you like to listen to music, read, and I think you've said even write sometimes?

Mary: Sometimes . . . I journal a bit.

Interviewer: I wonder if you try to write about how you're feeling and what you're thinking when you're at home, and bring the journal here so I can read it and we can talk about it. That might help us stay connected.

Mary: Well, it's a thought.

The session ends on this note. The interviewer has offered a tentative idea or plan that can accomplish at least two things for this client. First, the journaling might help Mary stay in touch with and get out her feelings, as well as bring this information back to the interviewer for further work in sessions. Second, this journaling might also serve as a bridge to keep Mary and the interviewer emotionally connected between sessions. Theoretically this could be considered a type of transitional object (Winnicott, 1971). The journal literally represents the relationship between the interviewer and client. It can become emotionally charged and act as a self-soothing mechanism for Mary. This idea might also minimize or even eventually replace some of Mary's destructive using.

The next session picks up several weeks after Mary has been journaling and discussing her writing in sessions.

Interviewer: Hi Mary. How was this week?

Mary: A little better, I think.

Interviewer: In what way?

Mary: Well, I think the journaling has really been helping me focus on my stuff, and I notice that I'm using less . . . I'm still using, but it's less.

Interviewer: Are you good with that?

The interviewer wants to remain nonjudgmental to allow the client to own the progress and decide for herself if the treatment is moving in a way that is helpful. If this idea comes exclusively from the interviewer, it can disrupt the client's ability to feel a sense of confidence about herself and instead incline her to rely on or look to the interviewer for acknowledgment or validation for progress. If the client is going to recover, she must be able to trust herself. This is the goal of all successful mental health treatment.

Mary: Yeah, but I want to stop using, and I'm not sure how to do that.

Interviewer: I know we've talked about this in the past, Mary, but have you reconsidered a recovery group like AA?

Mary [*angrily*]: I told you before, that crap doesn't work for me. I tried it a bunch of times, and it's always the same. I can't relate to the people, I don't like that expectation about a higher power, and it just seems superficial. I'm not doing that again.

Interviewer: OK, I get that. What about it seems superficial?

Mary: I just think stopping is more than just going to a group and talking about it. There's a reason I use, and I need to resolve that and I know the using will stop. I've already been able to cut back through our work together.

Interviewer: So you're feeling like the time here is enough to help stop the using?

Mary: I'm not sure; I just know that I feel better.

Interviewer: Mary, I respect your ideas. I was just thinking that maybe in addition to our work, a support group of some kind might help. I wasn't even thinking so much about the using as I was getting out and meeting new people, which is something you've also said you'd like to be able to do, isn't it?

Mary: Well yeah, but those people don't seem like my kind of people.

Interviewer: How so?

Mary: So many of them are so into that higher power thing and don't seem to work on themselves. They just seem to be using meetings to solve their problems. I think there's more to it than that. So, I can't really relate to them.

Interviewer: So maybe going to those groups actually makes you feel a little more isolated sometimes?

Mary: I think it does.

Interviewer: Well, I agree with you that things seem to be getting better. You've said the journaling has helped in our sessions and at home. You're not using as much, and you're also feeling good about that too.

This summary or paraphrasing is an intervention aimed at validating Mary's own approach to her healing, rather than suggesting that she adhere to any preconceived plan of action. Of course, Mary's objections to AA could be a form of resistance, but her obvious progress in sessions seems to contradict that idea.

Mary: I do want to start to get out and eventually find a way to get off disability and get a job. I'd also like to have a real relationship with a guy.

Interviewer: I know that's something we've discussed a lot. I think things are beginning to move in that direction. You've been able to work through a lot of your feelings, issues, and affects about your past, especially the abuse, and seem more confident and less anxious because of it. I also think we've been better able to manage your emotional reactions that contribute to the using, because of those important insights. Maybe now is the time to try and move ahead on some of these other issues.

This summary or interpretation is an attempt by the interviewer to help the client recognize that she has worked hard and is improving. It also provides some suggestions for moving ahead.

Mary: I want to do that . . .

This session ends with Mary feeling a stronger sense of self and better control over her addictive behaviors. One might say, from a psychodynamic standpoint, that this client has been able to repair aspects of herself that were damaged by her chronic childhood abuse through an empathic and nonjudgmental long-term relationship with the interviewer (McKenzie, 2011). From a neuroscience perspective, the interview relationship and interactions have helped Mary form new neural pathways that are a healthier way to function in everyday life. In fact, the effects of these new thoughts, emotions, and activities may be beginning to replace the more unhealthy, addictive aspects of this client's life (Cozolino, 2010). Some addictions experts would propose that a combination of surface-oriented cognitive-behavioral interventions targeted at altering behaviors (e.g., using), combined with psychodynamic methods aimed at repairing the emotional self (e.g., self psychology), is a more effective and comprehensive approach to successful dual-diagnosis addictions work (Levin, 1987).

THE DYING MAN REVISITED

In chapter 8, Al's case was presented as an example of working with general mental health cases. Al is dying, and working with a psychiatric nurse to examine his life and perhaps come to some closure with his estranged children. We revisit Al's case here because of his dual diagnosis: alcoholism in remission, depression, and narcissistic personality disorder traits. Working with clients who have comorbidity, such as Al, is a challenge for any interviewer because of the necessity to work on both the surface and intrapsychic levels in order to arrive at a successful outcome. The case example picks up after Al has begun to reach out to some of his children to try to repair some of the problems that he feels he may have contributed to in their lives.

> **Interviewer:** Hi Al. How have things been going with reaching out to your children?
> *Al:* Well, both good and bad.
> **Interviewer:** What do you mean?
> *Al:* I think I'm making some progress with some of my kids, but it's bringing up a lot of emotions for me and

reminding me of why I drank and even causing me to feel those urges to drink again.

Interviewer: Do you remember what kinds of issues are contributing to those feelings?

Al: Sort of . . . When I talk to my kids, they're pretty honest with me about how I hurt them. I mean, really honest . . . and sometimes angry. I didn't realize how I have affected their lives. When I let myself look at those things, I feel horrible about myself, and remember that I've always kind of felt insecure and inferior. I know that's why I started drinking.

Interviewer: When was that, Al?

Al: When I joined the navy at seventeen, in World War II.

Interviewer: That's a long time ago.

Al: Yeah, I know, but I still remember it.

Interviewer: Do you want to talk about it now?

Al: Sure. I felt pretty alone in the navy, even though I really wanted to be there. All the guys drank beer mostly, and I just joined in, you know, to be a part of the gang. I didn't realize it at the time, but I was becoming an alcoholic.

Interviewer: How do you know that?

Al: Because I used alcohol to cope with any kind of difficult emotions, instead of talking about them.

Interviewer: So you did that for a long time?

Al: Probably forty years or more.

Interviewer: But you don't drink or smoke now?

Al: I don't drink anymore, and my kids think I don't smoke, but I sneak an occasional cigarette once in a while.

Interviewer: Do you think you're still addicted to cigarettes?

Al: Probably.

Interviewer: How did you quit drinking?

Al: That's an interesting story. My drinking was getting so bad that I would just come home from work and start drinking my twelve-pack of beer. I wouldn't even have dinner with my wife and kids; I'd just sit in front of the TV and drink. I would get through the beer pretty quick, and then I'd start drinking straight bourbon. I would usually pass out on the couch, right in front of my kids. When it was bedtime for everyone, my wife would wake me up and we'd go upstairs to bed. I did this every night of the week, and even worse on the weekends. I mean, I did this all of the time.

Interviewer: Sounds like you were pretty involved with alcohol at the expense of everything else.

Al: Except my job. I never missed work, even though I was pretty hungover most days.

Interviewer: Some people might say you were a functional alcoholic.

Al: That's what I learned in AA.

Interviewer: When did you get involved with AA?

Al: Well, I'm getting to that. I guess my wife was getting really sick and tired of my drinking and the way I treated the kids. I never abused my wife, physically or verbally, but I was very rough on my kids. I think she finally couldn't take it anymore.

Interviewer: What happened?

Al: One night when I was really out of it, but not passed out yet, my wife came over to me and picked up the beer I was drinking and poured it over my head and went to bed.

Interviewer: That must have been a real shocker.

Al: Yeah, I was so embarrassed and knew right at that moment that things had to change. I apologized to my wife. We talked, and I started going to Alcoholics Anonymous meetings the next night.

Interviewer: So the experience with your wife was the powerful catalyst that helped you change?

Al: I think it was like the straw that broke the camel's back. Things had been building up for years. That incident just made me finally realize that things had to change. Remember, my wife is everything to me. I was afraid she'd leave me.

Interviewer: So how did AA go?

Al: It was great. I haven't had a drink in over fifteen years.

Interviewer: That's quite an accomplishment, Al.

The interviewer wants to validate Al's genuinely significant accomplishment, but knows that there are still, even after fifteen years of sobriety, a lot of issues with both Al and his family to be resolved. Professionals might say that Al is sober, but a "dry drunk," meaning he hasn't fully dealt with, worked on, or changed his behaviors. This is a difficult topic to broach with this type of client, but not at all uncommon.

Al: Thanks, I am proud of that.

Interviewer: How was the AA experience for you?

Al: Wonderful. I met a lot of good people who I could really relate to and talk about my drinking and other important things.

Interviewer: Sounds like it was a very supportive environment.

Al: Well, you know, your support group is really a lifeline. I talked out a lot of things with them. It kept me from drinking.

Interviewer: In some ways, that could almost be a substitute for drinking, couldn't it?

This is a risky intervention, but Al is trying to work on improving his relationships with his family. To do so, he will probably need to be able not only to talk with them, but also to understand the ways in which he may have kept himself from interacting with his kids, and utilized AA to contain and support him. This dynamic obviously has both positive and negative possibilities. On one hand, AA can be an important lifeline for people suffering from addiction. On the other hand, if AA is used exclusively, it can become a barrier to recovery and reconciliation with the client's significant others. AA is designed to help the addict stop using and to move through a series of steps toward working through significant emotional and personal issues (Kinney, 2012). If the steps are done successfully, the addict not only stops using, but is able to mend some of the complex problems that derived from the addiction. It is also usually recommended that the addict seek outside professional counseling to help repair the emotional difficulties that contributed to the addiction in the first place. Unfortunately, many people with addictions do not work through all of the steps. As in Al's case, they may use their AA group only for support and not "work the program." This results in the "dry drunk" syndrome, meaning that the using stops, but the behaviors and emotional difficulties remain frozen in time. The interviewer is trying to delicately negotiate this process with Al.

> **Al:** I hadn't thought about that, but I guess you're right. Was that OK?
>
> **Interviewer:** I think it was a lifesaver for you, Al. I'm wondering, though, how did things go in working on your twelve steps in the program?
>
> **Al:** I got through a lot of them, but to be honest, I don't think I did a good job making amends or even taking a personal inventory. I worked on all of those things with my sponsor and the group, but not so much with my family.
>
> **Interviewer:** So that explains a lot of the reasons for your genuine interest in doing that now with your family.
>
> **Al:** Yeah, I think it's going to be tough. I already am feeling urges to drink because of how bad I feel. I really don't blame my family for hating me. I was pretty horrible to them.
>
> **Interviewer:** Do you really think they hate you?
>
> **Al:** Oh yeah, some of them do, I'm sure.

It is very important at this point for the interviewer to help clarify and reframe some of Al's thoughts and emotions to help him proceed with his work. This could be considered a combination of narrative, cognitive-behavioral therapy, and education.

> **Interviewer:** Al, I think it's important to clarify something in all of this. Unfortunately you can't change what happened in the past. I know you have many regrets and wish

you could change things, but you can't. I also don't think dwelling on this in a self-destructive way is helpful. I do think moving ahead and working with your kids, as you and they are able, may have some possibilities for reparation and reunion. On the other hand, it may not. Despite your talking to them, some of your kids may never feel differently or may not be in a place that they can change right now. Maybe they will in the future. However, I don't think that means you should give up. Trying to work with your kids is going to be good for you. It's going to make you feel better about yourself. And that is so important in your life. Going through this process might just change some or all of the negative things you feel about yourself. That's what therapy is all about.

This powerful interpretation is clear, honest, supportive, and direct. The interviewer feels it is necessary if Al is to understand the process and move ahead. The timing is perfect. Any intervention of this type must be given at the proper time. Fortunately for the interviewer, it seems to be correct.

Al: I know you're right, and I know I really want to do this, whether things change or not. It's for me, but also for my kids. However things go, at least I will know that I tried and did the best I could.
Interviewer: You are absolutely right, Al.

With this understanding, Al continued to move ahead in his work with his children. Some of them reconciled with him, while others did not. However, that did not stop Al from moving ahead. He did not return to drinking, and he did begin to work his twelve-step program and continued in therapy until his death.

This particular case exemplifies the necessity of a two-pronged approach to working with clients suffering from a dual diagnosis. Al initially worked only on stopping his drinking, using his AA support group as an emotional substitute for alcohol. That helped stop the using, but Al was still emotionally wounded and vulnerable to seeking out alcohol as a self-soothing mechanism. The therapy with the interviewer also deterred drinking, but more importantly helped Al to repair his fragile sense of self and enabled him to reach out to his family for reconciliation and support.

RESEARCH IMPLICATIONS AND BASIS OF PRACTICE

The field of dual-diagnosis work is just beginning to enter into the validated knowledge area of research. Intuition, practice wisdom, and theory continue to inform all professionals working with this population. Fortunately there seems to be a growing realization that successful work with this population requires an approach that combines a focus on some form of sobriety along with deeper intrapsychic work to repair the emotional deficits that contributed to the onset of the addiction. Only this type of combined approach can combat the horrendous relapse percentage (Levin, 1987; O'Hare, 2005; PDM, 2006).

SUMMARY

Professional interviewing with dual-diagnosis clients can be extremely challenging. For years these two areas, addictions and mental health disorders, were treated as separate entities, resulting in faulty treatment outcomes and high recidivism rates. The two very different and complex case examples in this chapter demonstrate the trials and tribulations for the interviewer in successfully working simultaneously with both problems. Only a careful and informed interviewer can hope to help these troubled and vulnerable clients achieve a positive outcome.

RECOMMENDED READING

Kinney, J. (2012). *Loosening the grip* (10th ed.). New York: McGraw-Hill Higher Education.

This classic book on alcoholism has been used in addictions and alcoholism counseling training programs for generations.

O'Hare, T. (2005). *Evidence-based practices for social workers: An interdisciplinary approach*. Chicago: Lyceum Books.

O'Hare's work has numerous examples of evidence-based interventions with the dual-diagnosis population.

Levin, J. (1987) *The treatment of alcoholism and other addictions.* New York: Jason Aronson.

Levin's book on addictions treatment is essential for any professional interviewer looking to understand the complex and delicate combination of surface-oriented and intrapsychic approaches to working with this population. His emphasis on self psychology and addictions is especially compelling.

Psychodynamic diagnostic manual. (2006). Silver Spring, MD: Alliance of Psychoanalytic Organizations.

Part 3 of the PDM refers to contemporary research that is germane to understanding the neuroscience and empirical aspects of work with dual-diagnosis clients.

MULTIMEDIA SOURCES

Days of Wine and Roses. (1962). Blake Edwards (Director). Warner Brothers.

This is probably the most famous of all of the films on alcoholism. Jack Lemmon and Lee Remick are outstanding as a couple struggling with this horrendous problem.

I'm Dancing as Fast as I Can. (1982). John Hofsiss (Director). Paramount Pictures.

Jill Clayburgh is excellent in this film about a television producer addicted to tranquilizers.

Clean and Sober. (1988). Glenn Gordon Caron (Director). Warner Brothers.

Michael Keaton provides a powerful example of a cocaine- and alcohol-addicted personality.

When a Man Loves a Woman. (1994). Luis Mandoki (Director). Buena Vista Pictures.

This compelling film about a couple dealing with addiction in their relationship offers the professional interviewer a very realistic example of the challenges of this problem.

Leaving Las Vegas. (1995). Mike Figgis (Director). United Artists.

Nicolas Cage gives an Oscar-winning performance as an alcoholic wanting to drink himself to death. His desperate and self-destructive persona paints a true picture of how bleak late-stage addiction can become.

Alcoholics Anonymous Web Site, www.aa.org.

This is the official website for what has become one of the most important resources for people suffering from addictions. It is also an excellent resource for families and professional interviewers from any discipline.

Interviewing in Middle Phase and Termination

The same interventions and theoretical approaches used in the beginning phase of the interviewing process continue throughout the course of the work. As the relationship develops with the client, however, a stronger degree of trust and intimacy also develops. As a result, the interviewer and client form a relational bond that helps facilitate the therapeutic healing process, in the same way that family members, those in strong friendships, and couples usually get to know and trust each other more deeply over time. The interviewing relationship is different because it is not mutual and, as a result, can become even more trusting and intimate than many other relationships in the client's life. That bond is probably stronger in long-term work, but can develop significantly even in short-term work. Termination is actually the goal in any treatment and paradoxically should be considered and kept in the forefront of any professional interviewer's mind as he or she works with all clients. This chapter provides case examples of the middle and ending phases of the interviewing process.

MIDDLE PHASE INTERVIEWS

The case of Linda has been covered in chapters 2 and 5. This client came to therapy because of difficulties in her marriage. Over time, Linda revealed to the interviewer that she had been having an affair with a man from work. She has also discussed details of her unhappy marriage and her lonely and isolated childhood. Finally, Linda, with the help of the interviewer, is beginning to recognize that perhaps in some ways she is replicating aspects of her childhood, especially her estranged and inconsistent relationship with her father, in both her marriage and affair. The interviewer has been using a psychodynamic relational approach with Linda to help her uncover and repair the difficulties from her past that are interfering in her ability to live a happier life. The case example in this chapter picks up about six months after the sessions discussed in chapter 5. Linda has been in therapy for nearly a year by now. She is still in an unhappy marriage; she has recently managed, with the help of the interviewer, to end her unhappy affair with the man from work, but is still struggling.

> **Interviewer:** Hi Linda. How has your week been?
> **Linda:** Oh, OK I guess.
> **Interviewer:** You don't sound like things are going OK. Do you want to talk about it?

By this point in a longer-term relationship, the interviewer should be able to sense and pick up on even the subtlest of emotions and quickly respond in empathic ways to the client.

> **Linda:** You know me too well. I've met another man.
> **Interviewer:** Tell me about that.
> **Linda:** I don't work with him. I met him at a social event. He seems really nice. He wants to get together for coffee. Should I see him?
> **Interviewer:** Why are you asking me, Linda?

After so long in treatment, it should be obvious to the client that the interviewer does not provide this kind of advice, yet Linda seems to want approval.

Linda: I know . . . you're not going to tell me what to do. I'm still married, I know, but I really don't feel like I'm married, and this guy seems so nice. It's just having coffee.

Interviewer [*gently confrontational*]: But it sounds like you are having mixed feelings.

Linda: Well . . . he's married . . . just like the last guy.

Interviewer: And how are you feeling about that?

Linda: I have mixed feelings. I know it probably won't go anywhere, but part of me doesn't care. I just feel lonely, and he seems nice.

Interviewer: You've talked about feeling like he's nice a few times now. What do you mean by that?

Linda: He seems interested in me. You know . . . what I think, where I work. He also said I was pretty. I haven't heard that in a long time.

Interviewer: So he makes you feel good about yourself.

Linda: Yeah. Is that wrong?

Interviewer: I would hope you know by now, Linda, that I would not judge you. I can tell that talking with this man makes you feel good about yourself, and those are feelings that are few and far between. However, I can't help but see a possible similarity between this man and the other you were having an affair with just recently. Do you think that might be right?

Linda: Yeah, I've thought about that too, but this would just be coffee. I'm not sleeping with him or anything.

Interviewer: So you're feeling like maybe a friendship with this man might be a good thing for you?

Linda: I'm so lonely. I really think I want to at least meet with him in a safe place.

Interviewer: Like I said, Linda, I can understand your feelings, but as your counselor I also feel obligated to mention the possible complications here.

Linda: I know . . . I'll be careful.

The interviewer sees a possible difficulty here for this client. To the interviewer, it feels like a pattern and continuation of the kind of relationship that Linda has just ended. He carefully and in a nonjudgmental manner presents this possibility to Linda, recognizing that she may not be able to fully see it, or have much insight into the situation. It is not the interviewer's responsibility in this situation to judge or forbid Linda to meet with this man, but it is appropriate for him to point out the possible dynamics of a relationship, and how that might be a pattern in her life. Although the client is probably not ready to hear it, she appears to be entering into relationships with men who are unavailable. On a deeper psychological and attachment level, this could be seen as similar to what she experienced with her father. The interviewer will take these silent insights into consideration as the sessions move forward. The next session takes place about a month later.

Interviewer: Hi Linda. How have things been going?

Linda: Good news . . . I think.

Interviewer: What's that?

Linda: I asked my husband for a divorce.

Interviewer: Wow, that is big news. This has been coming for a long time . . . I mean . . . you have been thinking about approaching him about it for a while.

Linda: Well, I finally decided that the kids are older. I think they can handle it, and besides, I'm tired of seeing him treat them so badly. I also figured out that I think I can make it on my own financially.

Interviewer: Sounds like you have really thought this out. What did your husband say?

Linda: Almost nothing. He basically said OK, and that he would start looking for a place as soon as possible. That was relieving.

Interviewer: Yes.

Linda: I feel like a big weight has been lifted from me. We've talked about this since almost the beginning of our sessions, but I wasn't ready until now. You really helped me get here.

Interviewer: Well, thank you, Linda, but you have really done the work. I've just been here to help you explore the issues and make a clear decision.

Linda: I know . . . but I don't think I could have done it without you.

Interviewer: I think you've had the strength all along, it was just a process, but I'm glad to be helpful.

These statements by the interviewer are extremely crucial and important because they validate the client's process. It would have been easy for the interviewer to take credit for this work, or simply thank Linda for her gratitude, but clarifying that it was a mutual process and true work on her part that made things possible helps build a stronger sense of self and confidence in Linda. This is the hallmark of many of the psychodynamic and relational forms of practice. It takes time to build this type of character in the client through a patient, empathic, and nonjudgmental professional relationship.

Linda: Well, thank you. I have worked very hard.

Interviewer: You certainly have.

Linda: Oh, one other thing happened.

Interviewer: What's that?

Linda: You know that man I've been seeing?

Interviewer: Yes.

Linda: Well, we started having an affair. It just happened. We were just meeting at restaurants, then some bars, and one night we just got a room and it happened. I know you're going to think I'm bad.

Interviewer: Why are you worried about what I might think of you?

Linda: Well, I know you mentioned how the thing with this guy could turn out to be the same type of thing that I had before, but this time it's different.

Interviewer: How is it different this time?

Linda: He told me he's unhappy in his marriage and that he's going to leave his wife.

Interviewer: How are you feeling about this?

The interviewer can't help but wonder whether this situation is going to be a reenactment of her previous affair, as well as cause Linda more distress. However, he also recognizes that simply stating that will not change Linda's decision unless she has those same insights. At this point in time, that does not appear to be the case. The interviewer is feeling even more certain that timing and patience will be extremely necessary in this situation.

Linda: Well, of course I'm apprehensive, but he seems so good and honest. He talks about his marriage, and I get the sense that he's as lonely and unhappy as I am. I really think this could be a good thing. Please don't be upset with me.

Interviewer: I'm really not upset with you, Linda. However, I feel the same sense of cautiousness that we discussed when you first mentioned seeing this man. I want you to be happy. In my role as your therapist, though, I also feel it's my job to help you understand and explore these kinds of choices.

Linda: I know . . . we'll talk about it, and I'll be careful.

The interviewer is also beginning to recognize that Linda is looking to him for guidance in much the same way a child might turn to a parent. This could just be the nature of their interviewing relationship, or a form of transference. In other words, Linda may be using the interviewer as a substitute parent to help build the self-confidence she never received in her childhood. She may also be using the interviewer as a substitute father, one who can be reliable, caring, and consistent. These silent insights or hunches are carried into the next series of sessions. The following session occurs about two months later.

Linda: Things have not been going so well.

Interviewer: What do you mean, Linda?

Linda: You know I told you that the guy I'm seeing was going to leave his wife?

Interviewer: Yes.

Linda: He told me last night that she's pregnant. He also said that he doesn't think he can leave her now, not while she's pregnant. He said once the baby comes he'll be able to leave.

Interviewer: How are you feeling about this new development?

Linda: I don't know if I can trust him.

Interviewer: How do you feel about the fact that he obviously has been having sex with his wife while he's been seeing you?

The interviewer realizes that this confrontation is abrupt, but given his history with the client and the nature of their discussions around the relationship with this new man, it seems normal and appropriate.

Linda: Well, I didn't like it, but he told me that he had to have sex with her or she might suspect that he was having an affair. He thought she was using birth control, but obviously not.

Interviewer: But how did you feel about him having sex with his wife while he was seeing you, especially since he told you he was going to leave her?

Again, this is a very strong confrontation, but necessary given the client's avoidance of her feelings in the discussion. It is very important to remember that this case is in the middle phase of interviewing, where interventions of this sort are necessary and appropriate in the process. This type of discussion would be premature in the early phase of work.

Linda: Well, he is married, so I guess that's the normal thing to do.

Interviewer: So you aren't upset by this?

Linda: A little I guess, but if he leaves her, I'll be OK.

Interviewer: And given this latest news, how confident are you that he'll leave his wife?

Linda: I really want to believe him. Do you think I can?

Interviewer: I really couldn't possibly know, Linda, but I can tell this is very important to you.

Linda: I can't tell either. I am going to have to just trust him for now.

The sessions with the client continue in this manner, that is, Linda spending most of her time discussing her week and time with her lover. She continues to be reassured by him that he will leave his wife once the baby is born. The following interview takes place about four months after the birth of the baby.

Interviewer: How have things been going, Linda?

Linda: Not so good. We talked again about him leaving now that the baby has been born. It's been four months now, you know.

Interviewer: That long, huh? Well, how did the discussion go?

Linda: You won't be surprised to hear that he feels like he just can't leave right now. He says his wife really needs him to help with the baby. He says he feels too guilty to leave.

Interviewer: And how did you react?

Linda: I got really upset and started to cry like I usually do. He said he would definitely leave eventually, but it might not be until his child is in school now. He just doesn't feel he can leave his wife alone with a baby.

Interviewer: So now the timeline has been moved back even further.

Linda: Yeah, I don't know what to do. Part of me feels like I should either leave him or give him an ultimatum. Either he leaves by a certain time, or things are over.

Interviewer: And the other part of you?

Linda: I really love him and don't want to lose him. I think I can hold out for a while longer.

Interviewer: I don't think this is just me, Linda. It seems like this man's promise to you just can't be trusted.

This may seem like a bold, definitive statement, but the fairly long history of broken promises from the client's lover warrants it. The intervention is a confrontation of sorts and a clear reality check for the client.

Linda: But I really love him and want to be with him.

Interviewer: I can tell that you do, but it would appear that things may stay this way for a long time, maybe forever. How would you feel if he never left his wife?

Linda: I think eventually I would have to leave him. I don't think I could take it forever.

Interviewer: You know, Linda, we've been talking about this situation for quite some time. We've also spent a good deal of time discussing the other relationship you had, and the disappointment you continually felt when your father let you down and wasn't consistently available for you. I think there is a pattern going on here. That's not a criticism, Linda, I just think you are repeating and reliving something that is familiar.

This is a timely and necessary interpretation. Enough time has passed in the interviewing process, and the interviewer has been involved in enough discussions with this client to share this insight as a way of helping her resolve the situation.

Linda: Do you really think so?

Interviewer: Yes I do, Linda. Now that doesn't mean you have to change anything about this situation if you don't want to, but I think it's helpful to realize what might be fueling your continuation in this relationship, and what probably was involved in the other one.

Linda: So I should leave him?

Interviewer: I didn't say that. That is your decision. However, I think that you may continue to experience these sad and frustrating feelings as long as you are with this man. Do you think you could live with that?

Linda: I'm not sure, but probably not.

Unfortunately, the sessions with this client continue in this manner for several years. Linda's lover never leaves his wife, and Linda never leaves him. She leaves and returns to therapy over the years, always coming back with the same concern about her lover, and the sad feelings that she can't seem to resolve. The client becomes more and more aware that she is, in fact, reenacting the scenario with her father, but is willing to tolerate the emotional pain of it as long as she can continue the relationship with this man. Sometimes interviewing situations cannot reach a successful conclusion despite the best efforts and intentions. For Linda, this is one of those times.

SUCCESS AND TERMINATION

In chapter 9, Sandy's case was presented as an example of interviewing and treatment with a survivor of sexual abuse. Sandy is revisited here as an example of the middle phase and termination of interviewing. The case example picks up several months after Sandy's last session. The reader may recall that Sandy is a survivor of severe, chronic childhood sexual abuse perpetrated by her biological mother and her mother's boyfriend. Sandy is now thirty years old, and working with the interviewer on the repercussions of this horrendous abuse. She is suffering from panic attacks, which she experiences randomly, but especially after climaxing during sex with her husband. Sandy is also involved with many anonymous men whom she meets at bars, has sex with, and never sees again. She describes these events as compulsive activities, feeling strong urges to "pick up" these men. Ironically, when Sandy climaxes while engaged in sex with these men, she does not have a panic attack.

Interviewer: How's the week been, Sandy?

Sandy: Not so good. I've been having those urges again, and I had a horrible panic attack when I had sex with my husband this week.

Interviewer: I'm sorry to hear that, Sandy. How have you been handling these things?

Sandy: With my husband, I just have to be by myself and tough it out. I feel really suicidal and want to die, but eventually know it will go away.

Sandy talks about these events with little or no emotion, almost as if they are things she is witnessing, not actually experiencing. This might be called dissociation.

Interviewer: That sounds like a horrible experience.

Sandy: It is . . . but I'm not going to stop having sex with my husband.

Interviewer: How often do you have sex with him?

Sandy: Maybe every month or so. I get really whacked out when I do, so I don't do it very much.

Interviewer: You mentioned the urges. How have you been handling those?

Sandy: Pretty good so far. I haven't picked up any guys for about a month. But I'm really feeling like I need to get off and be in control, so it won't be long now.

Interviewer: What is the longest you have gone without having sex with strange men?

Sandy: This is the longest, I think. Hey, maybe this therapy thing is working.

Interviewer: That would be nice. When you experience these urges, do you ever try to do other things to keep yourself from acting on them?

Sandy: Sometimes I drink, but that doesn't really help much, or for long.

Interviewer: So eventually you give in to them.

Sandy: So far.

Interviewer: How have other things been going?

Sandy: Well, my kids are good, and I always like to work at the restaurant, but I think I'm going to apply for a new job.

Interviewer: Where at?

Sandy: As a cook at a day care center.

Interviewer: That sounds interesting. What do you like about it?

Sandy: Well, I certainly know how to cook, the money is much better, and the hours, and I kind of like being around the kids.

Interviewer: Sounds like it would be good all around for you.

Sandy: Yeah, I hope I get it.

Several weeks go by, and Sandy does get the day care job.

Interviewer: How are you this week?

Sandy: I got the job.

Interviewer: Great! How is it going?

Sandy: I really like it. I don't just cook, I get to drive their bus and pick up some of the kids. They also let me watch the kids sometimes when the child care workers are on break. It's only a few minutes, but I love it.

Interviewer: What do you like about it?

Sandy: I don't know, I just think I connect with kids, especially the infants and toddlers. A lot of people don't like that group because they're so high maintenance, but I just love to hold them and feed them and just be with them. It's a great feeling. They're so vulnerable, and it feels good to be able to protect them.

Interviewer: You certainly didn't get a lot of that when you were little.

Sandy: That's for sure. You know, I hadn't thought about it, but that's probably part of why I like it so much.

Interviewer: How have things been going with the panic attacks?

Sandy: Well, I did pick up a guy the other day . . . took care of the urge. I haven't been having sex with my husband lately though . . . I just don't want to get those horrible feelings.

Interviewer: I can certainly understand that.

The interviewer is intrigued by what appears to be a very positive event in the client's life, that is, the new job. This may actually present an opportunity for Sandy to find a healthy outlet for her emotions and perhaps even become a reparative activity of sorts. Some might call it sublimation, meaning substituting a positive activity for something painful or dysfunctional. In other words, by Sandy's caretaking children instead of hurting herself though random sex, she might be in a healing process. The interviews pick up months later.

Interviewer: How's your week?

Sandy: I'm not sure . . .

Interviewer: Something's not right.

Sandy: I guess so . . .

Interviewer: I can tell you're upset, Sandy. Can you talk about it?

Sandy: Well, work is going really well, but I've been having these dreams, or maybe memories, and I've been feeling really suicidal lately.

Interviewer: When you say suicidal, what do mean?

Sandy: I don't think I want to kill myself, but I just don't feel like living.

Interviewer: So you don't really have a plan, you are just feeling like you'd rather not be alive.

Sandy: Yeah . . . I guess that's it.

In any interviewing situation, suicide ideation must be taken seriously and explored with the client in order to determine if there is an actual suicide threat. In Sandy's case, suicidal feelings are common, as they can be for many survivors of sexual abuse. It does not appear to the interviewer that this is an actual threat, but it does sound like the feelings may be increasing for some reason.

Interviewer: You mentioned having dreams, or maybe memories? Can you explain that a little more for me?

Sandy: Yeah. I see myself as that little girl being sexually abused in all sorts of sick ways. I know it's me, but in the dream I'm not actually in my body. I feel like I'm floating above the bed looking down at everything. For the first time I'm really beginning to have strong feelings. I can tell I was terrified and feeling trapped. I think those were real feelings. I wake up in a panic and just want to die.

Interviewer: So maybe you are beginning to have some very clear memories and feelings about all that happened.

Sandy: I think so, but why now, after all these years?

Interviewer: I don't think that's unusual at all, Sandy. In my experience working with survivors of sexual abuse, memories and feelings can be out of awareness or emotionally hidden for years. It's the way your mind protects you from those horrible thoughts and feelings. I think you must be ready to deal with them now. We've been working on this for quite a while.

Sandy: I think you're right, but I still don't like it. Another thing . . . I've stopped having those urges. I can tell I'm not going to pick up guys any more.

Interviewer: How do you feel about that?

Sandy: Good, I guess, but it feels so strange. I feel like a different person.

Interviewer: Well, it does sound like you're changing.

Sandy: They asked me if I wanted to work at the day care center as a child care worker. They want me to work with the infants and toddlers.

Interviewer: And not be a cook anymore?

Sandy: Yeah, isn't that great?

Interviewer: I think it's wonderful. You really love working with those babies.

Sandy: I start next week.

Interviewer: I think I understand what you meant a while ago when you said it's been a mixed week. You've had some really scary times, and also some great changes in your life with work.

Sandy: Yeah, and they want me to go to school to study how to be a professional child care worker.

Interviewer: That sounds great. What do you think about it?

Sandy: I don't know. I've never been that good at school. You remember I dropped out of high school and got my GED. I want to go to college, I just don't know if I will be able to do it.

Interviewer: So you're a little unsure of yourself.

Sandy: Yeah, but I'm definitely going to do it.

The session ends shortly thereafter. Over the next year, Sandy continues to work on her abuse issues. She has successfully eliminated her urges to be with anonymous men; however, she continues to experience panic attacks and suicidal ideation when she climaxes during sex with her husband. On a more positive note, Sandy has been very successful in school and was promoted to a supervisor position at the day care center. She is beginning to feel better about herself and seems to have come to some psychological repair and reconciliation regarding her childhood abuse. Sandy continues in therapy to feel safe and secure through her relationship with the interviewer. The following session continues this process.

Interviewer: Hi Sandy. How are things with you?

Sandy: Pretty good. Work is really going well, and I'm getting closer and closer to finishing my program at the college.

Interviewer: That's wonderful news. You really have been successful.

Sandy: It never would have happened if it wasn't for you.

Interviewer: Well, that's very nice of you to say, but I think you had a very big part in all of this success. You've worked through a terrible life situation, changed your career, eliminated some self-destructive behaviors, and seem to be feeling really good about yourself.

Sandy: One thing I've learned is that you never get over the abuse. I think you have to accept it as a part of who you are. After all, those experiences don't define me, but they are a part of me and made me who I am. If I hadn't gone through the abuse, I don't think I could be as good of a child care worker. My passion for that work comes from what I've learned and gone through.

Interviewer: That's really profound, Sandy.

Sandy: Well, I learned it from you.

Interviewer: I think we discovered it together.

Sandy: Well . . . maybe.

Interviewer: How are you doing with the panic attacks and suicidal ideation?

Sandy: It's still there, but not as bad. I can handle it because I know the feelings won't destroy me, and that they will pass.

Interviewer: That's a really positive take on it.

Sandy: It is what it is . . . I can't do anything more about it.

Interviewer: It seems to me that you have come to some acceptance then.

Sandy: Yep. You know . . . I was wondering if we could try meeting every other week.

Interviewer: What makes you want to do that?

Sandy: I'm feeling better, and actually I don't really feel like I have a lot to talk about.

Interviewer: That's fine with me. I think it's a good idea.

Sandy: Now, don't get me wrong. I'm not stopping and I'm not going away. You'll still see me, won't you?

Interviewer: Of course I will.

The therapy with Sandy continued every other week for nearly a year. During that time, the interviewer worked with her to begin the termination process. They revisited the work they had done over the past years and the remarkable improvement that Sandy had made in her life. They also discussed Sandy's worries about leaving therapy. She had come to rely on it as a type of security blanket. She realized over time that there really was not much to talk about, but knowing the appointment was there was her hold on a secure reality. Winnicott's object relations theory would recognize this as a form of "transitional objects or phenomena." As Sandy became more confident and emotionally repaired, she was gradually able to relinquish the therapy in much the same way an infant abandons a teddy bear or blanket. Even after therapy ended, Sandy would occasionally call the interviewer just to connect for a brief moment. This was a truly successful therapy and termination. It wasn't perfect, and Sandy continued to experience panic and occasional suicidal thoughts, but she was generally happier and certainly not the tormented young woman who came to interviews years earlier.

RESEARCH IMPLICATIONS AND BASIS OF PRACTICE

Attachment and loss are interrelated concepts tied to termination, that is, separation-individuation. The recent advances in the understanding of attachment theory, infant research, neuroscience, and evidence-based practice have elevated the level of research to validated knowledge (Ainsworth, Blehar, Waters, & Wall, 1978; PDM, 2006; Bowlby, 1969; Stern, 2000; Cozolino, 2010). Intuitive knowledge has always indicated the importance of the development of healthy emotional relationships to the ability to function successfully throughout life. Practice wisdom further advanced those notions through years of interviewing experience in all of the helping professions. Finally, research is beginning to demonstrate a level of validated knowledge not only regarding interviewing of any length, but also the termination process with a variety of clients (Minnix, Reitzel, & Pepper, 2005; Shulman, 1999; O'Hare, 2005). The future of research in these areas continues to look very promising.

SUMMARY

The interviewing process is virtually identical in all phases of the professional helping process. However, the quality of the relationship between the interviewer and the client changes. Short-term work does not yield the same level of intimacy in the therapeutic relationship as does longer-term work. Time brings forth greater degrees and levels of emotional relatedness, as well as clients' personal history and their history with the interviewer. These nuances require the professional interviewer to vary the interviewing process.

The termination process is also influenced by the length and intensity of the interviewing process. Short-term work does not require the same type of careful and delicate processing of the interviewing history. Long-term interviewing, by its very nature, demands a longer revisiting of exactly what happened in the therapeutic relationship, and what needs to be done to help sustain the important gains that were made over that longer process.

The case examples in this chapter demonstrate some of the variations of the middle phase of interviewing and the termination process. These examples and interviewing techniques can be a helpful addition to any interviewer's repertoire.

RECOMMENDED READING

Walsh, J. (2007). *Endings in clinical practice: Effective closure in diverse settings* (2nd ed.). Chicago: Lyceum Books.

This book is one of only a handful on the termination process. It is an excellent guide for interviewers from any professional helping discipline in understanding and working through the termination process with their clients.

Psychodynamic diagnostic manual. (2006). Silver Spring, MD: Alliance of Psychoanalytic Organizations.

This important contribution is useful for understanding much of the key research on the validation of the need for long-term work in psychotherapy.

O'Hare, T. (2005). *Evidence-based practices for social workers: An interdisciplinary approach.* Chicago: Lyceum Books.

O'Hare's comprehensive work is one of the best on some of the most current evidence-based practice.

MULTIMEDIA SOURCES

Life as a House. (2001). Irwin Winkler (Director). New Line Cinema.

This poignant story of a father dying of cancer and his relationship with his young adult son truly captures the emotions and dynamics of the termination process. Although not a film on interviewing, any professional interviewer will glean a tremendous amount of knowledge from immersion in this film.

E.T.: The Extra-Terrestrial. (1982). Steven Spielberg (Director). Amblin Entertainment.

A classic film on attachment, separation, and loss, this movie brings home the dramatic importance of these processes and how essential they are in life and the interviewing process.

Ethical Interviewing

All of the interviewing professions have a code of ethics that prescribes certain behaviors for professionals working with clients. These codes of ethics are not all the same. Different professions may emphasize different ethical issues. Some professions vary slightly in their mandates. For example, the National Association of Social Workers (NASW) Code of Ethics in America strictly forbids social work interviewers to engage in any type of sexual and/or personal relationship with a client, even after services have ended. Some medical codes of ethics, on the other hand, allow physicians to engage in sexual and/or personal relationships with patients a certain number of years after they leave medical treatment. The Canadian Association of Social Workers (CASW) Code of Ethics specifically emphasizes this issue in value 2, "Pursuit of Social Justice." The NASW Code of Ethics has a similar mandate. The American and Canadian nurses associations' codes of ethics for nurses and psychiatric nurses, and psychological code of ethics all emphasize similar standards with regard to work with clients/patients. This chapter presents general case examples of the typical kinds of ethical dilemmas faced by most professional interviewers, regardless of discipline within the US and Canadian systems.

Kim Strom-Gottfried in her book *Straight Talk about Professional Ethics* (2007, p. 7) makes an important point regarding professional ethical interviewing: "Core ethical standards provide us the guideposts for action. Knowing what they are and what they mean is an essential first step in ethical practice. The challenges occur in those situations when standards collide, or when the standard fails to offer clear guidance for action." In other words, ethical decision making in the interviewing process is contextual. Decisions must be made on a case-by-case basis within the parameters of the particular professional discipline. This is a very challenging proposition. It takes years of experience for the professional interviewer to become relatively comfortable handling ethical dilemmas. This natural process is part of every interviewer's professional development.

It would be impossible to cover in one chapter all of the ethical dilemmas in professional interviewing. Instead, the case examples here describe some of the most common ones. Each case example has two scenarios. The first scenario demonstrates unethical professional interviewing and discusses its unethical aspects. The second demonstrates how the case could have been handled in a more ethical manner.

BOUNDARIES: PERSONAL/SEXUAL RELATIONSHIPS WITH CLIENTS

Most lawsuits against professional interviewers involve interviewers' having a sexual relationship with their client, either during or after treatment. The following case example demonstrates this issue.

Lisa, a thirty-five-year-old single woman, is seeing a forty-year-old male psychologist for relationship problems and anxiety. The psychologist is sexually attracted to Lisa, and Lisa feels attracted to the psychologist. The following interview occurs about a month into treatment.

Interviewer: Hi Lisa. You're looking very pretty tonight.

From the start of any interviewing process, the interviewer, regardless of gender or sexual orientation, should be cautious about making comments to the client that could be misconstrued as flirtatious or inappropriate. This first comment in and of itself may not be inappropriate; however, the interviewer should be very clear about the reason for it before making the statement.

> **Lisa** [*slightly embarrassed*]: Oh . . . Thanks.
> **Interviewer:** Is that a new dress?
> **Lisa:** No, I've had it for a while.
> **Interviewer:** Well, it looks very nice on you.
> **Lisa:** Thanks, I don't get a lot of compliments.
> **Interviewer:** I certainly don't see why not. You are a very attractive woman.

Now it appears as if at least two things are happening in this session. First, the interviewer is obviously leading the session's discussion to the client's appearance. In addition, he does not allow the client to have control of the subject matter, and she perhaps feels uncomfortable about where to go next. This would not be happening if the interviewer had not led the session with his opening comments about the client's looks.

> **Lisa:** Well . . . thanks again.
> **Interviewer:** So, how have things been going this week?
> **Lisa:** I've been kind of lonely and anxious this week.
> **Interviewer:** Why do you think you've been feeling that way?
> **Lisa:** Well, you know we've been talking about how anxious I get about dating guys. I haven't dated for months now. I just go to work and come home. I want to meet people, especially guys.
> **Interviewer:** I know we've talked about this, Lisa. Have you been visiting the online dating site I suggested?
> **Lisa:** Yeah, but I just don't feel comfortable e-mailing or chatting with guys I don't know. I wish it could be like I feel when I'm here with you.
> **Interviewer:** And how's that?
> **Lisa:** You know . . . very safe and comfortable.

Interviewer: Well, I'm glad you feel that way, Lisa, but I think it's because I'm your therapist.

Lisa: No, it's more than that. I think I'd feel this way even if I met you outside of here.

Interviewer: Well, that may be true, Lisa, but that is something we really couldn't know, could we?

Lisa: I guess not.

Interviewer: I have an idea though.

Lisa: What's that?

Interviewer: Well . . . it would be kind of an experiment.

Lisa [*a little hesitantly*]: What kind of an experiment?

Interviewer: Why don't we go out on a date together and see how you feel about it. That way you could see if it's me or not.

Lisa: I don't know, that feels kind of strange. Would I still be in therapy with you?

Interviewer: Of course you would be. This would just give us the opportunity to help you with your feelings and experiences around dating.

Lisa: OK . . . if you say so. It might be kind of fun. When do you want to go out?

Interviewer: How about tonight? You're my last appointment. We could go down to that little restaurant bar down the street. You're certainly dressed appropriately. I think I already told you how pretty you look in that dress. So what do you say?

Lisa: OK.

Interviewer: Great, let's go.

Lisa: Right now?

Interviewer: Of course, it's part of the therapy.

The session ends with the interviewer and the client going to the local bar. This situation is an obvious breach of the therapeutic boundaries. The interviewer has clearly been inappropriate by any ethical standards in asking the client for a date. He has taken advantage of the client's vulnerability by using his role as her therapist to persuade her to date him. The therapeutic relationship represents an uneven power differential that could be easily manipulated by the interviewer, as in this case example.

The following revised example demonstrates how the therapist could have handled this situation in a more ethical manner.

> **Interviewer:** Hi Lisa. How have things been going this week?

Notice that the interviewer does not mention the client's appearance at all, but instead begins to immediately express his interest in listening to her and helping her with her problem. This is obviously a much more appropriate way to manage the session.

> **Lisa:** I've been kind of lonely and anxious this week.
> **Interviewer:** Why do you think you've been feeling that way?
> **Lisa:** Well, you know we've been talking about how anxious I get about dating guys. I haven't dated for months now. I just go to work and come home. I want to meet people, especially guys.

By excluding the more personal interventions and comments from the interviewer, this case example becomes an entirely different scenario. The interviewer now seems to be clearly focusing on the client, demonstrating empathy, and following her lead, not his own agenda.

> **Interviewer:** What kinds of things have you been doing to meet guys?
> **Lisa:** Well, I looked into joining one of those online dating services, but I just don't think I would feel comfortable e-mailing or chatting with strange men. I certainly don't want to go to bars. I wish I could meet a guy like you, someone I feel comfortable with and not nervous.
> **Interviewer:** So what is it about me that makes you feel comfortable?

Lisa: You're so caring and understanding. I don't feel nervous around you, you put me at ease.

Interviewer: I'm glad you feel that way, Lisa, but do you remember how you felt when you first started?

Lisa: Not exactly.

Interviewer: Well, as I recall, you were very anxious, and it took awhile before you felt comfortable enough to open up to me. As much as I appreciate your feeling good about the therapy here with me, I'd have to say that for you to feel comfortable took some time.

Lisa: So you think that's how it might be with any guy, huh?

Interviewer: Well, I certainly can't be sure, but for you to be able to comfortable here was a process. We developed a therapy relationship over time. It didn't happen immediately.

Lisa: I know you're right. So maybe I could develop a relationship with a good guy.

Interviewer: I think you can. Let's talk a little bit more about ways in which you might go about meeting some guys.

Lisa: Sounds good.

This restorative example demonstrates how easy it can be to respond ethically and empathically to a client without imposing one's own agenda on him or her. Even though this interviewer finds the client attractive, he is able to silently acknowledge those feelings and not allow them to enter into or sabotage the process.

BOUNDARIES: INAPPROPRIATE SELF-DISCLOSURE

At times self-disclosure can be an invaluable intervention and source of support for the client. However, the interviewer needs to continually self-monitor in order to determine if, when, and to what extent information about self should be shared with the client. The case example illustrates the inappropriate use of self-disclosure, followed by a more careful and ethical approach.

A sixteen-year-old male client, Matt, is seeing a thirty-five-year-old male school social worker because of his concerns about his parents' divorce. This is the first interview.

> **Interviewer:** Hi Matt. I'm glad you could get out of study hall and see me today.
> *Matt:* No problem, I really wanted to come to see you.
> **Interviewer:** So I understand that your parents are going through a divorce.
> *Matt:* Yeah, it really sucks.
> **Interviewer:** Well, you know my parents divorced when I was your age, and I really had a hard time with it too. I know what you're going through.
> *Matt:* Yeah, what was your parents' divorce like?
> **Interviewer:** My dad was an alcoholic, and my mom couldn't take it any more so she started having an affair with one of our neighbors down the street. It was very awkward.
> *Matt:* Boy, that must have been a pretty tough thing. How did you handle it?

Already in this session, the interviewer has begun to steer the discussion away from the client's concerns and into his own past. Although it appears that the interviewer has the best intentions, he has not even gotten to know Matt's story or feelings about his parents' pending divorce. Many interviewers working with adolescents believe that self-disclosure is a way of forming a relationship with them. It is true that many adolescents want to know that the counselors they are seeing can relate to their experiences. Some general and carefully timed self-disclosure can be helpful in forming a trusting relationship with an adolescent. In this case, however, the interviewer is actually using the time to talk about his own painful experiences. It is an unethical way to manage the interviewing process, because it deprives the client of the opportunity to work on himself.

Interviewer: Well, I needed to get away from all of the craziness, so I started using drugs and drinking a lot.

Matt: Did your parents find out about it?

Interviewer: Eventually they did. They made me go to drug rehab. That was really intense and I hated it at the time, but when I think about it now, it might have been the best thing.

Matt: Well, my situation doesn't seem like it is anything as bad as yours. Maybe I should just suck it up and deal with it.

Interviewer: Everybody's life is different, Matt. Let's talk about your situation.

Matt: My folks just told me last week that they were getting a divorce. I didn't see it coming; I thought they were getting along.

Interviewer: Yeah, with my parents I wasn't a bit surprised. I just had a hard time being in the middle of it. You know, my mom wanted to talk about my dad, and my dad after he had been drinking would start crying with me about my mom. It was really tough.

Matt: Like I said, my situation doesn't seem anywhere near as bad as yours.

Interviewer: Well, maybe not, Matt, but tell me how you're feeling about it.

Matt: I'm confused right now, and sort of angry I think, but I'm not sure why.

Interviewer: I got real angry with my folks. I thought they were both acting kind of immature. Do you feel that way about your parents?

Matt: Like I said before, I'm not exactly sure how I feel, but I knew I needed to talk to someone about it. That's why I came to see you.

Interviewer: Well, I'm glad you did, Matt. Talking these things out can be really helpful.

Matt: I hope so.

Interviewer: Sure it will. Let's meet again tomorrow to talk about it some more.

Matt: OK. But what should I do about how I'm feeling?

Interviewer: Well, you know that I just used drugs to get away from the feelings. I wouldn't suggest that.

Matt: No, I'm really not into that at all.

Interviewer: That's a good thing, because it can really mess you up. It almost ruined my life.

Matt: So what do you think I can do?

Interviewer: Well, you said you were confused, right?

Matt: Yeah.

Interviewer: Why don't you think more about that, and we'll talk about it tomorrow, OK?

Matt: All right, I guess.

Interviewer: Don't worry about it, Matt, these things always work out.

Matt: I hope so. So I'll come by tomorrow at the same time then?

Interviewer: Yep, see you then.

The interviewer continued to use the time with this client to talk about his feelings, not the client's. As the session progressed, Matt appeared to be feeling worse, not better. He barely was able to talk about what he was feeling and dealing with in his life. Although the interviewer seems to have the best intentions, he is clearly not responding to the client, or building much of a relationship with him.

The next example demonstrates one of the many appropriate ways the interviewer could have handled this session with Matt.

Interviewer: Hi Matt. I'm glad you could get out of study hall and see me today.

Matt: No problem, I really wanted to come to see you.

Interviewer: So I understand that your parents are going through a divorce.

Matt: Yeah, it really sucks.

Interviewer: Can you tell me a little about that?

Matt: My folks just told me last week that they were getting a divorce. I didn't see it coming; I thought they were getting along.

Interviewer: So it was a real surprise to you.

Matt: I'm confused right now, and sort of angry I think, but I'm not sure why.

Interviewer: Can you talk a little more about the angry feelings?

Matt: I'll try. I feel angry with both of them. I wish they would have worked things out. Now I'm not sure what's going to happen. Am I going to have to move? Go to a different school? Lose my friends? I'm just angry with them for screwing up my life. Is that OK to feel that way?

Interviewer: I don't think there is a right or a wrong way to feel, Matt. Your feelings are your own, and they are what they are. However, it seems like you might be feeling bad about having them. Is that true?

Matt: I kind of do. I guess I think I should be more understanding of them.

Interviewer: But this is affecting you too, Matt. I think you are entitled to have your feelings, whatever they may be.

This approach to working with this client takes on an entirely different focus. The interviewer has not spoken once about his parents' divorce, but instead maintained a clear and empathic connection with the client. As a result, the session has become about Matt and his feelings. We are beginning to understand what Matt is feeling. This is a much more appropriate and ethical approach to working with clients.

Matt: Well, that makes me feel a little better, I guess.

Interviewer: You mentioned that your parents told you about the divorce. Do you remember what they said?

Matt: Kind of . . . it was sort of a shock and a blur. I think they said they were going to get a divorce because they hadn't been getting along for a long time. They said that it wasn't either of their faults, and it had nothing to do with me. They just weren't getting along and couldn't stay married anymore. They also said they were going to see an attorney next week.

Interviewer: Anything else?

Matt: Oh yeah, they told me not to worry, and that I would be OK.

Interviewer: So how has it been since then?

Matt: Like I said, confusing. Can you understand? Have you ever been through anything like this?

Interviewer: Well, Matt, actually my parents divorced when I was around your age.

Matt: So you can understand what I'm going through?

Interviewer: Matt, even though my parents also got divorced doesn't mean that my feelings were the same as yours. I believe that everyone has their own unique feelings about these kinds of things. I can tell you that I experienced difficult times too, but it's more important for us to focus on you.

Matt: Well, it's good to know that you went through kind of the same thing. That makes me feel less alone in all of this.

Interviewer: Well, I'm glad it does, Matt.

Matt: So what do I do now?

Interviewer: I'm not sure I know what you mean, Matt.

Matt: Well, all of these feelings. What do I do about them?

Interviewer: How have you felt talking about them here today?

Matt: Good, I think.

Interviewer: I think that's what we can continue to do, if you want to. This situation is going to be a process, Matt, and I think it's going to take some time. Maybe knowing you can come here to talk about it will help. I've seen this be very helpful for many teenagers.

Matt: So other kids have talked to you about divorce too?

Interviewer: Lots of them. Everyone is different, but they all needed time to work this through.

Matt: So I can see you again?

Interviewer: Sure. When would you like to come back?

Matt: Is tomorrow at this time too soon?
Interviewer: Not at all. See you then.

When the interviewer focused his attention on the client, the session changed entirely. The carefully timed use of limited self-disclosure clearly helped Matt feel comfortable and not so alone with his feelings and situation. The interviewer was careful to explain to Matt that all situations are different, but that they could be difficult. This was a helpful and ethical approach to the use of self-disclosure while maintaining professional boundaries.

SELF-DETERMINATION

One of the most important hallmarks of professional interviewing is upholding the standard of self-determination. It is crucial for clients to be able to make their own decisions regarding their lives. The interviewer's responsibility is to help the client negotiate this process. Sometimes there will be circumstances that warrant more direct confrontation, exploration, and education by the interviewer in order to help the client understand the entirety of the situation at hand. If clients are determined to be a threat to themselves or another, the interviewer is obligated by law to inform the authorities in order to protect those involved. Besides those caveats, however, it is the interviewer's role to ensure that clients are allowed to make their own decisions and not be hindered by the interviewer, whether or not they agree with the choices. For many professional interviewers, this can be one of the most difficult parts of the process.

The following case example involves a twenty-five-year-old male and a fifty-year-old female social worker. The client, named Eric, has come to therapy to work on his relationship with his wife. He is very recently married, and is having some difficulties surrounding the responsibilities that he and his wife share in the household, as well as his sexual relationship with his wife. This is the first session.

Interviewer: Hello, Eric, nice to meet you. I understand that you are here because of some difficulties with your wife.

Eric: Yeah, we've only been married a month or so, and already she's giving me trouble.

Interviewer: What do you mean by trouble?

Eric: Well, according to her, I don't do enough around the house.

Interviewer: Could you be more specific, Eric?

Eric: Sure. She thinks I should clean the house, help with grocery shopping, and make some of our meals. Listen . . . I work in construction, and I'm gone from 6 in the morning to sometimes 7:30 or 8 pm at night. When I get home, I'm beat. Construction is hard work. I make really good money. I don't think I should have to work all day, killing myself, and then come home and be expected to do household chores.

Interviewer: Does your wife work outside the home?

Eric: Nope.

Interviewer: So she works all day, every day, including weekends in the home. That's a twenty-four-hour job, Eric. I don't think it's unreasonable for her to expect some help from you.

Eric: Well, I disagree. There isn't that much to do around the house. I think she's being unrealistic. And then there's the sex. She doesn't want to be with me very much at all.

Interviewer: By very much at all, you mean what, Eric?

Eric: Maybe once a week. She says she's tired. I can't see how she can be. It's very frustrating.

Interviewer: Eric, I think it's important to understand that a woman's body is her own. You need to respect her decision and views about your sexual relationship together.

Eric: So I don't get to say anything about it? And on top of that I'm supposed to work more around the house. This doesn't sound like a fair arrangement to me.

Interviewer: Well, I can tell you're upset about this, Eric, but I don't think your wife is being unreasonable. Women today need to be respected. Some of your ideas sound very antiquated. That's surprising to me given that you're, what, in your midtwenties?

Eric: Twenty-five. I don't think I'm being old-fashioned at all. That's how I was raised. My dad worked hard, just like me, and my mom stayed home to take care of me and my sister. They got along just fine.

Interviewer: That was a long time ago, Eric. Things have changed with men and women.

Eric: Well, when we were engaged, my wife and I talked all about how married life was going to be. She agreed totally with me on this. Now she's going back on what we had decided on together. That's very frustrating.

Interviewer: I can see that, Eric, but again, I don't think your wife is being unreasonable.

The interviewer has made the ethical error of imposing her own belief system on this client. Her viewpoint seems to interfere in her ability to understand and demonstrate empathy for the client, even if she disagrees with his values. As a result, the interviewer has not really explored much of the client's feelings and ideas, but instead has chosen to argue with him and try to educate him to what she obviously considers to be the best way to handle this situation. The problem here is that although there may be many people that would disagree with this particular client's viewpoint, it is not the professional interviewer's role to tell the client he is wrong and that he should handle the situation her way. Outside of the session, the interviewer is certainly free to express her own opinions in any way she wants. With a client, the interviewer must demonstrate objectivity, understanding, and empathy in order to develop a trusting relationship and help the client make his own decisions.

The following example illustrates how the interviewer might have handled this situation in a more ethical and professional manner while subtly challenging some of the client's beliefs in order to help him work on the problem.

Interviewer: Hello, Eric, nice to meet you. I understand that you are here because of some difficulties with your wife.

Eric: Yeah, we've only been married a month or so, and already she's giving me trouble.

Interviewer: What do you mean by trouble?

Eric: Well, according to her, I don't do enough around the house.

Interviewer: Could you be more specific, Eric?

Eric: Sure. She thinks I should clean the house, help with grocery shopping, and make some of our meals. Listen . . . I work in construction, and I'm gone from 6 in the morning to sometimes 7:30 or 8 pm at night. When I get home, I'm beat. Construction is hard work. I make really good money. I don't think I should have to work all day, killing myself, and then come home and be expected to do household chores.

Interviewer: Does your wife work outside the home?

Eric: Nope.

Interviewer: So she is a homemaker.

Eric: Yep.

Interviewer: I can tell this really frustrates you, Eric.

Eric: Yeah, it does, and I'm glad I finally found someone who agrees with me.

Interviewer: I didn't say that I agree with you, Eric, but I can certainly empathize with your frustration.

Eric: So you think she's right.

Interviewer: I didn't say that either. You know, Eric, maybe I should explain how I do counseling. I see my role as being someone who helps a person sort out how they're feeling and find their own solution to the problem. I find that taking sides isn't really helpful. What is helpful is doing the best I can to understand things from your point of view, and help build a trusting relationship so together we can make things better. Does that make sense?

Eric: I guess so, but it would just be so much easier if I could go back home and tell my wife that you agreed with me, and then maybe she would come around a little.

Interviewer: I have a feeling, Eric, that even if I did that, your wife would probably not be very happy about it, and things wouldn't change anyway. This sounds like a relationship issue to me.

Eric: And then there's the sex. She doesn't want to be with me very much at all.

Interviewer: Can you help me understand what you mean by "not very much at all"?

Eric: Maybe once a week. She says she's tired. I can't see how she can be. It's very frustrating.

Interviewer: So let me see if I understand. You're feeling like you work very hard, and long hours every day, and come home to your wife who has unrealistic expectations of you, and on top of that she isn't very interested in having sex with you, at least not as much as you would like it. Am I getting it?

Eric: Exactly. I really love her, but I'm feeling so frustrated and lonely with her right now.

Interviewer: Eric, that's a very honest and vulnerable thing to say. Have you told your wife how you feel?

Eric: I can't, I'm not good at talking about my feelings.

Interviewer: Well, I don't know about that. You sure did a good job of expressing them right now.

The interviewer has begun to successfully engage this somewhat opinionated and defensive young man in the session. She does not share any of her own opinions about the relationship between a husband and wife, which would most likely derail any chance of building trust with Eric. Instead, she patiently focuses on his thoughts and feelings to demonstrate understanding and empathy, even if she disagrees with him. This is sometimes a very difficult thing to accomplish as a professional interviewer. As professionals, we are going to meet many clients with whom we disagree in the sessions. Religious and political viewpoints, life values, and many other complex issues will challenge even the best of interviewers. The ability to allow the client to have self-determination is the key not only to the development of a trusting relationship, but to the treatment as a whole. This interviewer is now on the road to that end.

CONFIDENTIALITY

The final ethical example in this chapter deals with confidentiality. The privacy of the client is an absolutely essential element to establishing the trust that it takes to ensure successful outcomes in professional interviewing in any discipline. If the client can't be sure that what he or she shares with the interviewer will remain private, how can the client feel safe enough to really open up about inner thoughts and emotions?

There are various laws regarding confidentiality. Generally speaking, if a child is younger than twelve years, the interviewer does not have any legal obligation to withhold information from the parents or caretakers. Most interviewers are tactful in this area, however, given the importance of trust for the young client and the need of the parents to know and protect their child. In my opinion, children younger than twelve typically don't seem to be bothered about this issue. For adolescents between the ages of thirteen and eighteen, the laws tend to be more obscure, leaving the decision to breach confidentiality to the discretion of the interviewer. Interviewers usually divulge confidential information to the parent when they decide it is in the best interest of the parent to know something that has a serious effect on the adolescent. Once again, however, discretion is crucial. Breaching confidentiality with an adolescent, even in the best circumstances, can irreparably damage the therapeutic relationship. Once the client has reached the age of eighteen, there is a strict code of confidentiality. Only situations that threaten the life of the client or others are a reason to violate the confidence of the therapeutic relationship. This can be difficult, as seen in the following example.

Joan, age forty-five, has brought her twenty-year-old daughter, Becky, to therapy because of Becky's recent breakup with a boyfriend. Becky has been very sad and somewhat depressed, and her mother is concerned about her. The interviewer is a thirty-five-year-old female social worker. The social worker has met first with the mother and daughter to get a sense of the overall concerns and to explain the nature of the interviewing process, as well as the limits of confidentiality. All parties have agreed that the interviews will consist primarily of individual therapy with Becky, and occasional interviews with Joan to get her opinions about how things are going with Becky and, with Becky's permission, to share a general sense of her work with the social worker. This is Becky's first individual session after the original joint interview with mother, daughter, and social worker.

Interviewer: Hi Becky. It's nice to see you again. I know we had the joint session with your mom last week, and I wondered if there were other things you might want to fill me in on that we didn't discuss with your mom.

Becky: Well, my mom really cares about me, but she doesn't know everything about my relationship with my boyfriend.

Interviewer: What do you mean?

Becky: Well, we had a pretty intense relationship. We were sexually active, and he was also very jealous.

Interviewer: Do you mind my asking if you used birth control?

Becky: No, not at all. I've been on birth control for a few years now, but don't tell my mom. She'd freak out. I think she still thinks I'm a virgin.

Interviewer: I won't, I told you and your mom that our sessions are confidential. It sounds like you were being very safe in your sexual relationship with your boyfriend.

Becky: I have always been that way with all of my boyfriends.

Interviewer: Have you had a lot of them?

Becky: No, not really, maybe a couple since I was sixteen. My mom doesn't know about them, though.

Interviewer: So what happened with your boyfriend? I mean, I know you broke up, but what happened?

Becky: Well, he wanted me to start using drugs, and that's just not something I'm into.

Interviewer: Can you tell me more about that?

Becky: There's not much to tell. He and I hang out with different kinds of people. He and his friends do a lot of drugs, and me and my friends don't. He kept pressuring me, and when I told him absolutely not, he said I wasn't his type of girl.

Interviewer: So it was kind of an ultimatum?

Becky: Yeah, I guess you could say that. I was pretty upset.

Interviewer: How long did you guys go out?

Becky: Almost a year. Mom thinks I'm all messed up about it, but I'm really not. I just miss him, that's all. I've had breakups before. I'll be OK.

Interviewer: You do sound pretty sure about that.

Becky [*sincerely*]: No, really, I know I'll be OK.

The session ends with the interviewer feeling fairly confident that Becky will be all right, and that this is a somewhat typical situation for someone her age. She also feels comfortable discussing the general thrust of the session with Becky's mom. In the following session, the interviewer meets with Becky and her mother to share her impressions about Becky's therapy.

Interviewer: Hi Joan. I'm glad we could all get together. I wanted to have a discussion about how Becky is handling this recent breakup with her boyfriend.

Joan: Me too. I've been so worried about her.

Becky: Mom, you don't have to be worried about me. I'm actually doing fine.

Joan: Well, I hope so. You're still so young and naïve. I worry that you won't be able to make good decisions when it comes to boys.

Becky: I've been dating since I was fifteen, Mom. I know what I'm doing.

Interviewer: Yes, Joan, Becky has shared with me that she has been very responsible in her relationships with boys. She's been using birth control for some time, and that's the sign of someone who takes their sexual relationships very seriously.

Joan: You've been on birth control? Why didn't you tell me? You know how your father and I feel about that issue. I'm extremely disappointed in you, Becky!

Becky: Thanks a lot. I thought you told me everything would be confidential in here. Now you go and tell my mom all about my sexual life. Great!

Interviewer: Becky, I didn't think your mom would get so upset. After all, you are twenty years old.

Joan: Yes. She's only twenty years old. That's so young.

Becky: You treat me like a baby. I can handle my own life. I'm never coming back here. I wanted a place where I could be safe and talk privately. That'll never happen here.

Interviewer: I'm so sorry, Becky. I can see that I made a mistake. Will you give me another chance?

Becky: Absolutely not. Mom, let's go.

Joan: I'm sorry, but if Becky doesn't want to be here, I can't force her.

Unfortunately, this ethical error in confidentiality, even with the best intentions, caused a rupture in the relationship between the interviewer and Becky. The interviewer assumed that sharing this information would help the mother better understand her daughter's maturity. However, the client had several times explicitly asked the interviewer to keep this information private. The trust was irrevocably breached.

The following example illustrates a more proper, ethical handling of this situation.

At the end of the first interview with Becky, described above, the interviewer continues, getting clear about what Becky would and wouldn't like to share with her mother.

> **Interviewer:** I think we should have a joint session with your mom to go over how you're doing. What do you think?
> *Becky:* That's fine with me.
> **Interviewer:** Now, Becky, I want to be sure that I don't share any information except what you want me to with your mom. What would you like me to tell her?
> *Becky:* You can tell her that I'm doing OK now. I've broken up with boys before, and I know I'll get over it. But don't mention that I've been having sex, or the birth control, OK?
> **Interviewer:** Got it. No discussions of your sex life or that you've been using birth control. Anything else?
> *Becky:* Just let her know that I'm old enough to take care of myself with these kinds of things.
> **Interviewer:** I think I know how to handle the session, Becky. However, I will check with you before sharing any information I'm not sure about. Does that sound OK?
> *Becky:* Sounds good.

The additional discussion helps the interviewer explore the parameters of the meeting with the client's mother, as well as clarify exactly what should and should not be discussed. After this bit of very important discussion, the rupture in the relationship with Becky probably would have been avoided. This final example demonstrates how things could have gone without the ethical breach.

> **Interviewer:** Hi Joan. I'm glad we could all get together. I wanted to have a discussion about how Becky is handling this recent breakup with her boyfriend.
> *Joan:* Me too. I've been so worried about her.

Becky: Mom, you don't have to be worried about me. I'm actually doing fine.

Joan: Well, I hope so. You're still so young and naïve. I worry that you won't be able to make good decisions when it comes to boys.

Becky: I've been dating since I was fifteen, Mom. I know what I'm doing.

Interviewer: Joan, when Becky says that she knows what she's doing, I get the sense that you don't seem to really believe her. Why is that?

Joan: It's not that I don't believe her, I just worry about her.

Becky: I know, Mom. But I'm over twenty years old now. I wish you would trust my decisions.

Interviewer: Becky, have you and your mom talked much about the breakup?

Becky: A little bit.

Interviewer: Is there anything that you'd like her to know about it that the two of you haven't discussed?

Becky: Well, Mom, he wanted me to do drugs, and I said no. That's why we broke up.

Joan: I didn't know that. I'm so proud of you. I guess you really do know what you're doing. I'm sorry.

Becky: That's OK, Mom. I know you love me. I just wish you wouldn't treat me like such a kid.

Joan: I think that's something I've got to work on a bit.

Interviewer: Well, it seems like this has been a good discussion for both of you.

This more careful and ethical approach with the mother and daughter led to a beneficial, mutual understanding about the nature of their relationship. The interviewer was careful to tactfully ask questions that helped the client decide exactly what she wanted to discuss. As a result of this trusting approach, Becky decided to share some personal information that reassured her mother about her ability to handle her life. Handling confidential material can be a challenging ethical dilemma even under the best circumstances.

THE IMPORTANCE OF SUPERVISION, CONSULTATION, AND CONTINUING EDUCATION

Any professional interviewer can benefit from ongoing consultation or supervision in order to ensure the delivery of ethical services. During professional interviewers' initial education and practice experiences, they are under the direct supervision of a professional within their discipline. Social workers are supervised by approved social work field instructors; nurses in behavioral health are supervised by their clinical preceptors in actual medical settings; psychiatrists in training are supervised by experienced psychiatrists in a variety of different medical settings. The list goes on and on. The important point to remember is that all professional interviewers go through a mandated period in their training in which their work is monitored and supervised in order to be certain that they are ready to practice in the public arena.

Supervision usually consists of the careful scrutiny of interviewers' work by a professional supervisor within their discipline. There are a variety of supervisory mechanisms. Some supervisors ask their students to write process recordings. Process recordings are written from memory by the student immediately after an interviewing session. The student must write, to the best of his or her recollection, the exact words of the interview. The supervisor reads the process recording before meeting with the student, and both of them discuss the strengths and weaknesses of the interview, as well as suggestions for future work. Some supervisors use summary recordings for the same purpose. Summary recordings are not as exacting as process recordings, but capture the student's best recollection of what happened in the interview. Still other supervisors video- or audiotape (with the client's permission) the interview and discuss it with the student. Finally, some supervisors sit in on sessions with the interviewer (again with the client's permission) to observe the actual process in real time.

All of these approaches can be extremely beneficial in helping students learn from their experience and have a set of more experienced eyes involved in their learning. From an ethical standpoint this is absolutely essential to helping the novice interviewer gain a solid foothold as a professional.

Most professional interviewing disciplines also require some type of postgraduate licensure before interviewers are legally allowed to provide professional interviewing in their discipline. For example, interviewers who have received their master of social work must be supervised by a licensed clinical social worker (LCSW) for a period of two years or three thousand hours of clinical work before they can sit for the LCSW exam (or equivalent) in their state.

Even after receiving a professional license to provide interviewing services, it is extremely helpful to continue to receive some type of occasional consultation with an experienced professional interviewer in your discipline. Some professional interviewers accomplish this by setting up peer consultation groups. This allows professional interviewers to discuss cases in confidence with their colleagues, in order to remain current and reduce the inevitable blind spots that occur in isolated practice.

The best consultant is someone with years of experience, who can be helpful to the new professional interviewer because of the sheer number and types of cases they have handled throughout their careers. Competent consultants are the best resources to use when the professional interviewer is struggling with an ethical challenge. It is highly likely that a good consultant will have had some experience with a similar situation and can help the interviewer sort through the subtle nuances that can be such a challenge in the interviewing process. It is never wise to go it alone in professional interviewing.

Another important source of knowledge and support is continuing education. Most professional interviewing disciplines require some form of annual continuing education in order to keep one's professional license current. In social work, for example, LCSWs (and their equivalents) must attend a certain number of continuing education events to attain a certain number of annual hours. Many states also require that a certain portion of these continuing education units (CEUs) must be in the area of ethics. That requirement ensures that interviewing professionals are continually involved in exploring the complex dilemma of ethics within their profession.

RESEARCH IMPLICATIONS AND BASIS OF PRACTICE

From a research knowledge base, ethics has certainly been a common-sense knowledge set since the beginning of human society. From a practice wisdom standpoint, professional interviewers have recognized and written about the myriad of ethical challenges for quite some time. Professional journal articles are full of perplexing ethical case studies that demonstrate the obvious and subtle quandaries that professional interviewers face in working with all types of clients in all types of settings. In recent generations, a great deal has been written about the necessity to codify professional ethics while recognizing the inevitable uncertainty of a definitive standard that fits all situations (Strom-Gottfried, 2007). Therefore, the area of ethics in professional interviewing has reached the level of theoretical knowledge.

Research studies in professional interviewing are just beginning. One can imagine that the reason for this may be, as it was in many forms of psychotherapy, that the study of ethics involves operationalizing many multifaceted variables that defy a clear and measurable definition. There are also moral and ethical challenges in the design of research that studies the professional interviewing process. For example, using a control group in an experiment on ethical professional interviewing could, in and of itself, be considered unethical. These methodological challenges can be overcome, but not without a great deal of scrutiny and rigor. Failure to do so could result in the same type of limited research results that came from some of the early clinical psychodynamic studies on complex variables such as transference, countertransference, and empathy (PDM, 2006).

SUMMARY

This chapter has covered the pervasive, essential, and fundamental property of ethics in professional interviewing. Several of the ethical challenges in professional interviewing are explored in examples of the right and wrong ways to work with clients. Both new and experienced professional interviewers are encouraged to pursue supervision, consultation, and continuing professional education in order to steer clear of the potential blind spots so common in isolated practice.

RECOMMENDED READING

Strom-Gottfried, K. (2007). *Straight talk about professional ethics.* Chicago: Lyceum Books.

Strom-Gottfried provides some of the clearest and most practical information on a topic that is difficult to define, let alone manage as a professional interviewer.

MULTIMEDIA SOURCES

The reader is encouraged to review the codes of ethics for US and Canadian professional disciplines of social work, nursing, psychiatric, psychological, and criminal justice. These can all be found online. These codes are an eye-opener in terms of the range and areas of ethics emphasized.

References

Adler, A. (1931). *Alfred Adler: What life could mean to you.* Center City, MN: Hazelden.

Ainsworth, M. D. S., Blehar, M. C., Waters, E., & Wall, S. (1978). *Patterns of attachment: A psychological study of the strange situation.* Hillsdale, NJ: Lawrence Erlbaum Associates.

American Psychiatric Association (2000). *Diagnostic and statistical manual of mental disorders* (4th ed., text revision). Washington, DC: Author.

Axline, V. M. (1947). *Play therapy.* New York: Ballantine Books.

Baldwin, S. A., Wampold, B. E., & Imel, Z. E. (2007). Untangling the alliance-outcome correlation: Exploring the relative importance of therapist and patient variability in the alliance. *Journal of Consulting Clinical Psychology, 75*(6), 842–52.

Bandura, A. (1962). *Social learning through imitation.* Lincoln: University of Nebraska Press.

Bandura, A. (1969). *Principles of behavior modification.* New York: Holt, Rinehart & Winston.

Beck, A. T. (1975). *Cognitive therapy and the emotional disorders.* Madison, CT: International Universities Press.

Blos, P. (1979). *The adolescent passage: Developmental issues.* New York: International Universities Press.

Bogo, M. (2006). *Social work practice: Concepts, processes, and interviewing.* New York: Columbia University Press.

Bowen, M. (1978). *Family therapy in clinical practice*. New York: Aronson.

Bowlby, J. (1969). *Attachment and loss*. Vol. 1, *Attachment*. New York: Basic Books.

Campbell, C. (2003). *Anti-oppressive social work: Promoting equity and social justice*. Halifax, Nova Scotia: Author.

Cozolino, L. (2002). *The neuroscience of psychotherapy: Building and rebuilding the human brain*. New York: W. W. Norton.

Cozolino, L. (2010). *The neuroscience of psychotherapy: Healing the social brain*. New York: W. W. Norton.

Egan, G. (2013). *The skilled helper: A problem-management and opportunity-development approach to helping*. Independence, KY: Cengage Learning.

Ellis, A. (1973). *Humanistic psychotherpy: The rational emotive approach*. New York: Julian Press.

Erikson, E. (1950). *Childhood and society*. New York: W. W. Norton.

Erikson, E. (1968). *Identity: Youth and crisis*. New York: W. W. Norton.

Freud, A. (1936). *The ego and the mechanisms of defence*. New York: International Universities Press.

Freud, S. (1940). *An outline of psychoanalysis*. New York: W. W. Norton.

Freud, S. (1960). *The ego and the id*. New York: W. W. Norton.

Gitterman, A., & Germain, C. (1980). *The life model of social work practice*. New York: Columbia University Press.

Halgrin, R. P., & Whitbourne, S. K. (2010). *Abnormal psychology: Clinical perspectives on psychological disorders*. Boston: McGraw-Hill.

Hartmann, H. (1958). *Ego psychology and the problem of adaptation*. New York: International Universities Press.

Heineman Pieper, M. B. (1981). The obsolete scientific imperative in social work research. *Social Service Review, 55*, 371–78.

Hepworth, D. H., Rooney, R. H., Rooney, G. D., Strom-Gottfried, K., & Larsen, J. (2006). *Direct social work practice: Theory and skills*. Belmont, CA: Brooks/Cole.

Hollis, F., & Woods, M. E. (1964). *Casework: A psychosocial therapy.* New York: Random House.

Horney, K. (1945). *Our inner conflicts.* New York: W. W. Norton.

James, R. K. (2008). *Crisis intervention strategies.* Belmont, CA: Brooks/Cole.

Jung, C. J. (1959). *The archetypes and the collective unconscious.* Princeton, NJ: Princeton University Press.

Kinney, J. (2012). *Loosening the grip* (10th ed.). New York: McGraw-Hill Higher Education.

Kohut, H. (1971). *Analysis of the self.* Chicago: University of Chicago Press.

Lacan, J. (1968). *The language of the self: The function of language in psychoanalysis* (A. Wilden, Trans.). Baltimore: Johns Hopkins University Press.

Lee, J. (2001). *The empowerment approach to social work practice* (2nd ed.). New York: Columbia University Press.

Levin, J. (1987). *The treatment of alcoholism and other addictions.* New York: Jason Aronson.

Lucente, R. (2012). *Character formation and identity in adolescence: Clinical and developmental issues.* Chicago: Lyceum Books.

Mahler, M. S., Pine, F., & Bergman, A. (1975). *The psychological birth of the human infant.* New York: Basic Books.

Maslow, A. H. (1943). A theory of human motivation. *Psychological Review, 50,* 370–96.

McKenzie, F. (2008). *Theory and practice with adolescents: An applied approach.* Chicago: Lyceum Books.

McKenzie, F. (2011). *Understanding and managing the therapeutic relationship.* Chicago: Lyceum Books.

Meeks, J. E., & Bernet, W. (2001). *The fragile alliance* (5th ed.). Florida: Krieger.

Miller, W. R., & Rollnick, S. (2002). *Motivational interviewing: Preparing people for change.* New York: Guilford Press.

Minnix, J. A., Reitzel, L. R., & Pepper, K. A. (2005). Total number of MMPI-2 clinical scale elevations predicts premature termination after controlling for intake symptom severity and personality disorder diagnosis. *Personality and Individual Differences,* *38*(8), 1745–55.

Minuchin, S. (1974). *Families and family therapy.* Cambridge, MA: Harvard University Press.

O'Hare, T. (2005). *Evidence-based practices for social workers: An interdisciplinary approach.* Chicago: Lyceum Books.

O'Hare, T. (2009). *Essential skills of social work practice: Assessment, intervention, and evaluation.* Chicago: Lyceum Books.

Pavlov, I. P. (1927). *Conditioned reflexes.* London: Routledge & Kegan Paul.

Piaget, J., & Inhelder, B. (1969). *The psychology of the child.* New York: Basic Books.

Powers, G. T., Meenaghan, T. M., & Toomey, B. G. (1985). *Practice focused research.* Upper Saddle River, NJ: Prentice-Hall.

Prochaska, J. O., & Norcross, J. C. (2003). *Systems of psychotherapy: A transtheoretical analysis.* Belmont, CA: Brooks/Cole.

Psychodynamic diagnostic manual. (2006). Silver Spring, MD: Alliance of Psychoanalytic Organizations.

Rank, O. (1936). *Will therapy.* New York: W. W. Norton.

Rogers, C. (1965). *Client-centered therapy.* Boston: Houghton Mifflin.

Rothman, J. C. (2008). *Cultural competence in process and practice: Building bridges.* Boston: Allyn & Bacon/Pearson.

Searles, H. F. (1959). Oedipal love in the countertransference. *International Journal of Psychoanalysis, 40,* 180–90.

Shebib, B. (2011). *Choices: Interviewing and counseling skills for Canadians.* Don Mills, Ontario: Pearson.

Shulman, S. R. (1999). Termination of short-term and long-term psychotherapy: Patients' and therapists' affective reactions and therapists' technical management (attachment style, therapy model). *Dissertation Abstracts International, 60,* 6B.

Siegel, J. (1992). *Repairing intimacy: An object relations approach to couples therapy.* Northvale, NJ: Jason Aronson.

Skinner, B. F. (1976). *About behaviorism.* New York: Random House.

Stampley, C., & Slaght, E. (2004). Cultural competence as a clinical obstacle. *Smith College Studies in Social Work, 74,* 333–47.

Stern, D. (2000). *The interpersonal world of the human infant: A view from psychoanalysis and developmental psychology.* New York: Basic Books.

Strom-Gottfried, K. (2007). *Straight talk about professional ethics.* Chicago: Lyceum Books.

Sullivan, H. S. (1953). *The interpersonal theory of psychiatry.* New York: W. W. Norton.

Tansey, M. J., & Burke, W. F. (1989). *Understanding countertransference: From projective identification to empathy.* London: Analytic Press.

Vygotsky, L. S. (1978). *Mind in society.* Cambridge, MA: Harvard University Press.

Walsh, J. (2007). *Endings in clinical practice: Effective closure in diverse settings* (2nd ed.). Chicago: Lyceum Books.

Wilkinson, J. M., & Treas, L. S. (2011). *Fundamentals of nursing:* Vol. 1, *Theory, concepts and applications.* Philadelphia: F. A. Davis.

Winnicott, D. W. (1965). *The maturational processes and the facilitating environment.* Madison, CT: International Universities Press.

Winnicott, D. W. (1971). *Playing and reality.* New York: Routledge.

Yalom, I. D. (1985). *The theory and practice of group psychotherapy.* New York: Basic Books.

Yalom, I. D. (2002). *The gift of therapy.* New York: Harper.

Zastrow, C. (2010). *The practice of social work: A comprehensive work text.* Belmont, CA: Brooks/Cole.

Index

About the Author

Fred McKenzie is university professor, director of the School of Social Work, and director of the Doctor of Social Work Program at Aurora University in Aurora, Illinois. Fred has been with Aurora University since 1991. He has also served as dean of the College of Professional Studies at Aurora University. Fred has been in private practice since 1982. He started his professional career as a youth worker in 1974 with Spectrum Youth and Family Services, and became the executive director of Barrington Youth Services in 1989. He received his master of social work degree from George Williams College in Downers Grove, Illinois, in 1982, and his PhD in clinical social work from Loyola University of Chicago in 1995.